DON'T ACCEPT ME AS I AM

Helping "Retarded" People to Excel

DON'T ACCEPT ME AS I AM

Helping "Retarded" People to Excel

Reuven Feuerstein
Yaacov Rand
and
John E. Rynders

Plenum Press • New York and London

Library of Congress Cataloging in Publication Data

Feuerstein, Reuven.
  Don't accept me as I am: helping "retarded" people to excel / Reuven Feuerstein,
Yaacov Rand, and John E. Rynders.
    p.   cm.
  Bibliography: p.
  Includes index.
  ISBN 0-306-42964-0
    1. Mentally handicapped children—Education—Psychological aspects. 2. Teacher-
student relationships. 3. Mentally handicapped children—Rehabilitation. I. Rand,
Yaacov. II. Rynders, John E. III. Title.
  LC4602.F47 1988   88-17618
  371.92'8—dc19   CIP

© 1988 Reuven Feuerstein, Yaacov Rand, and John E. Rynders
Plenum Press is a Division of
Plenum Publishing Corporation
233 Spring Street, New York, N.Y. 10013

Printed in the United States of America

To our wives:

Berta Feuerstein
Bilha Rand
Barbara Rynders

whose love, support, and wisdom
inspire and sustain us

Preface

We believe that the educator—parent, teacher, coach—should be, and often is, the most powerful force in a child's education. Sometimes, however, the educator has been cast into a role that de-emphasizes dynamic, strong educator–child interaction.

We contend that a dynamic type of interaction, which we call *mediated learning*, is essential for all children, at least at certain times. And, for those children who are neglected or disadvantaged or are termed mentally retarded, mediation is absolutely *essential*.

Consistent with our belief in the power of good mediation is our preference for the term *retarded performers* rather than the term *retarded persons*. The former implies, as it should, that a person's performance rarely reflects that person's potential.

Sincerely hoping that this book will be a source of hope, an agenda for action, and an outline for intervention, we stand committed to the proposition that intelligence and competence are much more modifiable than we often give them credit for being.

REUVEN FEUERSTEIN
YAACOV RAND
JOHN E. RYNDERS

Jerusalem and Minneapolis

Foreword

The Nobel Laureate Sir Peter Medawar once noted that natural scientists come in several varieties, including collectors, classifiers, and compulsive tidiers-up; detectives and explorers; artists and artisans; poet–scientists and philosopher–scientists; and even mystic–scientists. Unfortunately, no similar attempt has been made to label behavioral scientists according to the kinds of people they are or even to speculate on how their professional judgments and commitments may be flavored by the social values they embrace.

In this precious and highly readable book, Feuerstein, Rand, and Rynders take an important step toward filling the void. They distinguish clearly between passive acceptors and active modifiers, who deal with learning handicaps in strikingly different ways. People who are passive acceptors lovingly accept low-functioning children as they are; those who are active modifiers lovingly modify low-functioning children to realize what they can become. The passive-acceptant approach is basically fatalistic and patronizing. Those who advocate it are confident in their ability to assess learning capacities; they are prepared to help low-functioning children cope as best they can within their assumed limitations; and they are determined to protect these children from being victimized by a world that exploits individual weaknesses. The active-modificational orientation, on the other hand, is far more optimistic about children's potentialities than conventional measures would suggest, and it allows for enormous efforts to stretch seemingly stunted minds to unpredictable limits.

The authors describe the contrasting belief systems in detail and provide many examples of how educational policies and practices are affected by these differences. They also go a step further by implying that a sharp split exists even within the ranks of active modifiers. There are those who operate primarily with confidence and dedication, which they imbue in the children, thus creating a learning atmosphere in which teacher and pupil are both determined to do their best. In this instance, it is mostly heart that counts, rather than educational techniques, and some are persuaded that their success is inevitable because their hearts are in the right place. Others take the opposite view by opting for cold skill in place of warm good will and by expecting the special methods of assessment and instruction advocated in this book to make the big difference. They are scrupulous about keeping their science pure because for them science and faith do not mix.

But they have to mix, as the authors make so abundantly clear. Otherwise, we may be left to choose between some variant of faith healing and what may be described lugubriously as faithless healing, either of which leads to mediocre mediation, no matter how sincere the faith is in the first approach or how technically correct the healing efforts are in the second. Low-functioning children lack *both* self-confidence and clear pathways to learning, and the only way their needs can be met is if the two deficits are addressed simultaneously without splitting hairs on the question of how much each contributes to failure. Such pondering is as inane as wondering whether the left or right hand creates louder applause when it is obvious that neither hand, working alone, can produce the clapping sound at all. No wonder that the book stresses motivation no less than teaching/learning processes. The authors repeatedly insist that understanding the basic theory of mediated learning experiences and knowing how to apply it skillfully are necessary but not sufficient conditions for success in helping low-functioning children to outdo themselves. There is also a need for the teacher to be convinced that children's potentialities are indeed modifiable, and to be able to convince children of that fact as well.

The upbeat views of human capabilities expressed by Feuerstein, Rand, and Rynders might have struck the uninitiated reader as mere Pollyannaism if it weren't for the authors' own success in mediating children's learning experiences. To instill optimism in the reader, they cite poignant case histories of children who have benefited from such treatments, with special emphasis on persons who have Down syndrome. But the sober side of their message is that progress can be made *not* simply by a quick-fix, magical formula, but rather by huge investments of time, effort, skill, patience, commitment, and old-fashioned boundless love for children.

What makes the investment worthwhile derives from the authors' unconventional way of interpreting children's potentialities on the basis of past performance. Traditional measurement techniques seek to establish a baseline—or a level at which the child can perform repeatedly without mediation—as the best indicator of how well he or she can and will achieve eventually. In other words, only the successes that are *sustained* over several testings predict future performance, whereas one-time or even sporadic mastery is dismissed as simply a flash in the pan. Feuerstein, Rand, and Rynders acknowledge that the kind of problems children can solve over and over again today are the best forecasters of the kinds they can solve tomorrow. What troubles them, though, is that such a prophecy is self-fulfilling, since it applies only where the learning environments of today and tomorrow are unmediated or poorly mediated. Under mediational testing, the examiner is not particularly interested in baseline performance. Instead, he or she follows the "principle of the possible"; that is, whatever the child can be motivated and educated to do successfully just once—not necessarily again and again—becomes the level of reasonable expectation for the future. And even that level is not fixed, since the examiner is a *participant observer*, not an objective monitor, in the examining process, always providing the child with keys to learning and encouragement to improve performance in order to reach new heights of achievement that were never before deemed likely.

The "principle of the possible," in which a person's capacity is judged by his or her best effort—regardless of how rarely it is revealed—applies to all ability levels, even to genius. If an Einstein can posit a theory of relativity, that once-in-a-lifetime feat is the measure of his intellect, not his everyday problem-solving successes. Thus, the thesis comes full circle. The first impression it creates is one of faith-driven optimism about the psyche's plasticity and the power of human beings to effect dramatic changes in other human beings. Out of this conviction there grows a profound resolve to redevelop the potentialities of low-functioning children with Down syndrome. But in the last analysis, faith and hope are fortified by rationality, for the "principle of the possible" adds reasonableness to the theory of mediated learning experiences, while the success stories reported here lend vital supportive evidence.

ABRAHAM J. TANNENBAUM

Teachers College
Columbia University
New York, New York

Acknowledgments

Writing this book would not have been possible without the assistance and advice of many friends, staff members, and colleagues.

First of all, we wish to express our appreciation to our families, particularly to our wives: Berta Feuerstein, Bilha Rand, and Barbara Rynders, to whom this book is dedicated. This book could not have been written without their continuing support!

This book is also dedicated to the hundreds of children who have come to us for assessment and intervention. Some of them are described here. All of them were a powerful source of inspiration and learning for us. As one of the sages says:

> From all those who taught us—we become enlightened
> But from those whom we taught—even more so.

We acknowledge also the valuable assistance of a number of friends and staff members of the Hadassah–WIZO–Canada Research Institute and the Hasbro Paradigmatic Clinic for Down Syndrome in Jerusalem, Israel, for their special contributions to this book:

- Eitan Wig, graphic artist of the institute, for his inventive ways of translating ideas into graphics.
- Noa Schwartz, for her photographic talents and contributions, particularly the cover photo for the book.
- Ami Shitrit, for his photographic contributions and logistic efficiency.
- Yael Mintzker, M.A., coordinator of the Testing and Advisory Services at the institute, for her intensive work with children in need, particularly children with Down syndrome, as well as for her follow-up studies with persons who underwent reconstructive plastic surgery.
- Malka Hoffman, professor, for her critical comments, editorial advice, and insightful contributions.

- Miriam Cohen and Glenda Solski, speech therapists at the institute, who with their insightful work and persistence have improved the quality of life for so many.
- Miriam Hizkiahu and Hadassah Harkavi, for their efficiency in typing portions of this book.
- Gottfried Lemperle, M.D., from St. Anna Hospital in Frankfurt am Main, who introduced to Israel reconstructive plastic surgery to assist persons with Down syndrome.
- Hadassah Medical Center, and Professor M. R. Wexler, head of the Department for Plastic Surgery, for pioneering reconstructive plastic surgery procedures in Israel and adopting an Active Modificational Approach.
- The Hasbro Paradigmatic Clinic for Down Syndrome in Jerusalem, headed by Professor Harvey Narrol, and his collaborators, Dr. Theresa Sharav, Shuli Aviv, and Debby Zwiback, for their enthusiasm and innovative programming for people with Down syndrome.

Special thanks to Pnina Klein, assistant professor, Bar-Ilan University, School of Education, for her work in extending the theory of mediated learning to include young children with disabilities and their parents.

We would also like to express our gratitude to several organizations and foundations for their support of and faith in our work over many years:

- Hadassah-WIZO of Canada, under the presidency of Mrs. Cecily Peters, and the newly elected president, Mrs. Noemi Frankenstein, Canada.
- Hasbro Foundation, under the presidency of Mrs. Sylvie Hasenfeld, and director of Special Projects, Mrs. Evi Weiss, New York, USA.
- Deitscher Center, headed by Mr. Moses Deitscher and Mr. Meir Deitscher, Montreal, Canada.
- Berta and Alter J. Bessner Foundation, headed by Dr. and Mrs. William and Frieda Cohen, Montreal, Canada.
- Jenny and Georges Bloch Foundation, headed by Mrs. Jenny Bloch, Zurich, Switzerland.

To all of them we extend deepest feelings of friendship.

Our most sincere appreciation to the codirectors of the Hadassah–WIZO–Canada Research Institute, Professor David Krasilowski, director of the Talbieh Mental Hospital, Jerusalem, and

Mr. Shimon Tuchman, former director general of Youth Aliyah, for their encouragement and friendship during so many years, as well as for their wisdom and personal support.

In Minnesota, we wish to acknowledge the courage and skills of parents in Project EDGE who, along with their children with Down syndrome, have been a source of friendship and inspiration that is beyond estimating. Particular thanks are extended to Dr. J. Margaret Horrobin, pediatrician and codirector, Project EDGE, University of Minnesota Hospitals.

Our thanks to several University of Minnesota colleagues for working with us in developing and researching intervention techniques for people with retarded performance:

- Drs. Robert Bruininks and James Turnure, professors, Special Education Programs.
- Dr. Stuart Schleien, associate professor, Therapeutic Recreation Program.
- Drs. David and Roger Johnson, professors, College of Education.

Special thanks to Ms. Bonnie Warhol, office supervisor, Special Education Programs, University of Minnesota, typist of extraordinary talent, and valued friend.

Finally, to our publisher, Plenum Publishing Corporation, and most particularly to Linda Greenspan Regan and Victoria Cherney, editors, we extend our sincere gratitude for their faith in us and our work, their extraordinary patience, and their outstanding editorial skills.

Contents

DON'T ACCEPT ME
AS I AM

CHAPTER 1

You Are Human, You Are Modifiable

The Belief in Human Modifiability

Many letters arrive at the institute* asking for advice and help. One particular letter included a very peculiar request: Help to fulfill the will of a dying mother concerning her son Joel.† With all her heart she did not want her son to be permanently committed to custodial care in a large institution for people with severely retarded performance and behavioral problems. The boy had already been in and out of custodial care facilities many times. Each time he was released to his mother's care, Joel would make the family's life so difficult that he would be sent back to an institution. And yet, with the strong instincts of a mother who wishes to see her child happy, she felt that despite all the odds against the boy, her son could be saved from permanent custodial care.

Joel, age 16, was described as an "incorrigible" individual whose level of functioning precluded any attempts at independent living. Not only had he very little capacity for communication, his speech was very impaired. Furthermore, both his short-term and long-term memory were extremely limited, and he had little or no ability to achieve autonomy over his own actions. All this was complicated by his irrational behaviors, his inclination to steal stamps and bury them, or steal food and throw it away. His outbursts of anger made Joel

*The institute refers to the Hadassah–WIZO–Canada Research Institute in Jerusalem, Israel.
†All names and identifiable characteristics have been changed.

1

dangerous to have around, so much so that his intellectual impairments became secondary in importance to his aberrant behavior.

Yet at times this same boy could be docile and submissive, with a "yes" answer on his lips even before a question was completed. Joel also had some very interesting "islands" of competence. For instance, if given a drawing to copy, he would trace it on a transparent paper with speed and precision. Working in a totally unsystematic way, jumping from one detail to another, he produced a final product that was surprisingly good. But given even the simplest figure to draw from scratch, such as a human face or body, or a flower, he was totally unable to perform. The same was true if we attempted to overcome his limited verbal ability. Even verbal repetition was difficult for him and there were many words he was unable to produce even if they were voiced 10 or 12 times.

The letter written by several members of Joel's community that conveyed Joel's mother's wish emphasized that very few of them believed that anything could be done to change the course of Joel's life. Yet, sensing the urgency of his mother's wish, they made a final plea for help to the institute, Joel's last chance. In reading this letter, we had the feeling that all they really expected to hear was that there were no chances for Joel's care and treatment at the institute, especially after they had fully described the difficulties they had encountered in arranging for Joel's placement in a foster home and a youth village.

Despite the odds against Joel, we wanted to assess his modifiability. To the credit of the people of his community, they immediately brought him to us in spite of their grave doubts that there was any chance of helping him. Once we started to assess him, we began to appreciate the reasons for their doubts!

His birth history was enough to discourage any attempt to produce changes. Joel had been born prematurely, with a very low birth weight. Placed in an incubator immediately after his birth, he remained there for about three months. His vision, lungs, and brain were badly damaged owing to a combination of prenatal trauma, premature birth, and a prolonged period in the incubator.

After his release from the hospital, Joel lived in various institutions, separated from his mother and family. Custodial care continued throughout most of his life except for a period when he was cared for by his adoring grandmother.

When we started to assess Joel, it became clear that we were dealing with a multiply handicapped individual. His sensory, motor, and other modalities were affected, and, owing to a deficient environment, he was now severely disabled. We found in working with Joel that his attention span was very short, and even when he appeared to attend, he was extremely slow to respond. We had to repeat the same instruction scores of times in order to get him to understand and complete a task. Enormous effort was required to get him to learn and memorize the simplest word or phrase. He manifested very little ability to initiate any behavior. Joel's assessment by one of the authors and a number of teachers lasted 20 days. By the end of that time we were able to see small beginnings of change.

The belief that Joel was modifiable, despite all of his problems, enabled us to persist in our work. If it weren't for this belief, we would have given up.

Part of Joel's intervention program took him to a foster home program where he was given an enormous amount of individualized mediation, that is, sensitive, focused, dynamic, interactive instruction. His foster parents became intimately involved with him, using every possible opportunity to create stimulating learning conditions for him. They would point things out to him, repeating words that he learned once but couldn't repeat. Their work elicited responses that had not been forthcoming before. Months of work were invested to get Joel to remember the days of the week and the months of the year, and to tell time.

The joy we experienced when Joel was able to count, without error, up to 20 may have been comparable with the feeling of parents who see their child receive a high school diploma. When he was able to imitate or initiate multisyllable words or reconstruct experiences, we felt that a good part of the battle had been won. Not that there were no regressions. There were plenty. And regressions were sometimes very intense. For instance, one time, in an outburst of anger, he crushed some of his room's furnishings with his bare hands. During those times, it took a great deal of tenacity to make him aware of the damage he was inflicting on himself and thereby help him to control his destructive tendencies.

When spoken language became fluent, in part through development of his memory, a wealth of "souvenirs" came forth. One of the most amazing was that he started to vocalize in a foreign language, to which he had been exposed earlier in life. Reading was extremely difficult for him, but Joel reached a third-grade level eventually.

After a long period in the foster home group care program where he became well integrated with children functioning at a much higher level, he was transferred to Haifa and given a vocational apprenticeship with a carpenter.

A most important goal had been reached: Joel was able to function in a normal environment and proved to be capable of a fair amount of independence in terms of both work and social interactions. However, at least once or twice a year there were outbursts of maladaptive behavior, triggered by events that touched his increased sensitivity, and deep feelings of inadequacy and rejection that even an environment of acceptance could not blot out totally. After such episodes he would run away and climb into a trash bin. When found, he would say, "I'm garbage. I belong here." It was pathetic to see how his past experiences controlled and troubled him.

Following the foster home placement, he was placed with paternal relatives on a poultry farm where he, along with two other people, performed all the chores. He proved to be a responsible and efficient worker. Currently, Joel works in a small woodworking shop and lives in a community group home for young adults, where he is reported to be one of the most well-adapted persons.

The story of Joel is certainly a case by which the structural cognitive modifiability (SCM) theory (to be described further) is amply illustrated. The tremendous efforts invested in Joel's education were initiated basically through the will of his mother, who did not want to accept Joel as he functioned and believed that something could be done to modify her child. Without her will, the chances that his family or some organization would have initiated action to modify his level of cognitive functioning were close to nil. But, as the ancient Chinese saying puts it, even the longest trip starts with one little step. The mother's will was this "little step," ultimately determining the quality of her son's future.

None of us had any access to the mother's thoughts. None of us had ever discussed her hopes and plans for her son. We have no information about the kind of person she was. But we can be certain that, despite her extremely trying experiences with her son over many years, she held tenaciously to a belief that her child's severe problems were not necessarily immutable.

Joel's mother's belief in modifiability illustrates the importance of *belief* as an essential determinant in initiating and generating action. In fact, only a person strongly motivated by a belief will be liable to enter into and persist in an action. Why? Because belief is anchored in a need. Knowledge alone of a path or activity will not necessarily trigger action, because it is not anchored in a need of the individual.

Belief in human modifiability is equally essential to the full professional functioning of educators. Joining in with the spirit of Joel's mother's will, we offer five interrelated belief statements that are foundational to the theory and approach taken in this book. In a way, these five statements of belief could be a basic "litmus test" to see if a person who has been trained to be an educator of individuals with retarded performance is ready to assume that role.

HUMAN BEINGS ARE MODIFIABLE

This belief points toward the very nature of humankind. All human beings need to be considered as open systems, liable to be meaningfully modified by environmental intervention. Such a view contrasts sharply with the general hereditary view of achievement potential, which, in its extreme form, considers that the ultimate level of an individual's functioning is determined solely by his* genetic endowment. Consequently, little modifiability is expected.

Currently, there is an impressive body of evidence showing the vast possibilities of attaining meaningful alterations in the functioning of various groups of people, including those who have very severe disabilities. For example, data gathered by the authors in both clinical and experimental settings[1,2] demonstrate that the modifiability of people with many types of serious problems is possible.

THE INDIVIDUAL I AM EDUCATING IS MODIFIABLE

A general belief in human modifiability does not necessarily reflect an educator's similar belief as related to the specific child—or adult—with whom he is dealing. Sometimes the characteristics of the individual, his level of functioning, his resistance to various environmental interventions, his level of acting-out or disruptive behavior, may seem to be at odds with a general belief in human modifiability. The way in which a particular individual reacts to intervention may

---

*We will be using "he," "himself," and so on for expediency and grammatical purposes only.

cause the educator to consider modifiability as "nonapplicable" to the child with whom he is dealing. Such a negative belief may preclude the very activities needed to obtain modifiability. In order to activate and persist in long-term intervention, despite experiences of failure, it is imperative that the educator's belief in human modifiability be a strong one and refer to a specific child.

I AM CAPABLE OF MODIFYING THE INDIVIDUAL

This third proposition relates to the educator's feelings of adequacy and competency as an active, efficient force in producing modifiability in the student with whom he is dealing. Even when adhering to a general belief in human modifiability and to the modifiability of a specific child, some educators may find that the attainment of individual modifiability goals is beyond their own capacities. Such a perceived lack of competence can cause reformulation of the educator's general belief system about human modifiability. For instance, the child rather than the teacher will be "blamed" for lack of educational progress. Paradoxically, the teacher who feels inadequate may avoid referring the child to someone who might be of help because he does not want to reveal his incapacity. Occasionally, every teacher encounters a child for whom he must get help from another professional, or whom he must even refer to another teacher. But if this happens often, particularly after receiving additional training, the teacher should strongly consider changing professions.

I MYSELF AM A PERSON WHO MAY—AND HAS TO—BE MODIFIED

Full professional development can be obtained only by a long-lasting investment of the educator in his self-modification. Professional complacency is detrimental to the educational interventional process since it glosses over the differences among children, their specific capacities and conditions, as well as many other sociocultural factors that are pertinent to successful education. The lack of an educator's belief in self-modifiability often results in his placing excessive demands on the child to adapt and a lack of readiness on his part to adapt himself to the needs of the child with whom he is working.

SOCIETY—AND PUBLIC OPINION—ARE MODIFIABLE AND HAVE TO BE MODIFIED

It is perhaps unnecessary nowadays to note the impact society has on the development of educational attitudes and practices. But the educator does not always view society as a legitimate target for his educational activity. Society is often considered as a condition that must be taken into consideration as a determining factor, rather than as a target for intervention. We wish to point out that the individual's modifiability passes through the "filter" of social conditions. Modifiability of cultural attitudes, social practices and norms, as well as of general public opinion, is always a lengthy process. But each educator has to consider society as one of his main targets for intervention.

These five beliefs should be kept in mind as a context for appreciating and understanding basic concepts of the structural cognitive modifiability (SCM) theory. Let us now focus briefly on each of the three words in the theory's title since they stand for ideas that give the theory focus, dynamism, and power.

Modifiability

Modifiability is a central concept within the SCM theory. In order to better understand this term, a distinction needs to be made between "modifiability" and "change." Modifiability relates essentially to alterations that have occurred in the individual himself, his personality traits, his thinking ability and capacity, and his general level of competency. Changes are usually more limited in scope, more specific and localized, and very often show low levels of durability over time and weak resistance to the impact of environmental influences. People frequently experience changes, but changes often leave only minimal traces upon their higher functioning because they do not become an integrated part of their personality and structural cognitive endowment.

Modifiability is also a meaningful, substantial, and durable departure from a trend of development that has been predicted on the basis of the individual's traditionally measured level of performance. Only in rare cases do persons with retarded performance produce and maintain substantial modifiability on their own initiative. Such modifiability usually requires intensive and systematic intervention.

Considering the extremely low initial level of Joel's functioning, his almost complete lack of language and other communication skills, his lack of initiative, as well as all of his other disabling characteristics, one might have forecast a developmental trend that would not exceed his level of functioning at that time. In spite of all of the obstacles, Joel became significantly modified because higher-oriented goals were set for him and strong actions were taken to reach those goals. The independent and competent individual who emerged from this lengthy intervention process was radically different from the inactive and dependent person who began it!

The SCM theory postulates that modifiability is possible to attain despite severe obstacles in the individual himself or in his life conditions. The case of Joel does in fact reflect the overcoming of three barriers that are considered by many as powerful, permanent, negative factors that preclude significant alterations in the individual's level of functioning. These barriers are (1) age of the individual, (2) causes of the impairment, and (3) severity of the impairment.

Some consider the *age* of the individual to be a strong determinant of the success of environmental intervention. According to such views, the earlier intervention occurs, the greater its chances for success. This position is accepted by most psyhologists. But some also consider that beyond a certain age period, sometimes referred to as a critical period, meaningful alterations are no longer likely to occur through intervention.

There is no question in our minds as to the importance of early intervention. But the SCM theory challenges the critical period notion. While age is certainly an important determinant in the choice of interventional methods and modes of action, advanced age need not be viewed as an "invincible" obstacle. In fact, some intervention opportunities may be even more accessible at an older age when self-directed motivation of the individual may contribute to his own modifiability.

Sources of impairment, the second perceived barrier, may be divided into two broad categories: (1) genetic, hereditary, or congenital problems, and (2) environmental factors. The first category includes chromosomal problems such as Down syndrome. The second category, environmental conditions, includes such problems as poverty, parental abuse, and/or lead poisoning. Sometimes the two categories overlap and it is not an easy task to distinguish between them. For instance, mental illness can sometimes be linked to hereditary as well as environmental factors. And, according to some theories,[3] impairments of an environmental nature that occur during the first two or three years of life should be considered as constitutional, hence not liable to change.

The SCM theory challenges this position, asserting that intervention is possible, regardless of the nature of the impairment. Assuredly, the intensity of investment required for modifiability, the methods for intervening, and the techniques needed will vary in accord with the nature of the disability. But only in rare cases will the nature of the impairment preclude intervention.

Severity of the impairment is a third factor that some consider to be a strong barrier to intervention. According to the SCM theory, however, modifiability is possible even with persons who have very severe handicaps. Without question, the severity of the impairment affects the individual's accessibility to intervention but does not create conditions that should be considered as precluding modifiability altogether.

Joel's case illustrates this point well. One can hardly imagine a configuration of more adverse barriers than in his case. Meaningful intervention was initiated only toward middle adolescence; he showed extremely low levels of functioning even in the most rudimentary areas of activity; the sources of his impairment were multiple, including genetic elements, lack of appropriate early childhood experience, and a variety of family variables that made him at high risk from a developmental point of view. Moreover, up to the point when he came to us, environmental intervention efforts had been close to nil, since he was considered—except by his mother—as a severely retarded person who could not be modified and was destined for permanent custodial care.

Joel's mother's strong belief initiated intervention. On her initiative, a powerful individual assessment was done, uncovering some of Joel's true capacity. Modifiability not only was found to be possible but also, after many years of intervention, transformed Joel into a self-assertive, well-adjusted, and capable individual. His modifiability was a significant departure from the developmental trend predicted on the basis of his initial level of functioning.

Structural

A psychological structure can be viewed as a system composed of a number of elements that are interconnected and that mutually affect each other. Moreover, psychological structures are linked with a variety of other systems of the individual's personality.

As opposed to physical structures, which are static by nature, psychological structures contain dynamic components that are expressed through several characteristics: First, a structure is characterized by *strong cohesion between the whole—that is, the structure itself—and its components.* Consequently, experiences that relate to one or more components of a structure will affect not only the ones involved directly but also all the other components of the structure. For example, memory—which is one of the major cognitive structures—may include perceptual components (such as focusing), intellectual components (such as comprehending the content), motivational components (such as interest in the content to be memorized), and many others. All these components are interconnected and influence one another. Moreover, changes introduced in one of these components—such as raising the level of the individual's interest in content to be memorized—may affect all the other components considerably. In time, attention will be significantly enhanced and comprehension increased.

Second, a structure is characterized by *transformism.* Transformism refers to the tendency of the structure to change its ways of functioning. Such changes may, for example, be reflected in the rhythm of an activity. Tasks that previously required much more time may, through teaching, be accomplished more rapidly. Children may also show higher levels of intensity and flexibility in performing a task. These changes will ultimately affect the functioning of the structure.

The third characteristic of a structure is perhaps the most important one in the development of the individual's adaptational endowment. Owing to its energetic components, the psychological structure tends to act in a *self-regulating* and *self-perpetuating* way. This is expressed by its repeated use whenever the individual considers that the activation of such a structure may be helpful in solving a given problem or coping with a given situation. Precision, for instance, is one of the cognitive structures.

An individual who has integrated precision within his psychological system will tend to act in a precise and accurate way in all of his activities. He will collect relevant data in a precise way; he will register them (in written or oral form) in an organized and systematic manner; he may communicate the accumulated information to others with a high degree of accuracy.

With retarded performers, we often observe that structures that were almost nonexistent gradually become stronger through judicious repetition. After such systematic repetition, the structures become more autonomous—that is, they do not need to be cued by the teacher.

The successful use of a structure, while struggling to overcome adaptational difficulties, reinforces not only the structure itself but also the individual, both of which reach higher levels of proficiency.

The self-regulational aspects of the psychological structure refer mainly to the amount of energy needed to activate the structure.

Let's take the same example of precision. The student may have to use a lot of energy in gathering data pertinent to the solution of the task. But, after being successful repeatedly, and after gaining insight as to the contribution of precision in reaching his goals, he finds that acting precisely becomes easier, and he finally reaches a level of proficiency characterized by high precision and a low expenditure of energy.

Cognition

Cognition refers to a number of basic functions of the individual, such as perception, memory, learning, and thinking. The SCM theory emphasizes cognition for several reasons. First, cognition is of prime importance in most human activities and to the adaptational process of the individual. Few human activities do not have a significant cognitive component. Second, modern life, especially in a technological society, places heavy demands on the individual's cognitive functioning. The individual's educational, occupational, and socioeconomic status are highly correlated with his cognitive achievements. Hence, cognition is one of the most potent adaptational determinants. Third, cognition is a readily accessible avenue for environmental intervention. Structural modifiability does not, however, limit itself to the cognitive area but aims to affect other subsystems of the individual's personality as well. Cognition, by virtue of its flexibility, lends itself well to environmental intervention. In the realm of education, the great majority of programs that have been developed over the centuries have shown a cognitive orientation.

Although, in the last few decades, increasing attention has been given to the modification of the affective subsystems, the interventions themselves have been mostly cognitive in nature. Indeed, the cognitive subsystem of the individual must be considered not only as one of paramount adaptational importance but also as the "royal avenue" by which all other psychological subsystems can be reached and modified effectively.

The case of Joel illustrates in a most dramatic way that structural cognitive modifiability is in the realm of the feasible. Joel is a "representative" not only of so many who have benefited from meaningful environmental interventions but also of many more who were deprived of such an experience. The success we had with Joel poses a challenge for us concerning all those who, when denied SCM opportunities, may be condemned to continous dependency and low levels of life quality. Joel taught us what can be done and what has to be done even in the face of the most adverse conditions. He is no less a warning as to what the expected outcomes are, when appropriate intervention is denied to persons with retarded performance. Human modifiability is not only a belief but also a challenge and a responsibility.

CHAPTER 2

Human Modifiability
It Doesn't Happen by Itself

This book's title, *Don't Accept Me as I Am,* symbolizes an unvoiced cry of despair, the despair of thousands of people with retarded performance whose passive-acceptant (unchallenging/unmodifying) circumstances doom them to a relatively low quality of life. Out of love, parents may offer their child every type of comfort and pleasure in order to maintain his happiness. Anything that might disturb their child's placid environment is withheld. The child's comfort, complete peace of mind, feeling of being totally accepted, and even his ignorance of his being different, become all-important. Very little thought is given to the possibility of enhancing development in a substantial way.

The active-modificational (AM) approach, in contrast to the passive-acceptant (PA) one, reveals itself as an unwillingness on the part of the parent, caregiver, teacher, employer to accept the person's impairment—be it physical, mental, educational, or behavioral—as it is.

The SCM theory is anchored deeply in the AM approach, advocating the continual mobilization of environmental resources in order to enhance not only the individual's potential but his capacity to become modified.

Educators, social workers, parents, and others will vary greatly in their belief in the potential for human modifiability. This variance can be thought of as a position held on a bipolar continuum running between the passive-acceptant (PA) approach on the right and the active-modificational (AM) approach on the left end. In reality, though, these approaches can be described in terms of a spectrum of positions, each one closer to, or more remote from, one of these poles.

These two views do not refer to the quantitative aspects of educational intervention. Instead, they address its qualitative aspects, that is, its nature, goals, and direction toward which interventional energies and resources are directed.

In order to determine one's position on the PA–AM continuum, two interrelated questions should be asked: "To what extent is the individual's level of functioning, or impairment, considered immutable and consequently accepted as a given?" "To what extent are the social resources, interventional processes, and educational practices geared toward meaningfully modifying the individual himself as well as shaping his environment to be more modifying?"

In responding to these questions, whenever educational activities are geared toward significantly increasing the individual's modifiability and enhancing his adaptational capacities, we may consider them an active-modificational (AM) approach. Whenever an individual's modifiability is not the major objective of intervention, a passive-acceptant (PA) approach is reflected. Activities of a PA nature may be highly resourceful and varied and yet considered passive because they aim at adapting the environment to the individual's present level of functioning, rather than at enriching the individual's coping behavior for a better quality of life.

There are situations, however, in which a passive-acceptant approach is not only commendable but necessary, as for instance in building special ramps for people in wheelchairs. Even in this circumstance, though, it is important that the person himself commute from one place to another without requiring the direct assistance of someone else, if at all possible.

Acceptance does not refer to the emotional attitude that we may have, or develop, toward a person with a disability. It refers to the attitude we have toward that *disability*. Passive acceptance means to tolerate the impairment, considering it as immodifiable. To "live with" the impairment means that an investment is made not in the individual's modification but in his surroundings. Conditions are created for him that will not require modifications in his level of functioning. Thus, low-level or inappropriate functioning becomes reinforced and perpetuated.

HISTORICAL ROOTS OF ACTIVE MODIFICATION VERSUS PASSIVE ACCEPTANCE APPROACHES

The AM–PA controversy can be traced far back into human history. Its expressions are multiple in the chronicals of ancient history as well as in the transmission of culture across generations. Furthermore, certain cultural traditions have been marked more than others by the intensity with which they adhere to one or the other of these two approaches. We do not aim to present a thorough historical review here but will limit ourselves to a few illustrations that show how the AM–PA approach was reflected in educational practices.

Richard Scheerenberger, in his work on the history of mental retardation,[1] shows that from the earliest periods of recorded history, society developed highly diverse attitudes toward people with disabilities, ranging from fear to altruism, and from the attribution of "evil" to the attribution of "good" celestial forces to those so classified.

Ancient Greece, although emphasizing both intellectual and physical prowess, venerated the latter. Citizens of Athens were required to participate actively in social and military activities of the *polis*, and physical achievements were highly praised and rewarded. Intellectual achievement, although less rewarded, yielded a wide spectrum of philosophical schools and scientific achievements in Greece. But, as far as we know, no special treatment was given to the "feebleminded" or otherwise dysfunctioning persons who probably enjoyed special tolerance, that is, passive acceptance.

The Spartans carried the goal of physical perfection to an extreme, openly practicing selective infanticide. Physically weak and "feebleminded" babies were considered a burden to society, which had both the duty and the authority to allow them to die or to kill them. Spartan practices reflect an active-rejection attitude.

In Europe, the medieval age can be considered as a dark age for people with mental disabilities, a time of strong active rejection. Atrocious methods were employed in order to isolate and "control" people considered to be mentally retarded or mentally ill. Nothing was done to help them achieve a more adequate adaptation to life. Instead, they were condemned to live their lives under extremely adverse conditions, sometimes in complete darkness, and chained so that they could barely move.

In the 1700s, the well-known French philosopher Jean-Jacques Rousseau opened up a new era in educational philosophy with his ideas about "natural education." He argued that the individual is basically "good" and that "evil" is caused by negative social influences. Therefore, he advocated a "return to nature," claiming that children, if placed in a benevolent, beautiful, natural environment, would "unfold," that is, fully materialize their own potentials, becoming good human beings on their own. Unfortunately, this idealistic and appealing idea turned out to be very unrealistic.

It was only at the beginning of the 19th century that education started to replace treatment as the basic orientation in dealing with handicapped persons. Incarceration for life, under hostile conditions, was abolished. In France, Philippe Pinel (1745–1826) was perhaps the first to break the chains (actual chains) of the mentally ill and to introduce notions of human respect and dignity into their lives. Treatment in those days was strongly colored by an unusual form of passive acceptance mixed with active rejection, reflecting superstitious beliefs and ignorance. To some, abnormality was conceived of as a punishment of God for sins committed by the parents or by the entire community. Therefore, inflicting suffering on these "cursed" people was only to follow the "will of God."

The work of the French physician Jean-Marc Itard[2] is an illustration of progress made toward active modification. Perhaps for the first time in history, intensive educational intervention, in the form of sensory and movement training, was applied. Victor, also known as the "Wild Boy of Aveyron," was found naked, allegedly living with wolves, in a forest in southern France. He was described as not possessing even rudimentary socialization behaviors. Itard undertook the monumental task of trying to transform Victor into a "civilized" human being. While Victor's ultimate developmental outcome was disappointing to Itard (who had hoped to socialize him completely), Victor's progress was substantial when compared with his previous behavior and considering the obstacles faced by Itard.

Fortunately, Itard had an exceptional follower in the person of Edouard Seguin,[3] who, in France in the 19th century, established the first school for people with retarded performance. At that time, the idea of a *school* for people with mental retardation was revolutionary, as were Seguin's goals for the school. Developing the ability to think, enhancing abstract capacities, and teaching moral and social behavior were among the goals of his educational program. The techniques used to attain them were patterned after Itard's; that is, they emphasized education of the senses and of movement abilities. The work of Seguin and other educators opened the gates for the emergence of special education as a valued means for modifying the individual, an idea that eventually spread around the world.

The first special education school in America was established in Boston by Samuel Howe in the 1800s. Following a long history of mistreating people with mental illness and retarded performance, society had begun to relate to them as people in need, toward whom care and education were social obligations and whose abilities needed to be cultivated through special educational practices. It was not until the turn of the 20th century, though, that the education system started to accept the *rights* of children with retarded performance to an education. However, these rights were almost always delivered in self-contained schools and in special classes in those schools.[4] Then the "eugenics scare" occurred. Professionals who had adopted a philosophy of protecting the retarded performer from an uncaring society shifted their philosophy toward "protecting" society from the individual with retarded performance. For instance, in 1912, one professional wrote that people with retarded performance were "a menace and a danger to the entire community."[5] Passive-acceptant approaches found support in a variety of studies, such as Goddard's report on the Kalikak family,[6] which reinforced the hereditary hypothesis of the causation of mental retardation, or, in Goddard's own terms: "Feeblemindedness is hereditary and transmitted as surely as any other characteristic" (1912, p. 117). These opinions, flawed as they were, had a strong impact on educational thought and practices of those times. Segregation of people with retarded performance in large residential institutions, located in remote areas, became a prevalent practice.

Then, slowly, new voices were heard. Gradually, segregation in institutions was no longer considered to be the only way for serving people with retarded performance. Even Goddard changed his mind, writing in the late 1920s: "It is time to change several of our time honored concepts—first of all, feeblemindedness is not incurable. Secondly, the feebleminded do not generally need to be segregated in institutions."[7]

These changes in atmosphere and approach were not paralleled by immediate changes in daily practices. Most large residential institutions continued as before. Then, in 1942, a study by Harold

Skeels[8] on the development of children in two different institution environments threw new light on the possible impact of active modification on the development of people with retarded performance. Skeels's findings showed that favorable environmental conditions enhanced intellectual development, raising the IQ level, whereas adverse environmental conditions resulted in lowering the IQ level. His study had a strong impact on education, lending empirical support to a more optimistic view concerning the possibility of modifying retarded performance. The seeds for substantial change had been sown. However, education of persons with retarded performance continued to be strongly rooted in the categorizational system (e.g., "educable," "trainable") promoted by the traditional classification system built around IQ scores. It is only in the last few decades that special education has been provided for children designated as trainable mentally retarded.

In the 1970s, the person with retarded performance was no longer considered as an "outsider" from whom society had to protect itself. In fact, some people with retarded performance were beginning to be viewed as contributors to society. Legislation in the 1970s providing for early education, education in an integrated school if at all possible, supported work, and group home living arrangements attested to society's stronger commitment to people of all ages with retarded performance.

Educational Implications of PA–AM: Assessment, Referral, and Placement

Psychological assessment, guided by a PA approach and its belief in the immutability of intellectual and cognitive functioning, usually contents itself with a "one-time" assessment. No reassessment is needed where no change is expected. On the other hand, assessment anchored in the AM approach will require—and perform—more frequent reassessment so as to be able to evaluate changes that occur as a result of environmental intervention.

A PA approach is geared toward a product-oriented assessment, considering the individual's test outcome at a given moment as fully reflecting not only his present capacities but his future abilities as well. In contrast, an AM assessment is process-oriented, enabling a better understanding of the individual's specific ways of functioning, his difficulties and his specific capacities, so as to enable effective teaching.

The PA–AM difference can be seen also in educational procedures. To us, a basic question is: "What is the level and nature of psychoeducational difference that the regular classroom teacher considers as within his coping ability in school?" Educators who take a PA approach usually show low levels of willingness to cope with differences and deficits, especially since a child with problems is perceived as immodifiable. Furthermore, the "blame" for repeated scholastic and adaptational failure is usually thrust primarily upon the child in a PA-oriented regular classroom.

Strangely enough, despite the fact that disciples of passive acceptance do not believe in human modifiability, they often argue that if children with disabilities are mainstreamed, normal children could become "modified" negatively. The dictum "One rotten apple may spoil the entire barrel" reflects this unidirectional attitude, that is, that the environment is indeed able to affect an individual, but only in the negative direction.

Teacher preparation programs that do not prepare prospective educators to deal with students with differences reflect a passive-acceptant approach, one that perpetuates the perceived "break" in the sometimes arbitrary and often unnecessary distinction between children who are "different" and those who are not. Such a distinction often results in placing students with differences into segregated programs. Segregation, virtually by definition, promotes the *status quo*, that is, passive acceptance.

From a policy standpoint another aspect of the PA–AM issue refers to the possibilities of the special education child's being reintegrated into the regular class. Adherents to a PA approach usually create organizational and educational conditions that are unidirectional. A child with a problem readily gets into and is accepted by a special education class, but there is little possibility that he can move back, be reintegrated, in the regular education setting. Once special education, always special education! Conversely, educational settings characterized by an AM approach consider special education as a temporary arrangement. The ultimate educational goal is to have the child with a disability be returned to a regular class and to ensure his full participation in it.

PA–AM issues should be considered in light of the fact that many children, considered as nonadapted and highly "problematic" during their school years, succeed in adult life far beyond what was expected in light of their scholastic achievement. Under adequate conditions children with retarded performance can overcome their difficulties, crossing barriers that were imposed upon them by the educational system and its lack of belief in their modifiability.

PA versus AM Reflected in Choice of Educational Context

Educational curricula and teaching methods based upon the PA approach will usually be devoid of novelty and lacking in innovation, remaining in the realm of what the child has already acquired or what is nondemanding for him. Redundancy in curricula and classroom routine are often "justified" by the perceived need of the student to experience success, and only success, so as to bolster his self-esteem. Little attention is paid to the fact that such nonchallenging experiences of success usually do not attain the desired goals and are frequently counterproductive because they are continuously made obsolete by encounters with the requirements of real life.

A school system based upon the AM approach considers novelty and innovation as a necessity in order to enhance the individual's level of functioning. Obviously, to experience success under new and more demanding conditions requires more effort and more intensive work from both the educator and the student, but this goal is obtainable if appropriate intervention is introduced. Such experiences of "hard-won" success are very important to the development of feelings of competence and self-esteem; they are real, not artifacts.

Educators often make use of concrete teaching aids in order to illustrate new objects, concepts, or ideas. Such devices can be extremely effective in facilitating comprehension. For instance, medical students examine models of different body organs such as replicas of the brain or heart. Students learning auto repair take models apart in order to understand the mechanics of an engine. Elementary students study the passage between day and night and the relations involving the earth, the moon, and the sun using miniature three-dimensional models. Special educators are often especially inclined to use such devices extensively. In fact, special education students are sometimes perceived as being totally concrete-learning-oriented, that is, not capable of using higher-order mental processes to solve problems or to become oriented in the environment. Sometimes the atmosphere of the entire special school may become "concrete," manifesting a lack of programming to teach children to cope with life in more abstract terms.

Concretized educational practices are sometimes justified by claims that the students are being offered a world in which they are capable of acting adequately without having to experience continuous challenges, and perhaps failure and frustration. The problem is, though, that by binding the child only to a concrete world and by training him to act—even successfully—within the limits of concrete learning opportunities, not only are we not enhancing the individual's coping capacities, we are often reducing them substantially. Life's realities are *not* only concrete. On the contrary, adaptation requires a continuous activation of abstract thinking. Consequently, the continuous reference to concrete learning may cause the student to be incapacitated in real-life situations, incapable of coping with a constantly changing environment.

The AM approach also makes use of concretization in its educational and teaching practices, but its use is of temporary value only. The ultimate goal of the teaching process is to transcend the world of the concrete, to teach richer and more effective levels of abstract thinking rather than to create an "artificial world" to which the student may easily adapt. The following legend illustrates the differences between the two approaches as they relate to the use of concrete or abstract instructional devices.

Terah, the father of Abraham, was the owner of a shop that sold idols in Ur, the capital of the Chaldeans. One day Terah had to go somewhere, and he asked his son Abraham to look after the shop. After his father left, Abraham took a hammer and smashed all the idols in the shop. He broke them into small pieces, keeping only one of the idols "alive," the biggest one, putting the hammer in his hands. When Terah came back and saw his ruined shop, he asked, "What happened, my son?" Abraham replied, "A woman came in, bringing some offerings to the idols. All of the idols were very hungry, so they started to push each other as they rushed to the food. The biggest idol got angry at the others, took the hammer, and smashed all the rest. Then he ate all the food himself." Terah said to his son Abraham, "What are you talking about? Can these idols eat, do they get hungry, can they move?" Abraham replied, "Listen to what your mouth is saying. If they can't do anything, not even move, why do you consider them as gods and worship them?"

We may conclude that both Terah and his son Abraham used concretization in order to make their points and transmit their ideas. But Terah referred to a concrete world as something that must be continuously present and visible, without which he was unable to orient himself. Abraham, on the other hand, used concretization very powerfully to convey his ideas about the "value" of idols. And, immediately after demonstrating his idea, he transferred to the realm of abstract thinking: "Listen to what your mouth is saying. . . ." After which the means of concretization became completely super-fluous.

Another important AM–PA difference shows up in classroom management and is pertinent to regular classes containing special education children as well as to special education classes that are self-contained. The teacher taking a PA approach will orient his instruction primarily to higher-functioning students, ignoring the needs of those who have difficulties. For those with difficulties the message is "sink or swim." The AM teacher will tend to do more customized teaching, tailoring instruction to each student's capacity and need to become modified.

PA versus AM in Relation to Vocational Training

One of the most important areas of social intervention, especially with individuals having adaptational difficuties, is that of vocational training. The main aims of vocational training are to prepare society's future citizens for an active and autonomous life, to enhance their contribution to their own well-being and to society, and to preclude their becoming a burden on society.

The PA approach, with its inherent low expectancies for persons with disabilities, will set relatively low expectations in the area of vocational training as compared with the AM approach. For example, proponents of the PA approach will often advocate for the early intro-duction of vocational training because they believe that the current level of the individual's functioning fully reflects his future capacities. Thus, academic studies are considered to be not worth the invest-ment in terms of effort and time. Moreover, since individuals with disabilities usually require a longer time to acquire even rudimentary vocational skills, PA advocates will say, "The earlier we get started, the better off the student will be." Such a view may have highly detrimental effects. For not only will scholastic investment, even in the years preceding vocational training, be geared toward the lowest obtainable levels of functioning; vocational training also will be lim-ited to the most rudimentary working skills. After all, the individual is perceived to lack the necessary prerequisites for higher levels of employability if the PA philosophy is accepted.

The AM approach advocates that vocational training be postponed as long as possible, and that special efforts be made to offer the individual with retarded performance ample opportunities to raise his general level of functioning and his scholastic performance. By raising the individual's cognitive levels of functioning via intensive academically oriented teaching we may considerably increase his vocational options. By continuing to invest in the academic/scholastic areas and by delaying the onset of vocational training, or at least carefully meting it out, we may help the individual to increase the level of occupation for which he is eligible. (This point may be strengthened by comparing jobs that require reading skills with those that do not.) The impact that a higher-level job can have upon the self-esteem of the individual makes it worthwhile to invest extended and intensive efforts in academically oriented efforts so as to increase the individual's options.

Another interesting aspect of vocational training relates to the goals set for the individual's working life as an adult. The PA approach tends to carefully protect the individual from job frustration and failure. Consequently, training investments are oriented toward creating sheltered work conditions in which the individual can be accepted and will not need to compete to preserve his working place once he has one.

The AM approach advocates vocational training that directs students toward working conditions in which they will have to be able to compete with others, to assume responsibilities, and to perform complex tasks. More prolonged and intensive investment in the cognitive areas of functioning will help the individual to adapt to more demanding work conditions and to become integrated in more meaningful employment. At the same time, of course, considerable efforts will be devoted to developing social behaviors and work habits that will enhance the individual's adaptation and facilitate social interaction in his employment situation.

Preparing individuals with very retarded performance to do complex and socially desirable vocational skills under nonsheltered conditions has considerable research support.[9-11] The efficiency of such training depends not only upon appropriate goal setting but also on our ability to combine the work skills/habits and academic/cognitive skills required in a normalized vocational setting.

Vocational training based upon the PA approach will emphasize menial tasks such as those demanding little knowledge, even less

TABLE 1. Comparing the Passive Acceptance Approach
with the Active Modification Approach

Passive acceptance	Active modification
A. Early childhood period	
Mother says, "I won't wake him up even though he sleeps so much."	Mother says, "I'm going to wake him up even though he's sleepy, so that he can spend more time with me. We enjoy each other so much and he learns so many things when he is with me."
Father puts toys around room but leaves it to the child to become interested and engaged with them.	Father moves a toy truck within the child's reach, making sound of truck engine and helping child to move it around.
Finding that their child doesn't talk in one-word utterances at 3 years of age, parents put him in a preschool program with children who do not talk either so that their child will not be "frustrated."	Finding that their child doesn't talk in one-word utterances at 3 years of age, parents put him in a preschool with talking children, planning that he will benefit from imitating talking models.
Finding that their child is not toilet-trained at 3 years of age, parents keep child in diaper and put him in preschool where other children also wear diapers and where toilet training is not scheduled routinely.	Finding that their child is not toilet-trained at 3 years of age, parents find a preschool where children are being toilet-trained and where some have learned bladder and bowel control.
"We understand our child's speech. That's good enough."	"*Everyone* needs to understand our child's speech. We won't be satisfied if only we understand it."
B. Elementary school period	
Parents find a school where all other children are handicapped so that their child will be "safe" from possible ridicule by nonhandicapped children.	Parents find a regular school with a special class for their child so that integrated programming can be offered. Nonhandicapped students will be taught how to be friends of children with handicaps, how to interact cooperatively, etc., so as to minimize the likelihood of their acting inappropriately toward a handicapped child. Later, efforts will be made to have the child join as many regular class activities as possible.
Teacher emphasizes only "concrete" learning tasks.	Teacher introduces abstract as well as "concrete" learning tasks.

TABLE 1. (*Continued*)

Passive acceptance	Active modification
B. Elementary school period (*continued*)	
Teacher keeps the pace of instruction uniformly slow.	Teacher speeds up the instructional pace occasionally so as to have handicapped child "stretch" to keep up and improve his own performance.
Teacher avoids academic instruction because it's too frustrating for the handicapped children.	Teacher finds ways to introduce academic instruction to minimize frustration but also to keep the handicapped children moving toward literacy.
C. Secondary school period	
Teacher says that student with a handicap should be taken off any type of academic training and shifted entirely to the prevocational track because the student is 16 years old and "that's the right time for all mentally handicapped people to have vocational training."	Teacher doesn't remove student with a handicap from an academic program as long as the student is motivated in academics and making good progress in them. Teacher will often, however, introduce academics in the context of prevocational training.
Coach involves handicapped students in segregated recreation activities only, such as preparation for Special Olympics.	Coach creates integrated recreation groupings composed of handicapped and nonhandicapped who play cooperatively.
D. Vocational period	
Can't work at a machine (even though he's interested in that type of work) because it's too dangerous (his movement control is erratic).	Can work at a machine if equipment is modified and if cue training signals him that he is in a danger zone of the machine.
E. Independent living period	
Cannot take bus to work because he can't count change.	Investment is made in teaching those behaviors critical for independence, for instance, functional counting and reading, as well as the functional use of transportation.
Is placed in a residential institution for round-the-clock custodial care.	Is placed in a supervised apartment in his community where he will learn to live as independently as possible.

decision-making ability, and virtually no social interaction skills. In all cases, serious efforts should be made to move each person showing retarded performance to higher levels of vocational training and activity. In no case should we give up *a priori* without allowing for a fair chance to succeed.

The AM approach invests in teaching vocational skills that require more autonomous actions and decision-making abilities. Such jobs, being of a more complex nature, may create greater satisfaction and a higher level of self-esteem. This requires a different kind of training, though, one that includes promoting cognitive functioning in an atmosphere of active modification.

The PA versus AM approach can also be recognized by observing the reward and control systems used in vocational settings. A PA approach is usually reflected in systems based upon immediate gratification. This accords with the PA philosophy that immediacy fits the person's general way of functioning. With the supposed difficulties in transcending the "here and now," there will be little referral to self-regulatory systems.

The AM approach tends to use internalized psychological control and reward systems. Considering that an observed level of functioning probably does not reflect the individual's capacities, interventional activities are aimed toward activating "hidden" potential. Therefore, an AM approach limits the use of immediate gratification.

In this regard, the AM approach has found research support. For instance, in a series of studies done with people with retarded performance, it was found that self-activated internal reward systems were more efficient than externally determined reward systems.[12] And, in a recent study,[13] researchers reported high and durable levels of learning when behavioral control systems were self-regulatory.

Table 1, based upon a life task continuum, shows examples of PA and AM practices.

CONDUCTIVE EDUCATION[14]: AN EXAMPLE OF AN EMPHASIS ON AM

In describing active modificational approaches for people with retarded performance, we have always pointed out that modifiability is most accessible in the cognitive area rather than in physical conditions such as those found in cerebral palsy and severe motor disabilities due to brain trauma. In fact, in a paper published in 1970,[15] the senior author admitted the necessity of adhering to a passive acceptance approach in the treatment of certain serious motor and physical disabilities, owing to the severe limitations imposed by these conditions on the possibility and effectiveness of intervention. Obviously, wherever surgery or physiotherapeutic interventions can alleviate the impairing conditions, it is advisable. But to the extent that these interventions did not yield the hoped-for changes, passive-acceptant approaches such as building ramps for a person in a wheelchair were considered not only acceptable but highly desirable (even though it meant that the individual's disability was accepted passively). Indeed, on a worldwide basis, much of what has been done for people who have disabilities has reflected the passive acceptance philosophy. Zahi—to be described—appeared to have all the characteristics one would require in order to adhere to a PA approach.

Zahi was immobilized by poliomyelitis at the age of 1 and for a number of years lived in an iron lung. He was almost totally paralyzed. This situation did not substantially change despite physical therapy, surgery, and other forms of intervention, although eventually he was able to sit in a wheelchair if special postural supports were provided. Cared for by extremely devoted parents, Zahi developed cognitively in a most miraculous way. He finished high school at home with flying colors. And when his ability to sit in a wheelchair deteriorated, he continued university studies from his bed. Even as a child restricted to a limited number of movements, he learned to observe motion and registered it with keen insight. He observed, and then expressed graphically, movements of birds, animals, fish, human beings, and tree branches in the wind. All he had as a means of executing his drawings was a horizontal movement of his hand, restricted to about 15 or 20 degrees, holding the pen or pencil upside down. The boldness and expressiveness of his drawing at the age of 7 exceeded by far what one would expect from a normal or even gifted child of 12. With time, his need to express himself, especially in capturing movements that were inaccessible to him except in a visual way, became his passion, which he fulfilled in a diversity of painting mediums (see Figure 1).

One of the authors involved directly with Zahi considered this artistic accomplishment to be his utmost level of achievement and that his disability needed to be accepted as it was, that is, with full passive acceptance.

This continued to be our attitude until we learned that what we considered as unmodifiable had become the target of a direct attack

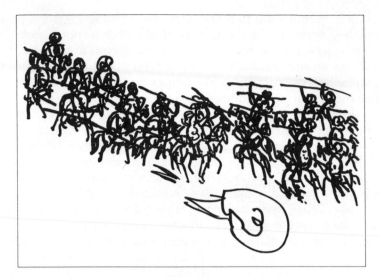

Figure 1. Zahi's drawing.

approach for rendering the individual with severe physical disabilities functionally mobile. This active modificational philosophy
had been advocated and practiced by the late Dr. Petö in Budapest.
His successor, Dr. Maria Hari,[16] who is now the head of the Institute
for Conductive Education in Budapest, carries on this exciting work.
Similar to what we advocate in our active cognitive modificational
approach, conductive education does not accept the physical condition of the individual as setting unsurpassable barriers to functional
change. The fact that certain central neuromuscular conditions are at
the basis of the disability does not, according to the Petö system,
automatically block modifiability. The fact that certain neuromuscular
reflexes are not present or are impaired is not accepted as an immutable condition. Modifiability is considered accessible provided that certain communicational, cognitive, and emotional abilities are present
to enable the child to cooperate. The most important dimension of
this approach is in the all-encompassing emphasis on the use of education and on the devoted instruction and guidance of the child's
teacher, called a conductor because of his special interventional involvement with the child. In turn, the conductor's intervention is
amplified by the group of children in which the conductive education
is operating, enabling the individual child to strive to perform tasks
beyond what his physical condition would seem to dictate.

In contradistinction to other methods, such as those employed by Berta Bobath and the French psychomotor reeducationalists,[17] which placed major emphasis on the affected parts of the body, in the Petö method the isolated function is of little or no interest as a target. Instead, the total functioning of the individual is the target. Another difference in the methods has to do with inhibiting defective patterns of movement by passive therapy. The Petö method mobilizes the child to active movement, using all the senses and creating all-encompassing motor functioning first by external means and then by consolidating it through constant use. In the Bobath method, individual therapy is considered the ideal, while the Petö method emphasizes therapy through the individual's involvement in group activities. In the Bobath method, the therapist takes the lead in treatment as the medical, orthopedic, and physiotherapeutic leader; the educator acts as a consultant at best. In the Petö method, it is the educator, the conductor, who takes the lead position, providing consultation to medical personnel.

The results obtained by the Petö method are remarkable, according to Gur's father. Prior to treatment in Budapest, Gur totally lacked control over his body, requiring that his head and torso be held up with straps in order for him to sit. Within a month after the beginning of therapy in Budapest, Gur was capable of sitting independently, holding his head erect, reaching out for food, and feeding himself with his own hands, behaviors that were previously nonexistent in his motor repertoire. These newly acquired behaviors indicated a wide array of possibilities for further development. The mere fact that Gur proved able to perform these things independently was a "seed" for the greater unfolding of independent behaviors. Other children are brought to functional levels of locomotion, discarding crutches or other supportive devices previously considered indispensable.

The Petö method passed unrecognized for almost 30 years. When "discovered" by the British, it was perceived as an eclectic way to handle children with severe movement problems. An attempted replication of the approach ended with disappointing results. It was then that a young psychologist, Professor Andrew Sutton[18] of Birmingham University, concluded that the replication had been done improperly because its major philosophical and educational orientation was totally misunderstood. Those who had attempted the replication had assimilated the method into other ongoing practices, not understanding that conductive education is a strong departure from more conservative approaches. Indeed, in order to become conductive educators, trainees undergo an intensive training program, eventually acquiring a level of skill that entitles them to be known as "conductors."

In concluding this chapter, we wish to emphasize again that the active-modificational approach is of paramount importance to the development of the individual with retarded performance, for both his present and his future prospects. The contribution of each person to his self-modification is of tremendous value and should be emphasized in all of our interventional endeavors. For all those who resonate positively to the title of our book, *Don't Accept Me as I Am*, we ask that they also adopt the challenge: "Make me a partner in this activity of modifiability. Do it *through* me, and *with* me. Don't do it *for* me."

CHAPTER 3

Structural Cognitive Modifiability
Outrageous Myth or Observed Reality?

The two mothers differed in many respects. Peter's mother made her way to the authors preceded by many letters of appeal since she was well aware that anybody acting on first sight would not become involved with her son, a seemingly hopeless case. A brief examination of the rich file of documents that Peter's mother brought showed many visits to clinics, pediatricians, and psychologists, all of which concluded with few words of hope for her son and even fewer recommendations for action. It is no wonder that the mother prepared herself with letters of appeal—pleas for help—some signed by family friends, some by prominent individuals, including one from a well-known official that sounded almost like a warning (You better help or . . . !).

Anne's mother needed no letters of referral, for two reasons. First, she herself was the wife of a well-known dignitary whose name opened doors everywhere, and second, she did not look for help but rather for advice in her search for a residential, custodial care setting. She did not bring a file to support her demand for advice; she considered her daughter's need for custodial care as self-evident, having concluded that Anne was a severely retarded child with little hope of developing beyond the trainable level. Placement outside the family was considered the only way to solve the problem of the family's inability to cope with the behavioral problems originating from Anne's cognitive deficiency.

The two requests could not have been more different. Peter's mother pleaded for her right to keep her son at home, vowing to do her best in order to promote her child's development. Anne's mother looked for the readiest way for her daughter and the family to separate.

Both mothers seemed extremely caring, but how differently their caring behavior manifested itself. One had only to visit Anne's room in order to sense the love that her mother felt, largely by dispensing pleasure to Anne. From wall to wall, her room was lined with shelves completely covered with a most beautiful selection of toys. Peter's mother chose a different route, making everyday household objects available to her son—pots, pans, and similar items. Anne's mother left her daughter to her toys for most of the time, whereas Peter's mother spent much of her time interacting with her son.

Were the differences between the behaviors of the two mothers dependent on the difference in family conditions and the nature of their respective children? We cannot answer this. If one were looking only at Anne and Peter, one would expect just the reverse relationship to occur. One would expect Anne's mother to behave like Peter's mother and vice versa. Anne looked relatively normal. She was somewhat heavy, with a blunt look and an open mouth, but otherwise without other physical signs that would indicate that she had such a low level of functioning. Anne was born prematurely; her low birth weight and bouts of respiratory distress required prolonged incubator treatment. Her speech, although relatively well articulated and intelligible, was extremely poor in vocabulary, in syntax, and, even more, in terms of content, which was highly stereotyped and repetitive. Her major activity, irrespective of where she found herself, was to push a little toy dog and endlessly emit barking sounds. The dog was selected from the very rich panoply of toys in her room, which for the most part she ignored totally. Her contact with adults was somewhat negative, especially when she was asked to do something. It required a great deal of persuasion to make her follow even a simple instruction, such as drawing a line or saying her name.

On the other hand, Peter's appearance, as well as the difficulties in establishing contact with him, were incomparably more discouraging. Peter had a birdlike face dominated by a large curved nose, large protruding squinting eyes, and a small mouth over a small chin. His hands were large, with elongated fingers. The fingers of his right hand were constantly making weaving motions, the only spontaneous activity noted during the hours of our observation. The rest of his body moved very little. Occasionally, when prompted, he would stand up and move toward the wall or a window and stand there motionless except for the incessant weaving of his fingers.

Peter was almost completely mute. The only sound he produced between long periods of silence was a shrieking cry with very little intonation. Eye contact was almost totally absent, and there was very little readiness to accept, much less respond to, physical contact. Eye contact was not easily elicited, even when his mother attempted to compel him to look at her by taking his head between her hands and imposing her gaze upon him. But what made it most difficult to work with Peter was his condition of passivity, which made interaction almost impossible. Any movement required an outside "trigger" in the form of a movement imposed upon him. Verbal instructions, even with accompanying gestures, were not sufficient. Furthermore, a behavior, once triggered, required continued stimulation in order for it to be maintained.

His condition paralleled very closely the symptom of aboulia (an incapacity to initiate volitional movements) often observed among individuals with central nervous system impairment or catatonic conditions. It was responsible for the despair of one of the authors during assessment; all of his attempts to elicit any response failed totally to penetrate the barrier of passivity and immobility.

How different was the first meeting with Anne. During our first few hours of work, she sat on the floor moving her stuffed animals back and forth while singing her animal-like song. After we had gained her confidence, Anne started to respond to some of our mediational interventions, which attempted to establish very elementary cognitive activities. Drawing a simple line between two dots was a real adventure into an unknown country of behavior. To produce a square was akin to the discovery of the wheel. The most elementary concepts of space—"down," "up," "near," "far," "big," "small"— were not easily understood because of her impoverished language as well as her difficulty in responding to our teaching efforts. But after these concepts were established through mediated interaction, we were able to make her repeat and consolidate these simple and yet important components in her behavior. What happened in the next 20 hours of work, spread over several days, seemed like a miracle. Anne leaped over many obstacles, first acquiring the capacity and the readiness to focus on a task and then acquiring the ability to match and distinguish between different figures. Her impulsivity was not due to hyperactivity (which had been one of the many claims made in order to explain her limitations) but was an expression of her limited knowledge of what is needed in order to solve as simple a problem as connecting two dots. But once she acquired these very basic skills, solving more complex problems became accessible to her, although she required continuous mediation in the form of teaching carried to the point of overlearning.

This produced in the examiner an increased readiness to invest time and effort in fostering Anne's capabilities. This was not the case with Peter. After a few hours of frustrating attempts to make him function, the examiner used up his entire repertoire of strategies to make Peter look in a requested direction, or fulfill an instruction as simple as to roll a piece of Plasticine with his left hand, or to continue to do alone what was at first performed with the hand of the examiner guiding his left hand. The examiner could not refrain from expressing to Peter's mother his despair and feeling of helplessness in attempting to mediate Peter's learning.

Anne's mother, on the other hand, reacted to the good news concerning her daughter's relatively high potential for change with what appeared to be almost discontent. It appeared as if the fact that Anne was given some hope for future cognitive modification not only was unexpected but created mixed feelings about its desirability. Following their decision to place Anne outside the family context, her parents had planned a long series of trips, and this suggestion seemed to be highly incongruent with these plans.

From the very beginning, the pessimistic assessment of pediatricians and psychologists, who diagnosed Anne as a developmentally high-risk child, made it difficult for her adoptive mother and father to become identified with their role as parents. Despairing of their small chance to have a biological child, and because of their sincere compassion for Anne, they suffered with her through every developmental challenge. This turned the relationship into one of mutual overdependency, with the mother showing that, in all possible ways, she accepted Anne as she was since her condition was considered as being immutable. Thereupon, choosing a passive-acceptant approach, she planned that everything would be done to make her daughter's life comfortable and pleasant, sheltered from any stress and competitive pressure. A great deal of ingenuity was used to create this protected environment. For instance, the mother used an oversimplified form of English that served to "insulate" Anne from the learning existent in an unshielded environment.

The years of delayed development in all areas—coupled with the interpretation of psychologists and educators who defined the central nervous system origin of Anne's problems, emphasizing that there was little if any potential to change—reinforced the parents' passive-acceptant approach. Still they were motivated to do their utmost to make her feel good about them and about herself. Very little was demanded of her and very little was denied her. Anne continued to play with her few toy animals, clinging to them as if they were the only sign of her identity.

No wonder that Anne's parents were somewhat shocked and confused when, following 20 to 25 hours of dynamic assessment with the learning potential assessment device (LPAD) (a dynamic, interactive, assess-mediate-assess approach, described in Chapter 11), the examiner expressed his firm belief that Anne could and should be educated toward an independent life. The mother did not know whether to cry, laugh, or just be angry. She quoted again the report from the pediatrician and the psychologist who had recommended custodial placement.

The reaction of Peter's mother to the subtle, and not so subtle, signs of the author's despair was radically different from that of Anne's mother. She openly declared her disappointment. "If you, known as the most optimistic of men, do not believe that something can be done for my son, then to whom should I turn?" Indeed, Peter's mother had hopes that appeared to all except her to be totally unfounded. She declared her belief repeatedly that much could be done, reiterating her firm decision to drastically modify Peter's functioning, his quality of life, and his prospects for independence. Hearing her speak about Peter, one could see that she had hoped that her son would become normal, even above average, and have the prospect of marrying and becoming a father. Even though Peter's mother made such projections guardedly, she pursued them with the kind of persistence that was regarded as totally unrealistic by social workers, psychologists, and teachers who were involved in her son's assessment. The pattern of confrontation had been consistent: Peter had changed schools many times, the major reason being that his mother would not accept that he be considered and treated as severely, and even profoundly, retarded (as he was classified many times). Each time a teacher related to him as a mentally retarded child, his mother would take him out of school. At the time of referral to the institute, Peter had been at home for about two years, having been taken out of school by his mother, who refused to place him in the special school for children classified as below the level of trainable, as had been recommended.

It is entirely understandable that Peter's mother, after having seen the agonizing failure of the author to make her son respond, could control her emotions no longer. She stood up and declared firmly, "You will teach me and I will do it! You will see I will do it! Peter will learn; he will read; he will write; my boy will *not* be an idiot!" Whoever saw Peter at that time—mute, autistic, immobile, unapproachable—would have considered custodial care to be a fully legitimate option and the mother's struggle as totally unrealistic and, indeed, extreme.

Well, the two, Anne and Peter, have developed mentally and socially far beyond what was expected even in the most rosy dreams of the author and the parents. Anne is now a noncertified nurse, a position she has held for the last 15 years. She is happily married to a normal-functioning man, has two capable children, and has established a wonderful relationship with her parents. Peter, much younger than Anne, has learned to read and write by using the computer. He still has a very long way to go, considering that he is still mute and has serious disabilities. But today, at the age of 22, disbelief in his cognitive modifiability is gone, making room for a much more optimistic outlook, and a great readiness to invest in teaching him.

This brief account of two dramatically changed destinies brings strong, albeit anecdotal, evidence to bear on the modifiability of individuals. What great changes! Changes in Anne's and Peter's cognitive structures are marked by an opening of new functional and behavioral vistas that may bring their developmental levels to even greater heights. Movement from Peter's total communicative isolation to an ability to express himself and involve himself in relationships and finally to a new ability to enjoy life is surely cause for optimism about his future. And Anne's expanded abilities have added richness and diversity to her life. The author himself experienced this tremendous change in Anne under sad circumstances. When the author attended the burial of his nephew, who fell in the Yom Kippur war, Anne, by then in the army, was among the flower attendants and in that role presented her condolences to the mourning family.

As she came toward him, the author hesitated, unable to believe that it was Anne. But she stepped toward the author with an expression of deep emotional empathy and words of encouragement. Both the author and Anne were deeply moved by the changed roles, from one who was being supported and comforted to one bringing comfort and support. Her official role filled her with a feeling of pride in being able to return, even though on such a sad occasion, something of what had been offered to her throughout many years.

Another case in point is Ruth, who has Down syndrome (a chromosomal disorder sometimes referred to incorrectly as "mongolism"). Ruth spent her days (actually years) dozing in front of the TV, her sole contact with "reality." She was completely illiterate and was diagnosed as severely retarded. No functional comprehension was considered possible for her. Indeed, for a long period Ruth resisted all attempts to modify certain aspects of her functioning. She insisted on traveling accompanied by her mother. She strongly resisted the idea of trying to learn to read. Each new task became a subject of negotiation that had to be faced prior to starting work. It was only after repeated mediated exposure to small successes that we started to see positive changes in her feeling about herself as a competent person.

After three years of intervention at the institute, her life became drastically different; she learned to read, write, travel by herself (buying her own ticket and sundries, which she liked to do), and even choose gifts for her mother. Her reading fluency and comprehension became so good that she became an avid reader. She gave up dozing in front of the TV in favor of learning to knit, cook, and perform many housekeeping chores. She started to work as an assistant in a kindergarten, where she was able to capitalize on the many books she read and her ability to tell stories to the children, who listened to her with great interest. Each evening, after work, she attended class. Upon the death of her father, Ruth, then 18 years old, became the source of emotional support and comfort for her mother. In fact, in some respects, she has become her mother's teacher since she is more competent in Hebrew than is her mother. For this reason, the author decided not to carry out his initial plan to place Ruth in an apartment with several peers in order to foster her independence. Instead, now that she has become a cognitively functioning individual, she provides very important emotional support to her mother.

Ruth has become a proficient individual, able to converse fluently on topics such as literature and art, citing the many books she has read. She does not hesitate to do things she previously considered inaccessible. She has opened herself up to a variety of learning opportunities and is active in pursuing them.

Cognitive development is not to be perceived as a luxury—gratuitous and of limited functional value—as seems to be the case in many of the programs offered to individuals with retarded performance. Many of these programs seem designed primarily to provide the individual with a good feeling about himself while giving up completely on teaching communication skills and literacy. Some of these programs emphasize music, dance, and other "muse"-like activities as the main focus of their curriculum, sometimes at the expense of promoting cognitive functioning. Thus, many children with retarded performance are taught to play the piano a bit or paint a little after many years of investment, but their mental functioning is not considered suitable for active modification. We do not object to introducing some "muse"-type activities for children with retarded performance. However, we would like to see much more investment made in programs that emphasize and modify cognitive abilities. Many cognitive deficits can be corrected, making a pronounced difference in the quality of life of the individual.

That such changes can be produced is well documented. What is unusual about the few cases described here, however, is their severity. At the time of referral, Anne, Peter, and Ruth were functioning in the range of severe retardation. Peter was once labeled as profoundly retarded.

The message we are trying to convey, and that these cases illustrate, is that people with retarded performance are much more modifiable than professionals and others ordinarily tend to believe. Nevertheless, whenever those who do not believe in the modifiability of the human being are confronted with changes like those described here, they almost always decide that the initial situation was just not as bad as had been thought. Those who do not believe in modifiability are ready to claim that the psychologist or pediatrician had misdiagnosed the cases. According to them, "Anne and Peter were not really seriously retarded, and Ruth was probably among those persons with Down syndrome who are just late bloomers." One such remark was offered when one of the authors described the outcome of a cognitive modificational program referred to as "the treatment group technique"[1-3] to an audience of professionals. At the end of the author's presentation, the leader of the group stood up and said,

"Either the children you describe were not as badly off as you describe them or their present condition is not as good as you tend to
perceive." This remark reflects the resistance to believe in the modifiability of the human being, a disbelief that is often strong enough to
defy even the clearest and strongest evidence.

By understanding the experiences of Anne, Peter, and Ruth, we
can appreciate how children with comparatively less severe conditions can be helped to change. The universality of cognitive modifiability as a unique human phenomenon is apparent when we consider the large number of people with retarded performance who
overcome the "retarded" label placed on them during childhood by a
school system that may have subjected them to watered-down educational programs. They frequently disappear from the "register" of the
mentally retarded upon reaching adulthood. Indeed, as adults many
of them function satisfactorily and, in some cases, much above what
was considered possible. However, not all of them prove able to
overcome the injuries imposed upon them by a restrictive education.
We ask: How much more would those who "made it" have achieved
if educators had joined them in setting higher life goals instead of
permitting them to accept a limited future?

Michael was 12 years old when he, together with many other
children living in an orphanage in India, was referred to a youth
group (Youth Aliyah) for immigration to Israel. For nearly all of his 12
years, he had lived in an orphanage after both his parents died. He
had no known relatives.

The conditions of solitude and emotional deprivation in which
Michael lived were pathetic. An underdeveloped child with small,
sad eyes dominating a small, dark face, he was illiterate, completely
without functional school skills, and disoriented in time and space. In
addition, his impoverished thought processes and vocabulary did not
allow him to comprehend his poor condition. When examined,
Michael showed a level of intellectual functioning typical of a 5- to 6-
year-old nonhandicapped child. Despite his desire to cooperate, he
was unable to respond to very simple tasks or questions, even when
they were presented concretely. For instance, he manifested great
difficulties in separating two rings by adjusting the indentation in one
ring to the opened part in the second ring. He tried endlessly, in a
perseverative way, to pull the ring through the thinner opening. He
could not put together the two sources of information available to
him, that is, could not relate the indentation in the one ring and the

width of the opening in the other. (This is a test of practical intelligence applied by one of the authors during his research with professor André Rey.[4,5])

Many of these deficiencies proved to be correctable once our staff began to show him how to look at the characteristics of objects, how to label the object at which he was looking, and how to make comparisons. He eventually showed such a good capacity to learn that we recommended him for immigration to Israel even though we knew that a very large educational investment would be required in order to capitalize on the modifiability observed during our assessment. Sadly, Michael was found to suffer from tuberculosis, which required preventive treatment. This delayed his immigration by a year, so that when he arrived in Israel he was 13 years old and very far behind in even the most basic schooling skills. Nevertheless, the author was able to place Michael in a regular Youth Village and established an intensive enrichment program to help him to progress rapidly.

Michael proved to interact well socially. He established friendships easily and knew how to turn them into long-term relationships, a characteristic not often found among emotionally deprived children. He also made good progress in prevocational training, although his reading ability remained at a very low level. (By the age of 15 he had barely mastered the most basic of reading functions.) When he reached the age of 17, Michael had to leave the Youth Village school and attend a vocational high school. However, his deficiency in academic skills made it very difficult to place him in an appropriate program, as we customarily did with many others in his condition. All of these children, like Michael, were monitored by a psychologist concerned with their development and welfare. The author was particularly interested in Michael, who had come to consider him as his foster father. The director of a very good high school specializing in horticulture was persuaded by the author to accept Michael and to offer him the help necessary to acquire a vocational diploma, which would allow him to work and become self-sufficient. Two days after placement, Michael said, "You know that I have no one to rely upon for help but you and Youth Aliyah. Do you really believe that I will make it in this school; and if I make it will I be able to support myself from this work?" It was the first time that the author had heard a direct question from this usually timid and seemingly helpless child. The author reassured him, pointing out the great progress he had already made, and promising continued support.

Despite his diligence, Michael had to repeat a year of school in order to consolidate what he had learned. Since then he has continued to develop emotionally and intellectually. After the two-year course in horticulture, he worked as a gardener's assistant. Later, he became a gardener for a wealthy family but then decided that he preferred work involving more person-to-person interaction. He even had aspirations of teaching children what he knew about horticulture. Michael recognized that he had received a good deal of special tutoring and wanted to reciprocate by supporting children who, like himself, were in need of special attention.

Although Michael's aspirations may have seemed dreamlike, his real life was fulfilling and showed that he was the master of much of it. He did indeed become a teacher at the school where he had previously been a student. It seemed paradoxical that Michael, the formerly illiterate, unschooled child, had become a responsible adult with the capability of passing on his knowledge of horticulture to others. Michael amazed all who knew him by becoming one of the best known specialists in plant breeding, winning recognition within his profession for the cultivation of flowers. After marrying (the author and his wife "stood up" at the wedding), Michael went on to further study and became qualified as a landscape architect. Settling down, he helped build a house for his wife and their three children, and took a leading role in the community.

What would have been the consequences if we had accepted Michael's low intellectual ability as immutable? The dullness and apathy he displayed were striking in those early years. The author's wife commented frequently on how little interest Michael showed in the variety of objects, books, and events he saw in the author's home. He never asked a question, never made comments, and answered questions only in an obtuse way.

How different Michael became! In the last few years, during his visits to our home, he brought news about the arts, science, and books—more than the author was ever able to follow. He became a highly cultured individual, knowledgeable about current events, full of readiness to help others, and a pleasure to talk with.

A follow-up of hundreds of children like Michael whom we examined during the early 1950s showed him to be representative of a large group of children who had been diagnosed as low-functioning, and who subsequently achieved relatively high levels of accomplishment. A sizable number even became involved in teaching and other helping professions. Among them were many who, like Michael, had very low prospects owing to little or no education, cultural deprivation, socioeconomic disadvantage, or membership in an oppressed minority.

It is interesting to note that Michael functioned as a moderately retarded child at the age of 15, an age considered by some developmental psychologists and behavioral scientists as "beyond hope." Some of them believe that effective intervention at that age is impossible since the development of intelligence and other traits of human personality is supposed to be limited largely to the first few years of life. As a result, disadvantaged, low-functioning adolescents and young adults have typically been offered very few opportunities for academic development. Instead they receive training in some menial, repetitious tasks, neglecting the development of the capacity to adapt to the ever-changing conditions of life. Even when they are temporarily functioning with the limited training given them, the first obstacle they encounter throws them off track. Each "wave" sweeps them away!

The pessimistic view about the effects of intervening later in life is frequently referred to as the "critical periods" hypothesis. Belief in this hypothesis has prevented many educators from providing intervention programs for large numbers of adolescents and young adults on the assumption that it is "too late" for them since they are beyond the so-called critical period of development. The thousands of files accumulated in the archives of Youth Aliyah and the institute, and the data we have gathered on the adaptation of these children 30 and more years after their initial assessment, demonstrate the pervasiveness of the modifiability of human beings at *all* ages. Indeed, the positive outcome obtained with older people with retarded performance is the ultimate rebuttal to those who are the "captives of their 'scientific' beliefs." Nevertheless, many persist in considering cases such as those described in this book as merely exceptional and therefore irrelevant to the issue of modifiability despite the strength of evidence presented. They seek only to affirm the "rules" of the immutability of intelligence, which forms the basis of the passive-acceptant approach described in the previous chapter.

The range of conditions described as modifiable points to one of the most characteristic and recurring changes produced in individuals such as Anne, Peter, Ruth, and Michael. In fact, these four individuals developed so far beyond anyone's expectations as to be barely recognizable after intervention had stopped. With mediated intervention they continued to develop in directions very different from earlier predictions. Thus, Ruth's level of functioning was expected to deteriorate considerably with age. (The IQ of many low-functioning individuals does often decline with age, probably as a result of the passive acceptance of the "inevitability" of decline.) The biological view of mental retardation regards this decline as a direct and inevitable outcome of the neurochemical characteristics of the retarded individual's central nervous system. Others, including ourselves, emphasize the importance of the individual's interactions with his environment, particularly with adults who mediate his learning, in affecting the quality of his mental functioning. We contend that the cases presented here support this emphasis. Not only did Michael and the others not regress as predicted by the "prescriptions" written in the textbooks and case files, they continued, and still continue, to grow and to develop new cognitive structures, diversifying their abilities into areas very different from those they were involved with before the intervention ceased.

When asked how far Michael will be able to go, the author is really at a loss to answer, and very happily so. He cannot predict because he knows with great certainty that Michael can develop new types of thinking and move in directions totally different from those he was traveling toward before.

Or take James. James was labeled and treated by all who knew him as a mentally retarded individual with a charming appearance and good social and emotional intactness, but whose functioning denoted a lack of comprehension of the most elementary relationships necessary for daily living. He had no concept of time. It was very difficult to help him organize his daily life. He would take meals at odd times, and any attempt to make him plan ahead, even for a short term, was met with a total lack of comprehension. Anything outside of his immediate visual perception was beyond his understanding. Indeed, the general picture was of a perpetually smiling but nonfunctioning boy. Then came one of the greatest experiences the author ever had, one that made him really understand the meaning of the passage from concrete thought to its symbolic substitutes. James had extreme difficulty in learning to read. For two years all attempts to teach him were in vain. His greatest difficulty was in his inability to master object–symbol correspondence, as is necessary in learning to read. Among several words, *table* (in Hebrew, *shulhan*) was one of the first words he encountered. We repeated the word a few times, and suddenly he stopped, pointed to the long table we were sitting near, pointed to the word *table* and to the actual table, and with an astounded expression on his face said in excitement, "What? Such a big table in such a small word?" To us this excitement represented his discovery of the written word as one of the substitutes for reality, that is, traces, symbols, and signs of which speech and the written word are a part. It took another year until James reached a relative level of efficiency in reading that enabled him to participate in school.

Against the background of such a low level of functioning, we considered it a very meaningful achievement that James became a skilled laborer in a body shop. When he finished his army service, he married, had children, and led a very comfortable life. We assumed that he had reached his peak level of achievement. Years went by and we had little contact with him. Then, recently, the author received a call from James. He said that he was speaking from his car and was concerned that he would soon be leaving the area within range of his telephone. The author was astonished. He had a phone in his car? He, James! (In Israel, having a phone in one's car is a luxury of the very elite and wealthy.) When we met he recounted the events involved in his marvelous transformation. He was now the director of a very large export company that handled the production, packaging, and distribution of food. James, who hadn't been able to plan the execution of three simple consecutive instructions, had become a highly skilled director of a large manufacturing program. In fact, when he showed the author some flow charts he had prepared for a new plant he was involved in establishing, he used terminology that was like a completely foreign language.

Despite the author's usual optimism, he must have appeared somewhat skeptical about James's achievements. But James supported his claims with solid evidence. The author even entertained a suspicion that some "nepotistic" maneuvers had brought James up to the top of the ladder. But no, he described his ascent as a slow process that started with a job as a truck driver, then moving on to become the personal chauffeur for one of the managers. This position gave him opportunities to learn about the business. Through careful listening, observing, questioning, and summarizing, James prepared himself for the future. All of this led to his eventually taking over a few managerial jobs, which, once successfully performed, opened the way to his becoming the overall manager.

His success story is important if only for its indication of how unexpected changes in areas such as planning, organizational leadership, and assertiveness can be achieved when all were previously out of reach. However, it was James's reason for visiting the author on short notice that revealed the most surprising change of all. James said that he was seeking advice on what can be referred to as an "existential crisis." "I feel I achieved the impossible. I raised myself to a high level of success, financially, occupationally, socially. I am well off. I have made many trips abroad both for business and for pleasure. I have a nice family with beautiful children who are also successful. But I feel I have not done what I would like to do most and that is to develop myself, to learn things I have never learned and become what I feel I could be."

James expressed in his words the longing for "being" as compared with the craving for "having," "becoming" as opposed to "receiving," seeking a higher form of existence. To see James, who had been so unimposing and inarticulate, now inspired by such a profound goal was a stirring experience for the author. Predicting a person's potential is a difficult task!

How far can James go? Who knows the ways of the human spirit and who can predict the extent of its development? His story illustrates more than anything the structural nature of change. The modifiability that started during adolescence and continued throughout James's life brought him to accomplishments far beyond those expected by most people who had observed him during childhood. The quality of life and the very nature of existence have taken on different forms in all respects for James. He has raised himself to the level of an abstract thinker, planning and setting important, long-range goals. The dull, obsequious, and unassuming person has become a competent, creative, and assertive adult.

The structural nature of human modifiability is best illustrated by the generalizability of a change, which, when produced in one area, tends to significantly affect other areas of the individual's functioning. Modifiability is also recognizable by the fact that the rhythm and amplitude of the change itself undergo important transformations. Thus, a change that required a very strong effort and a long-term investment initially is transformed in regard to the rapidity, quality, and ease with which it is produced, and "multiplies" itself at later stages. Think of how much more rapidly a child can learn complex rhymes once he has mastered the first ones. The change in the rapidity and skill with which the child learns, and the quality of his learning, demonstrate that the individual has changed in a structural way. The type of structural cognitive change we are seeking to produce is one that cannot be explained in terms of small increments in rate or precision but by change that appears to have "jumped the tracks," one that represents a radical transformation or a creative and productive synergism of thought. Indeed, the modifiability that James underwent brought him far beyond the goals at which the intervention was originally aimed.

Many of the usual educational practices for people with learning problems are limited to the act of dispensing information aimed toward the acquisition of modest goals by a process of overlearning. Far too little investment is offered for development of the learning-to-learn ability. In this regard, how much time and effort do we devote to our interaction with children with learning problems, guiding them in how to gather the information they need in order to solve a problem? How much do we instruct them in how to organize information so that they will be able to become, not just reproducers of information, but generators of new information, creative organizers and skillful modifiers of their environment? Unhappily, usually very little is done to foster such functions in individuals with retarded performance. While the effects of this lack of effort are not felt immediately, they become visible when the individual confronts conditions requiring adaptation. Lack of an educational investment in mediated learning experience (see Chapter 5), which would enable them to change in a structural way, will jeopardize their prospects for benefiting from whatever opportunities life offers. The passive-acceptant approach, as appealing and humane as it sometimes appears, orients individuals to a "dead end" in their development, demanding only that the environment, not they, be changed in order to render them more comfortable. In many instances, comfort now may mean discomfort later; a heavy price is paid by the child who is given comfort at the expense of his or her development.

This leads us to a very difficult question, one probably asked already by the reader: How were the described changes produced? How did Peter's mother succeed in doing what the author acting as an expert could not? How did she achieve what teachers and specialists constantly denied she would ever be able to attain? And Anne, who was offered so much in terms of therapy and remediation, what made her suddenly depart from her restricted course of development, emerging as a self-sufficient individual? An equally profound question is: What is it that makes human beings so malleable? How do we explain it? What is it in the human genes, in the human condition, in the person-to-person environment, that makes it possible for a person who functions at a low level of performance to change dramatically, reaching the opposite pole of the expected destiny?

That these are perfectly legitimate questions is clearly evident by the abundant skepticism that often greets the statement about such modifiability.[6,7] The chapters that follow will attempt to answer these questions and, at the same time, deal with the skepticism through showing evidence to back up our belief in structural cognitive modifiability.

The Influence of Mediated Learning

Adam wanders around in the large hall of a science museum. He runs from one exhibit to another, touches, pulls, looks, and runs again. His mother has long since stopped running after him. She hears his loud exclamations and is pleased to see her son busy with the rich and beautiful world displayed in front of him. Once or twice she attempts to explain to Adam how the ring turns above the magnet, but he is much more interested in making something happen than in understanding how it happens. The things he sees and experiences are stimulating. As long as he enjoys it, isn't that enough? The author didn't need much time observing in order to answer with a loud "No!" It is *not* enough to have a child exposed to a rich world of forms, colors, and movements, titillating himself through superficial interactions with them. The author approached Adam and began following him from exhibit to exhibit, observing his activity. He quickly realized that Adam's interaction with the exhibits was limited to sheer physical activity, leaving his thinking functions inactive.

As the author looked at Adam's "busybody" type of activity, it became clear that he learned very little from his encounter with the exhibits despite the fact that he behaved as if he were cognitively active and highly stimulated. When the author observed more closely, he saw that Adam paid attention only for a moment while pushing the button of one of the exhibits. His gaze rested only briefly on the button, and as soon as his hand reached out to it his eyes wandered to another exhibit. The author observed Adam as he turned the cranks of an exhibit that demonstrated the interaction of two connected vessels of water. He certainly didn't discern that the result of his cranking action was to raise the level of water in one of the containers but not in the other. As Adam ran around hectically touching things, he learned very little from his interaction with the displays. Consequently, for Adam, each time he did something it was as if it were the "first" time that he did it, acting as if all the moving objects were there to be touched, pulled, pushed, and beat upon, but nothing more.

Adam's mother hoped that her son would be affected by the experience at the museum, that through direct interaction with the exhibits he would learn the rules of cause and effect and other characteristics of the display. However, more is needed to learn these concepts than looking, turning, and running. Understanding requires the ability to compare two successive acts, such as turning the crank and perceiving that, as a result, the water level lowers. But what if Adam does not pay attention to what is happening? ("Which one of the cranks did I turn?"), then he does not learn about the relation between the original action and its result; not then; perhaps never.

As the author observed Adam's obvious enjoyment, he asked himself if one should interfere with the pleasure Adam derived from his activity or expect more of it than sheer enjoyment. Should we insist that Adam perceive, repeat, compare? Don't we remove his charming spontaneity by imposing an artificial condition of learning? Don't we take away the experience of discovery by interfering, by interposing ourselves between Adam and the observed world of stimuli? Indeed, certain educators have for many years held the view that such an imposition is not only unnecessary but undesirable and even noxious to the personality of the child, to his independence and his sense of freedom. A specialist in the training and certification of child care providers is quoted in a recent magazine article[1]: "A baby never needs to do any more than it can do because nature does a perfect job. . . . Carers should not assume they know better what the child should be playing with or how the child should be sitting or standing. Rather, they should allow the infant freedom to explore his surroundings with minimal intervention from adults." There are hints of Rousseau-type thinking in the belief that nature does a perfect job and that if adults try to teach a child something, they may only succeed in "messing him up." This approach, and others similar to it, assumes that direct exposure to stimuli without providing any mediated learning from an intentioned caregiver will lead to adequate cognitive behavior as a product of development and growth. We question the rationale for a "hands-off" approach in light of what we consider the way by which children develop the repertoire of behaviors that constitute intelligence.

But let us go back to Adam. From time to time, tired of his expeditions, Adam returned to his mother, seeking physical contact. She gave him a big smile and a warm hug, and asked him how he liked what he saw and what he did. Adam answered with a flow of superlatives. "I like it very much; it's great." His mother asked if he would like to see it again. "Yessssssss" was his answer.

However, no attempt was apparent in the mother–child interaction to elicit a more differentiated account as to *what* he had seen, the *reasons* for his interest, the *rule* that governs the flow of water from one container to the other. As Adam responded enthusiastically to the questions on how he felt about the museum, he accompanied his exclamatory remarks with noises and hand movements describing some of the startling and more conspicuous things he had seen. In particular, the movements of the pistons of a locomotive fascinated him. Although Adam described the movements of the pistons with repetitive, broad, pushing gestures, he did not go beyond the expression of his pleasure. He did not ask, "What makes a piston move?" "How does it happen?" "What is it for?" Nor did Adam's mother ask him these questions. She accepted the child's responses as they were. At first, observing the mother and the child separately, the author thought that their behavior might be a function of Adam's young age. Adam looked to be about 9 to 10 years old. He appeared able to read at least some of the signs of the exhibits, but he made little use of his ability.

Is Adam's minimal attention span and erratic behavior a manifestation of hyperactivity due perhaps to some minor brain damage? Or is it due to the nature of the objects of the museum, their novelty and diversity competing for Adam's attention? He appears to be unable to decide which exhibit warrants his attention and is torn away by each of them, looking at all of them rather than selecting one for focused attention. What enables a child to prioritize and select an object from a multitude of objects? And where does such a priority come from in the first place?

To begin to answer these questions, let us consider Youval, whom the author also followed and observed at the exhibits in the same environmentally rich science museum. Youval was somewhat younger than Adam and was accompanied by his sister, Ada, and by his mother, who carried a 12-month-old child.

The group proceeded from exhibit to exhibit in a way very different from that of Adam and his mother. Compared with Adam, who moved around like a butterfly, flitting unpredictably from object to object, Youval and his family moved along in a highly organized manner. The purposeful, directed nature of their route was clearly recognizable by Youval's pointing fingers and by his sister's signaling where to proceed, and which exhibit they would choose for in-depth scrutiny. Once they decided where to spend their time, a whole process of cooperation and sharing activity dominated their interaction with the exhibit. The family stopped before one exhibit that previously had caught their attention. The sign above the exhibit invited them to make a very large air bubble in a big bowl of liquid soap. Youval and Ada were obviously excited. They worked cooperatively, one raising a sheet of soap while the other blew the bubble in the sheet. Their mother stood by, guiding each one as to where to blow and how to regulate the flow of air. She put the children in front of her and, by protruding her mouth, demonstrated how to control the flow of air. She did her best to make both succeed, discreetly helping Ada (younger than her brother) more than Youval. She interpreted their success to each one of them as a sign of their competency and also as the result of their cooperation. Sharing was emphasized while competition was discouraged. When they arrived at the interconnected water vessels exhibit (see Figure 2) (the same one that interested Adam), the mother knelt down. Ada, guided by her mother, went to the left part of the apparatus, Youval to the right. What followed was a beautifully orchestrated interaction. It began with the mother's drawing the children's attention to the level of the colored water in each of the receptacles. Next, Ada turned the crank on the left, producing a lowering of the water level on the right, and then Youval turned the right crank, lowering the water level on the left. Their mother pointed out the changes produced in each receptacle and suggested that they let the crank rest, asking both children to think about what would happen once they let the crank return to its resting place. It was obvious that the mother was mediating to them an anticipatory mental operation. The children were both somewhat puzzled and did not answer immediately. The mother waited a while and then prompted them, "Think please." Youval thought the water

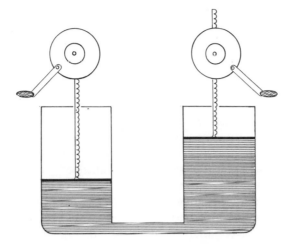

Figure 2. Interconnected water vessels exhibit.

would flow to his side for a reason he couldn't fathom. (Ada continued to look at each one of the receptacles hoping to see something happen.) The mother then asked, "Remember how the water level looked before you started to turn the crank?" Both children now recognized the answer; the water would return to where it was before they turned either of the cranks. Even the baby looked down from his position on her mother's back and followed the pointing fingers.

What was the mother's interaction meant to do? What was her intention in intervening the way she did? Was it accidental? It is impossible to know the thoughts of this mother, of course, but by observing the way she interacted with her children, the author concluded that she acted intentionally. She wanted her children to discover the workings of the interconnected vessels, but she understood that in order to make this happen she had to create the necessary perceptual and cognitive conditions. She drew her children's attention to the cranks, the nature of the vessels, the level of the water in each, and—describing all systematically—she became the means by which her children understood the workings of the exhibit's mechanisms. The change produced by Ada as she turned the crank was followed by a change by Youval. The mother then attracted the attention of both children to the changes produced consecutively by each of them. She had them recall the level of the water as it was before they turned their cranks and then asked for an anticipatory response: "What will happen if the movement is stopped?" As the children hesitated in their response, the mother didn't "jump in" with the ready-made solution, as some parents would be tempted to do. Rather, she gave them time to think. When she felt that there was need for some help, she suggested to both children that they compare the present level of the water with the initial one—helping them bring together the two sources of information necessary in order to discover the concept behind what they saw.

How different was the quality of the interaction between the children and their environment in the two cases of Adam and Youval? Did Youval perceive more than Adam? In sheer sensory terms, probably not. Did Adam manipulate less? Certainly not; Adam was much more active than Youval and in the same span of time covered more ground. But, since no one restrained Adam from surrendering both to the attraction of each exhibit and to his need to experience novel things, his experience was superficial. His pushing and pulling did not require that he take the time or the effort to look at what happened in the exhibit, and therefore he did not understand the relation between what he did and what happened. The benefit Adam derived from his interaction with the exhibits was limited to the immediate gratification derived from his activity. In contrast, Youval learned *how* to look, *where* to look, and *how* to gather data that would lead him beyond the sheer registration of facts, toward the interpretation of their causes. Confronted with new tasks of a different nature, Youval will probably continue to observe carefully, compare, reason, and search for meanings, and therefore learn more and become more affected by his experiences.

Adam, having had superficial experiences, runs the risk of deriving little intellectual benefit from future exposures to educational opportunities. Very little of what he has experienced has prepared him for a better understanding of life's deeper challenges and pleasures.

What makes the two children function so differently when exposed to the same types of stimuli? We contend that the difference lies in the nature of their experience: Mediated Learning Experience for Youval versus direct, nonmediated exposure alone for Adam.

Adam is exposed to stimuli (S). He responds (R) in ways that the stimuli allow and/or even call for. Some learning specialists consider this exposure, and the resultant response of the child, to be a sufficient condition for many areas of the child's cognitive development. Thus, chains of stimulation events and responses are considered by some scientists as the source of learning, especially when the child's behavior has resulted in particular effects. The child, considering the results of his behavior, establishes a relation between S and R, which then becomes the source of reinforced behavior. This can happen in the direction of either avoiding the repetition of a behavior if its effects prove to be undesirable or repeating a behavior if its effects prove to be desirable. Under this model of learning, singular behaviors eventually become a part of the repertoire of the individual. But the question is, does it really happen this way? After repeated interactions with the exhibits, Adam was unable to point to the crank that made the mechanism run one way or the other, or even the one that made it go or stop. The reason for his inability occurred because when he turned the crank he looked at neither *where* it was nor *how* it compared with the second crank, or *what* happened *when* one was turned but not the other. Repetitive manipulation without *thinking* and *understanding* did not result in a learning experience. Each time Adam approached the machine he had to find out anew which crank caused what response by trying and erring, again and again. Similar to the fox in Aesop's fable, Adam came out of the vineyard as lean as he went in.

Don't we regularly witness such "flitting" behaviors with children and adults who exhibit retarded performance? How many teachers are puzzled by certain children's inability to become affected by the learning processes to which they are exposed? Some children with retarded performance seem to repeat the same errors and show the same incapacity for learning even after having been exposed to cause-and-effect conditions numerous times. As Adam illustrates, the ingredients necessary to turn an experience into a source of learning are found in prompting the individual to label, compare, group, categorize, and give meaning to the present experience as it relates to former ones. This active way of experiencing the world is the product of a second form of interaction, which we refer to as mediated learning experience (MLE) (see Figure 3).

In a mediated learning experience, the organism (O) exposed directly to stimuli (S) receives and responds (R) competently and fully to them only after features have been selected, framed, modified, by the adult human (H) mediator. In MLE, things to be learned are subjected to an order imposed by the adult mediator, who assures

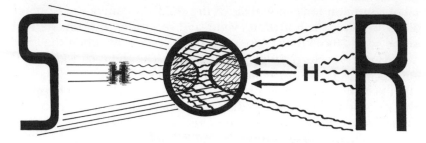

Figure 3. Mediated learning experience (MLE) model.

that relations between certain stimuli will be experienced in a certain way. The order of appearance, the intensity of given stimuli, the changes that occur in all these are grasped by the child through the intentional behavior of the mediator. The reasons for the observed changes become the object of examination by the mediator, who points to the crucial events and their critical aspects.

By the same token, the H interposes himself between the organism and his responses to the perceived reality, shaping the responses so that they will have a cognitive and social meaning and rejecting those that fail to communicate adequately or to adapt themselves to the particularities of the experienced stimulus.

Without an adult mediator interposing himself between Adam and the source of stimuli, the child developed very few of these prerequisites for learning. And so his experiences, as rich as they were, left him unaffected. He displayed a mix of deficient cognitive functions typical of children who have had no MLE or a very limited amount of this type of interaction. Inadequate instruction (in reality, virtually no instruction at all) leads to a passive way of experiencing the world, which isolates each event that is experienced as an episode having very little relation to what has gone before and even less to what will follow.

Evelyn, the daughter of an illustrious family known for its high cultural standards and its contributions to charity, was deprived of MLE, possibly because she had a nonobvious genetic disorder that was thought to block growth. Hence, her parents filled the environment with exciting stimuli but did not mediate them to her. When we first saw her she displayed infantile social behavior and showed an astonishing lack of information and an even greater lack of adequate thinking activity.

Evelyn received extensive mediated learning experience, including intensive instrumental enrichment (IE) (see Chapter 12), after which her level of functioning was well within the average range of intelligence and the achievements typical of a ninth-grader. She is able now to be reflective about the reasons for her having lived in the state of mind of a retarded performer for such a long time. She often describes her upbringing, telling of being left alone with her toys— TV, hi-fi, computer—which were dispensed generously but without mediation. Life went by, registered only as a series of images, with no one to help link (mediate) the images to her surroundings in a meaningful manner.

Youval's way of experiencing the exhibits differed substantially from Adam's. Upon repeated encounter with the stimuli, not only was Youval able to manipulate the apparatus and repeat his previous result, but he could anticipate certain outcomes resulting from changes in the way he turned the crank. His mother, as a mediator, produced in Youval what the encounter with the stimuli and its manipulation alone would have never produced, knowledge of and motivation to learn more about the relations between certain parts of events, which—in turn—are characterized by succession, order, contingency, cause and effect, and other factors. It was the mother's mediational interaction that enabled Youval and Ada to go beyond sheer recognition of cranks and receptacles to the understanding of their functions and the way these functions relate to other similar functions, and to them as individuals. The effects of the mediational interaction increased the thinking capacity of Youval to benefit from each of the tasks, becoming more experienced, motivated, and competent. Furthermore, the mother, as a mediator, having interposed herself between Youval and his responses, shaped the pattern of his response by accepting one response and then demanding that he add more responses. For example, when Youval used gestures to describe the relation between the turning of the crank and the changes in the level of the water, his mother gently encouraged him to respond verbally. In contrast, Adam's mother did not interpose herself between her child and the stimuli, did not encourage verbal description or elaboration. Although Adam's exposure to the stimuli was an exciting experience that did affect his motivation in a general way (he wanted to return), he experienced little or no cognitive gains or cognitive motivation as reflected in his unchanged level of competency in handling the tasks.

The more a child is subjected to mediated learning experiences, the greater will be his capacity to benefit from direct exposure to learning. On the other hand, a lack of MLE will produce an individual who will benefit very little from direct encounters with learning tasks. Moreover, his modifiability will be seriously impaired, leading to a lack of flexibility in adapting to unfamiliar and complex situations.

It is our contention that MLE is a uniquely human condition and that its importance cannot be overestimated. In this regard, Jerome Bruner,[2] the world-renowned developmental psychologist, said recently, "MLE is not only for the handicapped, it is for all of us since it's MLE which makes us human!!!"

CHAPTER 5

Mediated Learning Experience
What Makes It Powerful?

Those who hear about the theory of mediated learning experience (MLE) often wonder if *all* interactions—adult–infant, teacher–pupil—are not of mediational value. They ask us what the theory of MLE offers that is new, and why one should ascribe special importance to it.

These questions are certainly legitimate. In responding to them, let us consider a situation that all parents face: A young child is about to touch something dangerous. A concerned parent cries out loudly, "No, don't touch." Is this interaction considered an MLE? The parent has, after all, interposed himself or herself between the child and the source of danger. In doing this, hasn't the parent mediated the concept of danger to the child and produced in him the types of changes that will affect his behavior permanently?

Well, not all interactions, no matter how important they are to the individual, have mediational value. The "no" of the parent, which has made the child remove his hand from the source of danger, will produce the desired response for the moment, but it will not help the child decide when and where touching is dangerous and, therefore, forbidden in the future. Mediated learning experience orients the child to seek out and make the important connections between a currently experienced dangerous event and other similar experiences to which he has been exposed, and to anticipate what he will experience when he encounters something similar in the future.

Mediated learning experience does not refer primarily to the "what" of the interaction, where the interaction takes place, or when it takes place. It is rather *how* we interact with the child that characterizes an MLE. We can communicate units of information to the child. We can give him instructions. We can tell him a story. We can offer him food, sing a song, or talk about clouds without necessarily mediating to him, even though all these acts do represent interactions between an adult and a child. In order to turn this interaction into a mediated learning experience, we have to give the interaction a special quality, one that is necessary in order to affect the child's cognitive system and produce a higher level of modifiability in him. But before describing what this particular "how" is that turns this interaction into a mediated learning experience, it is worthwhile to describe what conditions are *not* necessary to turn an experience into a mediational one.

Mediated learning experience is not dependent on the language in which the interaction takes place or on the content around which the interaction between the mediator and the child is based. One can mediate in any language, English or Chinese, gestural or verbal, symbolic or mimicry. What is even more important is that if the mediator organizes the life of the child, schedules it, and selects certain stimuli (even without directly addressing the child), he is mediating by producing a certain order and organization in the events to which the child is exposed. By this, he mediates the reality which the child is experiencing in a very meaningful way.

In fact, in the early childhood period, when interaction is preverbal, a major form of mediation is through the organization of the environment and experiences. Selecting, scheduling, organizing the succession of events, modifying the intensity of certain stimuli, repeating certain stimuli, regulating their appearance and frequency—all of these precede verbal interactions. Yet their power as a determinant of the plasticity of the child's cognitive system is very high.

Mediated learning experience is not limited to people who have a rich language or whose level of communication is extremely sophisticated or organized. Mediated learning experience occurs with people who have very little verbal interaction ability or a very minimal mode of direct communication. Remember the account of how the teacher of Helen Keller made the whole world penetrate the barriers of Helen Keller's sensorial deficits solely through a tactile mode of communication. The power of this nonverbal communication produced Helen Keller's world of knowledge and intelligence, influencing her total personality in a dramatic fashion. Since mediated learning experience can be produced in a universe of contents, the Bushman, mediating

Figure 4. Mediation of a need for precision.

to his child how to make an arrow, is no less effective a mediator than is a master teacher who mediates the use of a computer. The Bushman is as concerned with the precision of the result as is the teacher of geometry in Western society (see Figure 4).

If it is not primarily language or content that distinguishes MLE from other types of interaction, then what are its distinguishing features? The following 11 attributes can, at least for the present, describe interactions bearing the stamp of MLE:

1. Intentionality and reciprocity
2. Transcendence
3. Mediation of meaning
4. Mediation of feelings of competence
5. Mediated regulation and control of behavior
6. Mediated sharing behavior
7. Mediation of individuation and psychological differentiation
8. Mediation of goal seeking, goal setting, goal planning, and achieving behavior
9. Mediation of challenge: The search for novelty and complexity

10. Mediation of an awareness of the human being as a changing
    entity
11. Mediation of an optimistic alternative

The first three—intentionality and reciprocity, transcendence, and meaning—must all be present in an interaction in order to assume that the "how" of the interaction bears the mark of MLE. These first three attributes characterize the universal, yet unique, quality of the human condition: its modifiability and autoplasticity. The other attributes, largely culturally and situationally determined, are responsible for the development of differences in cognitive style, creating great diversity in human existence. (Criteria and categories of mediated interactions appear in Appendix A.)

INTENTIONALITY AND RECIPROCITY

The most important difference between a mediated and a nonmediated interaction lies in the fact that MLE is marked by an intention animating the mediator (e.g., a father), as he interposes himself between his child and the sources of the stimuli. Conversely, a nonmediated task would be one that is supposed to "teach itself" through direct exposure alone. In a nonmediated case, there will be little possibility of determining if the exposure has had a significant effect on the individual or not. Has the child perceived it? Did he have enough time to grasp its meaning? Was the child attending to it at all? Has he seen the most relevant attributes of the task or has he registered only its global dimensions? The intention of the mediator affects the three partners involved in the interaction: the stimuli to be perceived, the child, and the mediator.

All of them are changed by the intention to mediate. MLE encourages the child to perceive things with clarity and precision. A father, motivated by an intention to have a particular thing perceived fully, transforms the stimulus, rendering it more salient and attractive to the child, changing its amplitude (e.g., loudness, brightness), its frequency, and the duration of its exposure. Furthermore, the mediator will change the "state" of the child, rendering him more vigilant and positioning him so that he is more ready to attend. By contrast, direct exposure, in the absence of such intentions to mediate, does not assure that a situation will be perceived or will penetrate the thinking apparatus of the child.

As the child is transformed, that is, made more alert, among other things, the mediating father transforms himself in order to achieve his goal. For instance, a father, attempting to make a child see something, chooses the object according to the effect it may have on his child and according to reasons he holds for its importance, which may transcend the immediate goal. He learns to recognize his child's way of signaling a desire for engagement and puts the thing to be seen at an optimal distance. In trying to make his child imitate his verbal or gestural behavior, he makes sure that the child hears what he desires and sees what he sees. He will do everything possible to maintain his child in a state of alertness. Any manifestation of fleeting and sweeping perception will be corrected by making changes in the volume, distance, or visibility of an object, "running after, and capturing," the wandering eyes of the child through pointing, masking a portion of a task, or perhaps underlining or highlighting a part of it (see Figure 5). And, if this is not enough, the father will intensify and repeat certain aspects of an act to be imitated, perhaps slowing down his movement, repeating an associated word rhythmically, reevoking it after a while, or using baby talk as a way to elicit certain behaviors. All of this occurs in an interaction that features intentionality and reciprocity.

Intentionality transforms the triangular relationship (father,

Figure 5. Mediation of focused, purposeful, perceptual behavior: "Don't look at the sides, look here!"

stimulation source, child), creating within the child the prerequisites for cognitive modifiability. Intentionality also reflects the desire of the father to shape the child's functioning in a direction consonant with his culturally determined values, goals, and habits, all of which express themselves in the content of the intentioned act. For example, choices of books, photos, TV shows, schedules, and events presented to the child will reflect the father's cultural, religious, personal, emotional, and cognitive values that he wishes to transmit to his child as an extension of himself. Furthermore, the child's physical, sensorial, and mental condition will itself become a potent determinant of choices of stimuli and produce types of intentional interactions that will reflect the parent's desire to cater to the child's particular needs.

That this does not always happen is apparent from the cases presented earlier, and can be seen in the following incident. A mother of a child with Down syndrome probably delayed her child's speech development because she did not adapt her speech pattern to her child's pattern. She did not modify the rhythm of her speech until we suggested that she intentionally do so. Later, she and her son had mutually satisfying mother–child communication. At the time we came into contact, this mother had been resistant to the idea that her child's condition required adaptation on her part.

This brings us to another characteristic of MLE that distinguishes it from direct exposure learning: Mediated learning is present whenever there is a strong, clear loop between the sending and the receiving ends of the communicational process. In fact, a mediated learning experience is not considered to have occurred unless the mediator is sure that the message reached the intended receiver. The fact that some mediational interaction has been attempted does not mean that it has indeed taken place. In many cases, the reasons for a gap lie in the sender; in other cases, the barrier is in the behavior or condition of the receiver.

TRANSCENDENCE

An MLE interaction is never limited to the immediate need that elicited it. The emotion-laden "no" the mother shouted toward her child when he was on the point of touching something hot was meant to fulfill an urgent immediate need: to save the child from harm. However, since nothing in this message goes beyond (*transcends*) the immediate need to save the child, no meaningful long-term effects will likely be produced by it. Will the child to whom this "no" was addressed know when and where he should not put his hand the next time danger occurs? Has the child who has responded to the loud admonition become modified in some way by doing so? Has his repertoire of knowledge—necessary for making his own future decisions—been enriched by this order? Has his need system become modified or expanded by it?

In an MLE situation, the instruction "no" would be complemented with a series of explanations of the reasons behind this "no," which are not necessary in terms of the immediate need to save the child's hand but are crucial in terms of the goal of the MLE, that is, to have the child become modified in a structural way. So, a mediating mother, after her "no!" has pulled the child back from harm's way, explains the reasons for alerting him. She makes the situation calling for his action distinguishable from other situations where the alert is not necessary, and produces a state of awareness in the child, an emotional and cognitive condition that will transcend this particular situation.

It is the transcendent nature of the interaction that produces flexibility in the child's thinking. Additionally, the transcending elements produced by the mediator address culturally determined goals in which the mediator acts as a transacting agent of his or her own culture. Thus, a mother feeding her child has his survival as her main goal initially. However, feeding the child after certain preparations, such as cleaning, changing, and bathing him and then preparing a particular place for him to eat that she has cleaned carefully and arranged attractively, is transmitting something beyond survival. For survival he can eat anytime and anywhere. Transcendence, established by cultural imperatives, preferences, or styles, enriches the mediational interaction with components of time, space, succession, order, culture, and other dimensions that have importance to the development of the child's cognitive structures.

Of the 11 components of MLE, it is transcendence that is the most humanizing. It is also the component that is probably the most neglected nowadays with the decline in promoting cultural richness and transmission as both a societal and an individual goal. Mediating transcendence is particularly difficult for those who have to use all of their energy for sheer survival, as is the case with economically poor people. For them, the "here and now" of survival are of prime concern; very little energy is left for the less urgent matters. This is also frequently true for persons who are educating retarded performers, who are said not to benefit from having long-term goals set for them. Even a casual analysis of a curriculum offered to people classified as educable mentally retarded, and even more for those classified as trainable mentally retarded, will reveal how little emphasis is given to teaching cognitive strategies that make the individual able to reach higher levels of thinking through using a transcendent mode of interacting.

MEDIATION OF MEANING

The mediation of meaning represents the energetic, affective, emotional power that will make the mediational interaction overcome resistance on the part of the learner and thereby ensure that the stimuli mediated will indeed be experienced by that learner. Meaning, mediated verbally, gesturally, or by mimicry, and reflected in the organization of the universe of objects and events, assures that the child not only becomes receptive to the world but also is engaged in a mutual and reciprocal interaction with it. Meaning is mediated in a great variety of ways. In early mother–child interactions we observe expressions of meaning, which the child learns amazingly fast. The mother's expressions of joy, excitement, or sadness (often subtly expressed) are readily comprehended by the child and become powerful in determining further interactional patterns (see Figure 6). At later stages in development, meaning becomes related to culturally determined values, allegiances, and attachments as the mediator endows various objects, events, and relationships with personalized

Figure 6. Nonverbal mediation of negative meaning.

meaning. This exposure to the reason for behavior creates an orientation in the child toward the search for meaning and significance, which manifests itself eventually in a variety of situations beyond those elicited by the interaction. The questions "why" and "what" are frequently heard from children who have been exposed to the mediation of meaning.

A most important factor in the process of mediating meaning is the affective tie between the mediator and the child. Some developmental theorists consider that the emotional tie is a sufficient condition for fostering the child's cognitive development. This has sometimes produced the dictum that "all a mother has to do is love her child, and if she does so, his developmental needs will be met." This has not proven itself to be as true as some hoped. In one large study of child-rearing patterns in two groups of high- and low-functioning children, it was found that in the first year of life the low-functioning children functioned normally and even appeared to have a certain advantage over their more advantaged peers. But in kindergarten, and even more so in later grades, a decline in the level of cognitive functioning became apparent, with a large increase in the gap between the two groups.[1] The interpretation of that study's findings is complementary to the theory of MLE inasmuch as the mother–child interactions in the lower-functioning group were marked by a high degree of physical closeness and other manifestations of love but few of the qualities of MLE (e.g., meaning, intentionality, and transcendence) in the interactions. Again one has to agree with a prominent psychologist and educator[2] that "love is not enough." On the other hand, although affectionate interactions are not a sufficient condition for structural change, at certain stages in development they may become the *raison d'être* of the MLE and become necessary for the effectiveness of the interaction. For some children there may be no other motivator than the bond the child has with his parents. Even at later stages, in order to accept the adult as a mediator, affective ties will play a crucial role.

Which brings us to a very important question: Who is the optimal mediator? There is no simple answer to this question because there is no mediator who will be equally valuable for everybody in all places and at all times. The mediator accepted at one time may become unacceptable at another time in the development of the child. Yet we can single out a few characteristics of a strong mediator that have nearly universal importance for the success of MLE.

The first characteristic has to do with the motives for acting as a mediator. If we try to understand the reasons why humans—for example, parents—mediate, intergenerationally as well as intra-generationally, we cannot escape the feeling that there is a deeply ingrained, though only dimly perceived and even less admitted, need within them to "live on" mentally, behaviorally, and even spiritually beyond their biological existence, through their children. This "hidden" motive for mediation ensures that the optimal mediator will be the one for whom the process of mediation or cultural transmission responds to his need for continuity and for projecting himself into the future. This motive will make the mediator manipulate objects and events of his past so that they not only will be accepted but will become a vital part of the life of the child and will eventually become the object of transmission to future generations. Thus, it is very difficult to recommend as mediators individuals who are not committed to their own values, mores, goals, styles of life, past heritage, and future goals that represent intergenerational imperatives. By implication, parents and other agents of a given culture should not rely on a noncommitted stranger to mediate their particular culture to their children.

Similarly, the need to ensure the continuous existence of an ethnocultural group cannot be achieved without creating the conditions for the cultural transmission of that particular group. In fact, cultural institutions established for this transmission are (or should be) animated by the awareness that it is only through transmission of the past, and creation of the conditions for identification with it, that continuity of the group will be secured.

Larry W. Emerson[3] of the Navaho nation speaks of many cases in which the Native American individual or community is experiencing a sense of cultural loss, a loss of identity and self-concept. He attributes this partially to the break in the cultural transmission process. Native American leaders had viewed education as the key to their survival. They had hoped that the educator would have an intrinsic desire and appreciation of Native American culture and would look to new ways of incorporating the educational process into their ways so that Native Americans could maintain their language, culture, and heritage throughout the many changes (e.g., technological, cultural, linguistic, political) that lay ahead. Unfortunately, the dream failed.

Emerson attributes many of the cognitive deficiencies of the Native American child to the cultural deprivation produced by the discontinuity of cultural transmission. Thus, he sees MLE as a means of reviving the process of cultural transmission, affecting not only the identity of the group but also the cognitive modifiability of young children, adolescents, and even adults.

In a somewhat parallel fashion, both the nuclear and the extended family receive support from the cultural group(s) to which they belong. Cultural transmission, taking the form of mediation through a one-to-one relationship, becomes a vital tool for enhancing the adaptability of both that individual and the group to which he belongs.

Cross-cultural studies concerning the adaptation of individuals and groups to an unfamiliar environment have shown that the more a group has preserved its cultural values (often through preservation of its language), the more it has been able to maintain a high level of cultural cohesiveness, and the greater has been its capacity to cope successfully with the unfamiliarity and the complexity of a new environment.[4] A dramatic example of the relationship involving cultural transmission, mediational interactions, and successful adaptation to an unfamiliar situation is demonstrated by the Jewish Ethiopian immigrants who recently arrived in Israel and were suddenly confronted with the extremely different occidental 20th-century culture of Israel. Although the majority of the immigrants were illiterate, they displayed considerable adroitness in learning reading, writing, and arithmetic, often adapting more rapidly than some other groups of immigrants that were far less distant culturally, linguistically, and technologically from Israeli society. The reasons for this adaptability seem to be due to the quality and the large amount of MLE offered, both within the nuclear family and through the other agents of society who are charged with the transmission of culture in a manner that will ensure its continuity under adverse and hostile conditions. This group of people, identifying themselves as Jewish by origin, had to live for two millennia in total isolation. They had to use creative and powerful means to transmit their cultural identity to their children and thereby survive as a people. The mediational tool that enabled them to pass on their identity was the extensive use of the oral tradition, both in the family and in the community, since they were devoid of other means.

We have dealt at great length with mediation of meaning in order to emphasize that this component of MLE is essential to ensure that the MLE will be used and accepted by the partners of an interaction, thus enabling groups to adapt to new situations and preserve their identity. We trust that parents will now understand more fully the legitimacy of their right to mediate, not only because it has its origin in their often unconscious need to continue their existence through their children, but also because it is vital for the development of the human as a flexible, adaptable, and modifiable being. And it is also understandable why in our S-H-O-H-R diagram (Figure 3) we cannot accept the possibility of substituting the H (human) for an M (mediator) because this might allow others to replace the M with a C (computer). The human mediator, while he may make effective use of a computer, *cannot* be replaced by it.

MEDIATION OF FEELINGS OF COMPETENCE

Competence can be acquired in a variety of ways, including direct, active interaction with stimuli. Adam, described earlier, became a master in turning on and turning off a variety of science exhibits. He may have even improved his finger dexterity through his manipulations. In the future, he may also learn to drive a car and master a number of other tasks through direct exposure to various activities. In some cases, competency can be achieved through direct exposure to activities without mediated learning experience. However, such achievement is not always accompanied by feelings of competence. We are often surprised at how many highly competent people are tortured by a profound feeling of inadequacy. Some feel that they are basically incompetent but that they have fooled everyone; they feel like impostors. No evidence of their achievements will alter their feeling of incompetence. Each success, rather than reinforcing their confidence, is interpreted as a sign that they are closer to being "found out." Being good reasoners (otherwise they would not be as successful as they are), they find dozens of ways to explain their success without ascribing it to their intelligence or their competence. "It is sheer luck that I have succeeded." "This task I took on didn't demand any intelligence or any competence; therefore I succeeded."

This lack of association between *competence* and the *feeling of competence* strengthens our contention that direct interaction with tasks alone, even when followed by success, and even mastery, does not necessarily engender a true feeling of competence. Rather, competence depends to a large extent on the presence of a mediator, interposing himself between the individual and the task, mediating the feeling to the individual that what he or she has accomplished does indeed indicate genuine competence.

This type of mediation entails two steps, both of which start in early childhood. The first mediational step is to help the child succeed in a task in which he previously was not successful. The struggle of the child with a certain task is "made successful" by the mother's discreet intervention. She may carefully construct the loop through which the child learns to tie his shoelace, or lend a supporting finger to the underside of a spoon, permitting her child to successfully transport the soup to his mouth. She will bring together those components of a task that are requisites for its successful mastery. Thus, making Youval, described earlier, reevoke the initial level of the water allowed him to anticipate the outcome of a future encounter with the water apparatus. It is important, however, that the mediator keep his assistance within the strict limits of what is necessary in order for the child to succeed, not to offer more lest the child become too dependent on the mediator. We have to keep in mind that MLE is considered to be effective in producing structural cognitive modifiability, but it is only one of two modalities by which the human interacts with the world—the second, and usually most pervasive, being direct exposure to stimuli. A mediator who obstructs direct access to the world through "smothering" a child with MLE doesn't really mediate but rather offers him reality ready-made. The sad outcome of such an "oversized" mediating H is an individual incapable of benefiting from direct exposure to stimuli, remaining at a level of MLE dependency. Not only is the feeling of competence itself nonexistent in such an individual, but competence itself is nonexistent.

The case of Josh is pertinent here. Josh is a boy with Down syndrome who was raised by a father who devoted his every waking moment to his son, allowing very little space for the child to experience life by himself. If we were to represent graphically the position of this father as a mediator, we would have the following: S-H-O-H-R. Such an "overgrown" mediator leaves very little learning responsibility to the child. Everything experienced by the child has been preselected, digested, and elaborated for him by the mediator—in this case his father—who, literally, chewed the food for his son so that all that was left for him to do was to swallow it.

The father took Josh out of school at an early age, claiming that he wasn't learning anything because his teachers taught only overly simple subjects such as the alphabet (which the teachers claimed Josh had not mastered). The father contended that Josh read poetry fluently and, furthermore, was able to copy and even write poems himself. On one occasion, the author asked Josh to read a simple sentence, whereupon the father intervened immediately, requesting permission to give Josh a particular text he had brought with him, claiming that Josh knew the more complex texts better than the simple ones. Josh sat near his father, who pointed to every word and sounded out the first syllable of each one. Josh then completed the word. After this had continued for a while, the author asked the father to let Josh start the words by himself. Josh could not. At this point the two—Josh and his father—broke down, crying. The father, recovering his composure, decided to refer Josh for remedial teaching under the direction of the author. It took us more than a year to shake Josh out of his dependency, which manifested itself in many spheres of life—feeding, dressing, counting, talking. Anything demanding autonomous effort was literally unavailable to Josh.

After the year of work, and a great deal of investment in encouraging him to react more spontaneously, Josh began to read. He had to learn from scratch, but after a need for competence was mediated to him, he started to want to read by himself. Recently we witnessed the emergence of a rebelliousness never seen before in Josh, and we had to work with his father in order to help him understand the meaning and importance of this spontaneous and independent behavior, that is, Josh's developing a higher level of functioning.

This case is illustrative of misjudgment on the part of a parent. But it also reflects upon practices employed by other parents, and by educators and caregivers who believe that applying huge doses of help is the only way to achieve a training goal.

Related to this point, in a survey of tasks offered to young adults with Down syndrome who were ready to enter a semiindependent living situation, we found that none of them had been taught to strike a match to light a stove. The reasons invoked by parents were multiple: It is dangerous; they may not know when to do it (deficient decision making); they cannot blow it out (supposedly because of the poor muscle tone of lip and tongue); they don't know how to hold the match so it won't burn their fingers. As we demonstrated to parents how easily these difficulties are overcome (teaching the child to keep the flame upward when igniting, or to blow it out by moving the hand), we witnessed the joy their sons or daughters experienced in mastering this task as well as the boost in their feeling of competency.

The mediator must select the task and the manner of presenting it to the child so that it will enhance not only his competence but also, by interpreting to him the meaning of his mastery, his *feeling* of competence. In the case of striking a match, the immediate goal is competency in the task; the transcendent goal is the feeling of competency that will promote more independent living.

Offering the individual an opportunity to learn tasks in which he or she is already relatively skilled is not conducive to a feeling of mastery or competence. There is an optimal degree of novelty, complexity, and challenge that is required in order to experience a feeling of competency. Consider how little challenge is given to a child with retarded performance when the main concern is to make him feel relaxed, free of the stress that is involved in confronting new things and in facing the frustration of possible failure. As we said earlier, the feeling of competence cannot be acquired without the interpretation given by the mediator as to the meaning of an achievement. This implies a number of things. First, some children with retarded performance may not understand the difference between success and failure and may tend to underestimate or overestimate the meaning of their achievements. The feedback offered by the mediator, including the interpretation of the meaning of the achievement as evidence of competence, may prove to be critical for the child's evaluation of self. In certain cases, the interpretation of an achievement will demand an adaptation to a scale with unfamiliar values that the child cannot attain by himself. A child lifting a 2-kg weight who sees his father lifting 20 kg with less effort will experience a feeling of inferiority and incompetence unless the father helps his child understand that, for the child, lifting 2 kg is a fine achievement (see Figure 7). Indeed, interpretation is often the key to enhancing the feeling of competence and its direct result, that is, enhanced motivation to perform in new areas of learning.

An individual considered by others to be mentally and physically handicapped often feels that environmental conditions, especially a physical condition, set insurmountable limits to his competence. This feeling is all too often transmitted to the individual, who may then avoid areas of challenge. Ruth, described in Chapter 3, became able to talk about her feeling of avoidance. One day, when one of the authors

Figure 7. Weight lifter.

presented her with a task involving an analogy, she burst into a loud and irrepressible laugh. When asked why she was laughing, she blurted out, "You are *meshugge*" ("crazy"), accompanying her words by moving her finger in a circle beside her head. When asked what made her think that, she said, shaking with laughter, "You think that I can do this?"

MEDIATED REGULATION AND CONTROL OF BEHAVIOR

Regulation of behavior is the means by which an individual uses various sources of information to decide *if*, *when*, and *how* to respond to a given situation. For example, when confronted with finding geometric shapes in an amorphous cloud of dots, the student will need to ask himself: "Do I recognize these figures, their names, the number of dots necessary to draw them?" "Do I know how they look when they are turned upside down?" "Do I have information about the distances between the various lines?" Regulation of behavior embodies two opposing aspects: the control of impulsivity and the initiation of behavior. Impulsivity is seen in a child who is unable to regulate his own behavior; he may be asked a question and actually give his answer before all of the question is verbalized. An inadequate response may also be due to impulsivity in gathering the information necessary to provide an appropriate response. Many children who manifest impulsivity fail in tasks even though they know what they need to do to respond correctly. Impulsiveness is amenable to change, but a high level of investment is required to do so. A mediator can restrain the impulsiveness by demanding that the individual devote more time to studying the task and then by creating conditions under which an answer will not be accepted unless controlled behavior occurs.

At certain stages in the development of control over impulsivity, the mediator may need to use physical means to keep the child from impulsive responding—perhaps holding the child's hands (or asking the child to sit on his own hands)—so that he won't point to an answer before looking carefully at the situation and thinking about it. However, the most important way to regulate the behavior of an impulsive individual (and to help him regulate it himself eventually) is to make him aware of the requirements of a particular task in terms of perceptual investment, precision, comparison, learning of relations, and other factors relating the requirements of the task to his present level of competence.

The second aspect of regulation of behavior is the acceleration of the response by overcoming inhibition, which is often due to an individual's lack of knowledge or lack of confidence. An individual may have perceived the problem adequately; he may even have a proper answer, but he is unable to answer either because of inhibition due to feelings of incompetence or because of difficulties in initiating a specific behavior. Thus, Peter, described in Chapter 3, could not initiate behaviors he had in his repertoire unless his mother manipulated his arm. Peter's behavior stands in sharp contrast to the behavior of the impulsive individual who gives very little time to inspecting and organizing a task before responding. Thus, the double process of becoming aware of the nature and complexity of the task and one's own level of functioning produces a structural change in the individual's propensity to act in a regulated way (see Figure 8).

Figure 8. Mediated regulation of behavior: "Please do handle it with care."

MEDIATED SHARING BEHAVIOR

Mediating sharing behavior, both by manipulating situations and by creating models of sharing, stimulates a child's socialization and animates two people's interactions, fusing their attention and creating a common experience. The major source behind sharing is the need to produce a kind of unity and pleasure between two individuals. This need is an extension of the early mother–infant bonding process. Indeed, it is amazing to see how early a child is able to share with his mother, following the mother's eyes as she focuses on a toy. Sharing becomes even more obvious once the child has learned to point with his finger, indicating his intention to share what he sees with his mother. As the child matures, his mother mediates the need for him to share with other children, pointing out how she feels when he shares his feelings with her, making sharing an extremely important reciprocal experience (see Figure 9).

The author mediates sharing when he distributes candies, usually selecting one child to serve as his "agent" to distribute the candies among the other children. Young children learn to enjoy this sharing experience. They choose those with whom they want to share (and, naturally, those with whom they do not want to share), giving the author an opportunity to mediate sharing behavior in terms of the importance of fairness and respect for individual rights. Sharing, becoming cooperation, is observed frequently in large families where the parents make the parceling out of household responsibilities an essential way to cope with the heavy homemaking and child-rearing

Figure 9. Sharing behavior.

burden. In large families, sharing becomes a vital element in ensuring family harmony, often contributing meaningfully to the enhancement of cognitive, emotional, and communicational functioning of the individual and his family as a group of individuals working together in harmony.

Parents usually attempt to protect children who have disabilities, judging them to be too fragile to share stressful experiences with them. This can create conditions of emotional and cognitive impoverishment, hampering the child's (and parents') development. The father of Rene, one of the autistic young adults at the institute, did his best to shield his daughter from the final stages of his wife's death, seeking to protect her from experiencing stress and grief. But this protection, which extended itself over Rene's entire life, deprived her of the vital opportunity to learn to experience sadness and grief, as well as joy and happiness. She didn't know how to describe such emotions or even how to mimic them. We intervened and, through an intensive process of mediation to both father and daughter, Rene became exposed to the experience of grief. By the sharing of his emotion, her father opened up a whole new world of feelings to his daughter. This brought about an important change in her interaction with her father. In many respects, it is this experience of intensive sharing that has become the vehicle by which we have been able to integrate Rene into the community, not just as an accepted individual but as an active, sharing and contributing member.

MEDIATION OF INDIVIDUATION AND PSYCHOLOGICAL DIFFERENTIATION

Mediation of individuation and psychological differentiation is, in some respects, the opposite of sharing. Sharing is fusion between two people; individuation and differentiation put the emphasis on how we distinguish ourselves from others. In educational systems it is very important that teachers mediate to the children how to perceive themselves as individuals, distinct from others. Such mediation takes place not only when children learn how to be individualistic but also in the ways by which a teacher becomes a model for the children, portraying himself both as having an authoritative position and as reflecting the possibility that others' views have a legitimate place in classroom discussions. In some teachers, we see a tendency to downgrade those children's views that do not match their own. It is essential that the individuality of the student be respected. Assuredly, it is a given that a student has to conform to the discipline of instruction, the mores of his community and of his teachers, and his social group. But, while a certain degree of conformity is necessary to maintain order, at least some expression of the legitimacy of different feelings, views, styles of expression, and modes of experiencing must be encouraged from an early age.

In an outburst of anger over her failure to peel a potato, Tamar, aged 4½, said the following to her grandmother:

> I am not you
> and you are not me.
> Your hand is not mine
> and my hand is not yours.
> And you can't do things like me
> and I can't do things like you
> and that's it.

In her outburst, Tamar expressed not only her frustration but psychological differentiation, comparative behavior on a number of distinct parameters; differences resulting in failure to do certain things are understood as subclasses of other, more substantive, differences that one must accept as existent.

MEDIATION OF GOAL SEEKING, GOAL SETTING, GOAL PLANNING, AND ACHIEVING BEHAVIOR

This type of mediation widens the individual's thinking in terms of time and space, creating in him a future-directed orientation. Goals are sought with the help of the mediator, who points out the alternate ways of reaching a goal.

Choosing a specific goal from a number of alternatives demands cognitive abilities such as an adequate perception of the goal and its attributes, the extensive use of representational types of thinking, and an understanding of the kinds of demands it places upon the individual's problem-solving ability. Mediation of goal seeking can begin at a very young age. Even before a child learns to speak, we can observe goal-oriented responses in the child and build on them. But goal seeking will be more easily mediated later, when the child interacts verbally. Children with retarded performance, in particular, will benefit from mediating goal-seeking behavior, enriching their cognitive structures with comparative and representational types of thinking. Unfortunately, sometimes we limit goal seeking when dealing with individuals who have retarded performance. We presume that they are unable to use representational modes of interacting and therefore cannot think in terms of the future. It may be that these children show little orientation toward the future because we do not mediate to them the world of imagination through representational modes of relating to reality!

MEDIATION OF CHALLENGE: THE SEARCH FOR NOVELTY AND COMPLEXITY

Parents, caregivers, and cultures differ widely as to the extent to which they mediate challenging behavior. Indeed, there are cultures that discourage their members from seeking out challenges and responding to them. In a nonchallenging society, education will lack spark. Overprotective parenting and oversystematized teaching present barriers to accessing challenging and novel tasks. Thinking proficiency itself generates a need in the individual to look for more challenging experiences. However, an individual will seek out a new challenge only if, after having struggled in order to reach some degree of competency, he is enticed to pursue greater achievements. Even normal parent–child interactions may be debilitating if independence is not encouraged through mediation.

The mediation of challenge is even more important when parenting a child with retarded performance with whom creating overdependency seems so natural. Indeed, preparing such an individual to be exposed to challenging circumstances requires courage on the part of the parent. In many cases, it will even require mediating the right to fail temporarily, as a way to become more proficient and to reach out to higher levels of functioning. Encouraging children to start tasks that they know they will not be able to master immediately is a very important element in widening intellectual, language, motor, socialization, and other competencies.

The story of Debby, who has Down syndrome (presented in Chapter 7), is instructive here. She learned how to accept failure and in doing so learned how to cope with more challenging tasks. For example, even though she was hesitant in walking up stairs as an adolescent because she was not proficient in doing so, she walked with her group of normal friends up mountains and down through valleys. She knew that she needed to participate in these activities in order to belong to the group. She went on these treks even though she would sometimes fall, choose an incorrect trail, or need her friends' help in some way. We noted, however, that she would not accept the help of her parents in performing these challenging tasks. Instead, by accepting the help of her peers, she felt much less dependent than if she had relied on her parents. And her peers, rather than discouraging Debby, created new challenges that she faced with their help. Today, as a young adult, there are few tasks she will not attempt, and she has a sound sense of what she can and cannot master herself. Unfortunately, many parents of children with retarded performance protect them from difficult tasks, assuming that they will never be able to accomplish them. Many children (not excluding those who are considered normal), when asked to do something, will say, "But I haven't learned it. How can I do it?" "If you won't try it, you will never learn it" would be the appropriate answer. But in many cases, a negative response from the child is accepted, resulting in even greater reluctance on the child's part to involve himself in challenging tasks. Thereafter, the task is modified, usually "watered down," which renders it uninteresting and meaningless from the standpoint of learning. In other words, parents reduce the challenge residing in the complexity and novelty of the task in order to adapt it to the present capacity of the child rather than modify the child in order to render him able to cope with the novelty and the complexity. Without question, the concept of "matching" the task to the capacity of the child, as professed by well-known educators,[5] is a sound in- structional practice; however, it sometimes results in a static concep- tion of the individual's functioning—for example, a belief that stages of development must be attained in a fixed succession. A fervent follower of Piaget (the world-renowned child development theorist) once formulated the instructional consequences of such a theoretical stance as follows: Either the individual is at a maturational stage that enables him to grasp a given concept and solve a given problem, whereupon he doesn't have to be taught, or, if he is developmentally not ready to grasp it, then teaching him will not help.[6]

One of the most important conditions for successful mediation lies in the belief that the individual *can* go beyond his present observ- able level of functioning. Without such a belief, very little of the mediation of challenging behavior is legitimate. The absence of this belief may be one of the reasons few children with retarded perfor- mance are confronted with challenging situations or are even allowed to become aware that goals and tasks exist that extend far beyond what they know or are able to do at present.

Asked what he knows in arithmetic, a retarded performer who has mastered simple addition and subtraction says proudly, "I know it all." Unrealistic competency perception is another problem that many retarded performers, both children and adults, manifest. It is the outcome of lack of mediated confrontation with appropriately challenging tasks.

Sue, 28 years old, possesses strong motivation and a very rich vocabulary but is impaired by severe stuttering. One day, her mother brought her to the author to be examined. Standing near her daughter in the author's office, the mother implored, almost in tears, "Please don't teach her things she is not able to do," revealing that she was afraid that anything her daughter did not know already would become a source of frustration. The author responded, "I won't teach her anything she already knows. I will teach her only things she doesn't know, and I will also teach her how to master

Figure 10. Mediation of challenging behavior (preference for complexity and novelty over simplicity and familiarity).

them!" During the 14 hours of assessment and instruction he did indeed teach Sue several new and highly complex things.

The success of mediation of challenging behavior is dependent on the mediator's belief that important changes can be produced and that confronting the individual with tasks more complex than he is accustomed to handling will enhance his adaptive behavior. Needless to say, the mediation of challenging behavior requires that parents and teachers also mediate the necessary cognitive tools along with the desire to engage in more challenging tasks (see Figure 10).

MEDIATION OF AN AWARENESS OF THE HUMAN BEING AS A CHANGING ENTITY

This domain of mediation is extremely subtle and requires a very cautious approach. It is the way by which new cognitive structures become active in the individual, making him able to produce changes in himself on an intentional basis. To exist means to have an identity that stays the same, beyond any changes we might produce in ourselves; to live, on the other hand, is to be in a constant process of change. These two antagonistic needs—to exist, i.e., to stay the same, and to live, i.e., to change—require a constant balancing act, requiring that the individual reconcile these two antagonistic needs in order to achieve fulfillment.

Often, the need to change is not encouraged (or even deemed desirable) for a person who is a retarded performer. Change is approached with extreme caution, particularly if it is targeted toward the social realm of the individual, such as bringing about increased assertiveness and claims for greater independence. Society may not always be receptive to such change. But the onset of assertive behavior in an individual with retarded performance who was previously behaving in a conformist way is to be encouraged, not discouraged.

In our practice, we have seen many individuals who underwent substantial, meaningful changes in their levels of functioning. But often these changes were not accepted (or sometimes were ignored) by the "establishment," particularly by the school, as being valid and durable. Enlarging the individual's capacity to learn, his repertoire for functioning, and, especially, his aspirations to function on higher levels can create uncertainty about accepting the modified individual, especially when he rebels against an unyielding environment, trying his best to escape from it.

Our involvement in the assessment of a few of these "rebellious" youngsters led us to identify these symptoms as the "King Solomon and the Cobbler" syndrome. According to legend, Satan turned Solomon into a cobbler. Solomon, knowing his real identity, protested and cried loudly, "I am King Solomon!" The people of the village mocked the "imposter" who, dressed in the clothes of a simple cobbler, claimed to be the splendid king. Similarly, many individuals with retarded performance cry out, "I am not retarded. I want to be more than what you consider me to be. I want to do much more than what I am asked to do. I can make it. Let me out!" Ironically, the establishment often views this as a prime symptom of disability, believing that the individual is not able to make a real judgment of his deficient capacities and has adopted aspirations that are unrealistic.

This approach to the individual as an unchangeable entity is reflected in the well-meaning attempt by some professionals to alert parents to the worst that can be expected from the child's condition, ignoring a possibility that the predicted destiny may not materialize if powerful intervention takes place. The belief in the predictability of certain biopsychological signs is so strong that some professionals think they can (and must) precisely forecast the whole life trajectory of a young child with retarded performance, going out of their way to make sure that the parents understand that nothing can be changed. Something can be changed! The possibility for change needs to be understood clearly by professionals and must be actively pursued through their mediational efforts.

Needless to say, one has to make sure that the change is consonant with the need of the individual to preserve his identity. An interesting dilemma occurs in maintaining a reasonable balance between a person's identity and change of appearance in the consideration of plastic surgery for children with Down syndrome (discussed at length in Chapter 10). People who hear about plastic surgery often ask: "How will the child feel about himself if his appearance changes significantly? How will this affect his identity, the continuity of his self? Will he not in some way become alienated from himself?" These are legitimate questions that signal a need for caution in order to prevent identity traumas from occurring. But caution must not become so strong that the possibility for positive change is ignored or abandoned too quickly.

Individuals must learn that by becoming modified they will have to assume different roles according to situations presented. Thus, a change in the role of the student with retarded performance produced by his being shifted from a special educational environment to a regular one may be accompanied by stress. The mediator, aware of these changes, will help the student to anticipate the stress and will ensure that there is support and feedback for him at every step of the process, to make it possible for him to cope and become integrated in his new environment. Change and awareness of being modified is certainly a source of stress but need not become a source of distress.

MEDIATION OF AN OPTIMISTIC ALTERNATIVE

This type of mediation emphasizes the way the individual views the future and is an important determinant of cognitive modifiability. Confronted with a number of alternatives as to what will happen in a given situation, the individual may choose an optimistic alternative or a pessimistic one. A variety of factors determine one's choice.

We consider mediated learning to be very important in the particular way by which the mediator helps the child choose one alternative among many. The effect of mediating the choice of a pessimistic alternative may be very harmful to the individual's cognitive functioning. Adhering to a pessimistic alternative, as is the case in cultures that adhere to a fatalistic view of life, can engender a passive approach to reality; in essence, since there is no hope, the activity necessary to pursue a positive destiny may appear futile. Such a culture does very little cognitively and technically to change the course of an impending disaster, accepting it as unavoidable. Choosing an optimistic alternative, on the other hand, tends to mobilize all of a culture's resources—physical, emotional, and cognitive—to make a positive outcome happen. Mediating an optimistic alternative implies acknowledgment of pessimistic alternatives, signaling that if an optimistic one is chosen, mobilization will be necessary to make it become a reality. Mediating a positive choice to a child involves mobilizing him to search for those elements in the situation that will substantiate the positive choice. A negative alternative requires little or no mobilization.

In an art museum the author and two children, aged 6½ and 5, viewed a large painting depicting a horse-drawn wagon about to go over a precipice. Only the back end of the wagon was in view. The children anxiously asked questions in an effort to better understand the danger depicted in the painting. The author helped them see those details that showed the danger that the wagon was in. In the painting, two men were straining to hold the wagon back, pulling with all their strength on a rope attached to the rear of the wagon. The children were helped to see that the men were strong and were pulling with all their might. One of the children, engrossed in the situation, started to encourage the men in the painting, shouting in a loud voice for them to pull harder. Both children were extremely immersed in the situation. When the author asked whether the men would succeed in pulling back the wagon, Abner, the older child, after a renewed inspection of the painting, answered with great confidence, "Of course they will succeed." When Abner was asked to give the reasons for his belief, the author expected to hear him repeat some of the reasons discussed previously. But no, having studied the picture for a long time, Abner brought a reason to light that the author himself had not perceived. He said, "See, there is a pulley." He pointed to a barely visible rope, linked through a pulley and tied to the wagon. The boy's earnest, solution-oriented search paid off. It enabled him to find the half-hidden rope attached to a barely visible pulley. Surely, this would save the wagon (see Figure 11).

Choosing an optimistic alternative will sharpen the thinking pro-

Figure 11. Mediation of an optimistic alternative.

cess, orienting an individual to search for the cognitive support needed for testing his optimistic hypothesis, a process that may be particularly important for the high-risk child. A belief that an intervention may change the child's course of life can play a determining role in the decision to intervene.

TWO MODALITIES OF MEDIATION

As was said earlier, MLE may appear in two forms: a direct form in which the mediator interposes himself, sometimes physically, between the child and the stimuli, pointing, focusing, selecting. Or it may appear in an indirect way: The mediator, animated by his intentions, creates conditions that will endow the chosen stimuli with the power to penetrate the child's cognitive system, shaping the presentation of a situation so that certain things are registered and the relations between them will be discovered and then learned.

A combination of direct and indirect forms of mediation is considered by us to be the most effective way to create flexibility of the mind and in the self-changing ability of the individual. In the instrumental enrichment (IE) program (to be described in detail in Chapter 12), direct and indirect thinking exercises are forged into a powerful system of mediational interaction. Thus, the IE exercises are structured, organized, and endowed with meaning. Mediation by the teacher, who is aware of the characteristics of the IE tasks, their goals, and the intentions underlying their structure, becomes the "voice of the silent exercises."

This is true also of what may happen in an interaction that is meant to mediate a focusing activity to the child. Focusing is an extremely important condition of the interaction between the child and the world since it enables him to gather the data necessary for elaboration. It is focusing that ensures the sharpness of what is to be perceived and that will permit the recognition of the stimuli under a variety of conditions later. The sharper the focus, the greater the investment in an initial perception, and the better will be the chances that the individual will recognize the same stimulus even when it is presented in a different way or when it appears in adverse conditions of perception, such as reduced cues or under conditions of extreme transformation. Take, for instance, the IE task of Organization of Dots, in which the individual is asked to find a square, embedded in a cloud of dots, that is intersected by other geometric figures, and that appears in an atypical orientation (see Figure 25, p. 213). These adverse conditions make it difficult for the individual to see the square, but if he has been helped to focus (invest) in the perception of the figure and is assisted to add some cognitive components of the task to it, he will be in a good position to explore and find the transformed square, despite the confusing condition in which it is presented.

In what way does a mother affect the focusing capacity and focusing readiness of the child? Since she is the first "object" with whom the child interacts, the tendency—probably innate—exists at a very early stage in the perceptual activity of the child to prefer his mother's face to other objects. At an early age, the child focuses on the mother as a revered object to which he acts as if he were addicted. He looks at her as if he could literally "swallow" her face with his eyes. Who has not seen a child turn himself 180 degrees on the lap of the mother in order to capture her gaze? This purposeful behavior shows how much investment the child may make in order to have eye contact with the object that is both familiar and beloved. The mother's face, so attractive to the child and so frequently attracting his eyes, is a mutually reinforcing focal point.

Several well-known psychologists[7,8] have shown that the perceptions of children living in orphanages, who have had very little opportunity to focus on stable mother figures and other objects of love, have abilities marked by a fleeting and blurred quality. Furthermore, these children show little readiness to invest the amount of time and active exploration necessary to have an exhaustive view of the object to which they are exposed. Some of these children look through a person as if he were made of glass. Their gaze runs around in an unorganized and fleeting way (recall the story of Adam in Chapter 4).

How does a mother affect the focusing capacity and focusing readiness of her young child? As mentioned earlier, at a very early stage in the perceptual activity of the child, the mother becomes a revered object to which the child acts as if he were addicted. Similarly, the child's attraction to her face is extremely reinforcing to the mother, who creates new and better opportunities to see her child's face above and beyond the times when the child needs her. The transcendent nature of this interaction creates a degree of familiarity that will also become a source of additional experience, leading eventually to the child's learning about transformation. A transformation occurs when an object changes some of its characteristics while keeping others constant. In order to comprehend a transformation, the child has to have a good knowledge of the constant characteristics of the object that maintain its identity even after certain of its dimensions have undergone change. It is within the framework of the familiarity of the mother's figure that the child learns that she can be sad, joyful, angry, cheerful, lovable, or distant, can change from crying to laughter, and still be herself—his mother. Soon he will learn to relate these changes to other phenomena that occur in the same way. And he will learn that the reasons for the observed transformation in his mother's mood can be read from her face. This may well become the model upon which the search for causal relations may be based at later stages in the life of the child.

Events experienced through direct exposure will become meaningful through the mother's intervention, too. For example, holding her toddler in front of a photo, the mother observes his preferences in looking toward certain things, and then makes these things more available to him. These activities enhance the child's perceptual habits and his efficiency in gathering the data necessary for elaborating them.

The propensity to focus is affected by very early child–mother interactions in which the mother creates the prerequisites for effective problem-solving behavior and for hierarchically higher mental functioning in the child. If this does not happen, one will see the ill effects of the child's being exposed to unselected sources of stimuli, that is, a lowered capacity to give priority to one stimulus as compared with the many others competing in his perceptual apparatus (recall Youval's story, Chapter 4).

We often tend to explain the hyperactive behavior of certain children by speculating that some brain injury has occurred. We do not take into account that an unorganized environment may also create inattentiveness and inability to handle a task in a more focused and accurate way. Children who live in a "mindless" or chaotic flow of stimuli, not regulated by them or selected for them—such as those who sit for long hours and view frivolous television programs—are often actually "tuning out" mentally.

By contrast, mediational interactions, directed, guided, and shaped by the intention of the mother, endow a situation with certain meanings, as compared with others that become ignored, creating conditions that impose direction on the mental processes. The mediation of long-term memories may illustrate this direction process. Children often do not consider their memory as an area that they can dominate, retrieving from it, at will, a given piece of information. If a memory is there spontaneously, they have it, they can express it. But if it is not there, they cannot do anything to make it happen. (See the works of John Flavell and David Elkind in this regard.[9,10]) The mediator who makes the child recall his past experience creates an awareness in him that he can, on his own, retrieve the information from where it is stored by a process of reconstruction.

Cognitive operations become, then, the support system for construction (e.g., filling in or excluding details according to rules) of principles that govern the individual's mental life. How different it is when a mediator requires the child to produce something by active construction as contrasted with the situation where the child is given a ready-made answer, or where the child's mental activity is limited to that of simple reproduction, devoid of the mental effort involved in the application of retrieval through active reconstruction strategies. Mediators, interposing themselves between the child and his responses, shape those responses, give them an active rather than just a passive characteristic, turning the child into a generator of information, not just a reproducer of ready-made or stored information.

Another factor in mediated interactions is the transmission of the past and projection of the future. Transmission of the past has its greatest importance in the fact that the life space expands through transmission. Here the mediational interaction fulfills two distinct roles: First, it has a formative value inasmuch as it produces new modalities of interacting with the world, such as using representational thinking with a degree of vividness very similar to the sensorially experienced. Second, MLE has a role in the transmission of information that would never become available were it not for the specified conditions of mediation. What would we know of the many things totally inaccessible to our senses if there were not mediators who make the knowledge of their existence available to us?

Unhappily, transmission of the past is much rarer nowadays. The retarded performing child is seldom offered more than a very brief glimpse of his parent's past. Yet many of them could become greatly enriched by articulating their lives with components of the past and through participation in the planning and shaping of their future.

Creating a life space extending from the immediate here and now requires a special code, made of a substitute reality such as words, symbols, and concepts, and a special orientation in order to enter it, sense it, experience it, with the vividness and the meaning that characterize our immediate experience (see Figure 12).

A mother who keeps a certain consistency, a scheduled way of interacting with her baby, may enhance the development of a whole repertoire of cognitive functions that then serve as enablers for problem-solving behavior. Scheduling such activities as feeding and toileting may reflect the mother's being taught by parents and neighbors, but it also corresponds to her sensitivity (she can't stand the child's crying) and environmentally determined constraints. Scheduling is an intentional act on her part. A mother who keeps a fairly constant schedule is often heard to say, "I want my child to learn that there is an order in his home. He will need this later in life."

Scheduling, or the mediation of a temporal order, is important not only at home but also in school. The organization of a sequence of acts requires planning behavior, representation, and an anticipation of the future (see Figure 13).

Imitation is certainly the prime way by which the individual's repertoire of behaviors is mediated. Imitation can, of course, take place (and it usually does take place) through direct exposure to stimuli. The child observes the model to which he is exposed and reproduces the observed behavior in an immediate or deferred way, in a precise or modified way. Deficiencies in imitative behavior can be observed in many children with retarded performance. For example, children with Down syndrome are often portrayed as great imitators. But, to the contrary, we know that many of them have great difficulty in imitating models, especially complex models, to which they are exposed. In order to render them able to imitate, behavior has to be mediated to them. In doing so, the model for imitation will not be presented in a casual way but will be animated by intention. The mediator will make sure that the child preceives the model in a sharp way and focuses on the behavior the mediator exhibits, changing the amplitude and frequency of an experience to facilitate imitative behavior. All this will make the child observe, repeat, and consolidate the behavior newly acquired through imitation. Thus, learning to learn will be established through mediational interaction (see Figure 14).

Another powerful way of mediating to the child, utilized by cultural agents throughout the generations, is the provocation of a child's need for mediation. One such purposefully shaped "provocation" experience can be found in the way the night of the Passover is

Figure 12. Mediation of symbols.

Figure 13. Mediation of a temporal order.

shaped. One mediation strategy is to make the child ask those questions that will allow the older generation to reevoke the story of the
Exodus, its meaning, and its purpose. The preparations that precede
the evening (a very hectic one) reach their climax in the realization of
the night's difference, of its newness, of its being special. Difference
becomes emphasized when the child is asked not only to perceive but
to constantly compare the nonfamiliar events occurring during this
evening with what he knows to be normal, regular, and familiar.
Why unleavened bread and not the regular kind; why the unusual
food as compared with what is normally eaten during the year; why
the unusual seating arrangement on pillows; why drink four cups of
wine? Special arrangements are made to keep the children alert
throughout the whole night of the Passover with its long hours of
reciting the story of the Exodus. Children are encouraged to stay alert
by introducing rewards to keep them asking questions. For example,
to make sure that they will not fall asleep before the end of the
evening, they are encouraged to "steal" a well-hidden piece of matzo
(an unleavened cracker) from their father and then negotiate a reward

Figure 14. Mediation of imitative behavior.

as a condition for returning it at the end of the dinner when it is needed as a part of the blessing of the food (see Figure 15).

In summary, mediated learning experience, as a theory and as an operational system, allows us to understand human plasticity and modifiability. Furthermore, it serves as a powerful guide in shaping the interaction of the growing human being in a way that will permit him to increase his modifiability wherever this has not developed owing to a lack of MLE.

Figure 15. Mediation of perception and definition of a problem (dealing with the incompatible).

CHAPTER 6

Why Does Mediated Learning Fail to Occur?

There are two broad categories of reasons for the lack of MLE in both the group and the individual situation. The first is that MLE is not offered by those social, cultural, or family agents who are supposed to do so. The second category of reasons for the absence of MLE resides in the incapacity of a particular individual to benefit from the MLE offered to him because of barriers inherent in his physical, neurological, cognitive, or emotional condition at a given time in his development. The first category is best illustrated by the state of poverty, often cited as the major reason for absence of mediated learning experience. Indeed, poverty can be a powerful inhibiting factor. An economically impoverished parent who has to make sure that the child's survival needs are met has very little uncommitted energy and few resources with which to mediate the child's learning experience. However, this is not always true. Indeed, if the economically poor family is living in a culture that sets a high priority on cultural transmission, parents will often defer even basic necessities in favor of mediating their cultural heritage. This was the case for many Jews in Poland who were literally on a starvation level of subsistence but who, in order to pay a teacher or to maintain time themselves to interact with their children in a mediating way, were ready to reduce their personal material subsistence.

Sometimes, a lack of mediated learning experience may be due to an overloaded family structure where parents cannot fulfill a mediational role because of being overburdened with the care of too many children. However, in a family where MLE is the prevalent mode of interaction, the existence of several children actually produces an amplified form of mediated learning experience (as noted in Chapter

5), one that under the parents' careful orchestration will even accelerate the development of their children because they capitalize on the forms of mediation provided by one another.

A beautiful example of the amplification of mediated learning experience was described by a mother of 11 children who, shortly after she gave birth to her 11th child, wrote an excellent paper about raising a large family. She had encouraged and prepared her older children to share with her in mediating to the younger ones, and through this feels that she helped them to attain high levels of academic and social achievement.

Another reason for the failure of some cultural agents and parents to offer MLE is the discontinuity in the life of groups or individuals, as can occur in conditions of immigration where the past is "left behind" and in certain cases even cast aside. Some immigrant parents, disadvantaged by their uprootedness and suffering from the fact that their past culture did not prepare them for confrontation with a new, technologically advanced one, may try to prevent their children from appreciating and even learning about their heritage. "Don't be like me" or "You're better off not knowing who I was or how I was living" is the implicit, or even explicit, message. In many cases, this represents a real sacrifice on the part of the parents and is done with a great deal of pain and sadness, even to the point of jeopardizing their own mental health. This unfortunate condition of "rejection" of one's past affects communication between parents and children, restricting it to the here and now and depriving it of the richness that mediating a past cultural experience can add to the child's functioning. A striking illustration of the effects of lack of mediation of the past can be found in the case of Helen.

Helen is the daughter of parents who, because of a dramatic change in their religious beliefs, decided to negate their past heritage along with rejecting all the objects, attitudes, customs, and other reminders of their former life. Indeed, music recorded by her father (a renowned jazz and rock composer), and the type of communication at home (both parents used prayer in their language and writing), changed radically or disappeared in efforts to obliterate the past. Both parents did show interest in transmitting their new beliefs and living practices to their children, but it was not easily done because of their own ambivalence toward their new life.

When brought to us, Helen had been described as a mentally retarded child with an IQ of 56, displaying an antiintellectual, rebellious attitude toward all attempts to teach her to read and write. Her psychological report said that she showed strong signs of an attentional deficit and that an organic condition might be responsible for her low functioning. The experiences to which her parents had exposed her, rich as they were in terms of music, left few marks on her repertoire of knowledge or her ways of interacting. Any attempt to make her think about the future was futile. It took us a long time to discover the person who was living behind this mask of passivity, an uprooted/unrooted adolescent with a very limited sense of reality, but with a very rich fantasy life.

Shortly thereafter, Helen started to display aggressive and delinquent behavior, and we suggested that she be placed for a while in a foster family. This failed totally; she became even more rebellious. Then, her parents turned again to the author, searching for another solution. She was again assessed, but this time with the learning potential assessment device (see Chapter 11). During this more productive assessment, partly owing to a much better level of cooperation (we found out later that she disliked her foster home and was eager for a change), and partly because we used mediated learning in a very intensive way, the results changed drastically, moving her from an IQ of 56 to an above-average level of intelligence as reflected in her behavior and thinking. Helen accepted mediation, enjoyed her success, and spontaneously proposed that the author allow her to live with his family (which the author did).

Mediational interaction with Helen helped change her whole style of thinking and way of life. However, it took years before her true personality and capacities became functional. Ultimately, because she became so interested in her studies, she received a degree from a university, married, and became a relatively well-to-do banker. Interestingly, she continued the interest that her parents had shown and included music in her life, both as an amateur musician and by making substantial monetary contributions to her city's orchestra.

Cultural minorities, often oppressed and deprived by a sudden and uneven encounter with the dominant culture, may discontinue their traditional forms of cultural transmission. This subsequently affects the readiness of the members of the nuclear family to mediate to their children. Such a discontinuity has happened to groups, such as groups of Native Americans, and its effects on both the culture and the individuals in it are deleterious.

Another reason for ineffectual or absent mediated learning experience, again involving cultural transmission, is the constant shrinking of the family to the restricted frontiers of two-parent and single-parent families. Industrialized societal conditions often weaken the relationship of people in the current generation to their ancestors. Family get-togethers and visits to the homes of grandparents, uncles, aunts, and cousins occur less and less and are often diminished in their importance. Intergenerational integration occurs far less than in the past, too. At best, there is a very restricted field of encounters that contribute little to maintaining the link between the past and present, and a projected link to the future. This limitation to a present orientation gives a unidimensional character to the existence of a large number of individuals. Devoid of the richness of the past, their orientation to the future becomes seriously impoverished.

Another factor that contributes to the lack of MLE in Westernized societies is the current emphasis on "rugged individualism" and "self-realization." The contemporary parent often devotes a great deal of time and energy to materialistic goals, which sometimes results in less opportunities for mediated learning experience with their children. The emphasis on individualism can affect the ability of men and women to function as effective mediating parents. Indeed, the trend toward individualism is pushed to the extreme by some of the existentialists who question the extent to which we have the right to impose our own culture on the next generation, and the right to shape the child's cognitive and personality repertoire to suit a particular culture.[1] Such questioning points to the weakening, sometimes even the total loss, of one of the most basic needs of parents in general: to perceive their children as extensions of themselves. Carried to an extreme, such an attitude may cause parents to relinquish the right to "impose" their values on the development of their children cognitively, affectively, behaviorally, and spiritually. A weakening of the desire for mediated learning experience is but one symptom of the loosened relationships between generations. To make matters worse, such loosening weakens parents' feeling of responsibility toward the next generation and presents a threat to the continuity of cultures themselves. The general disintegration of cultural transmission efforts may, in turn, further reduce mediation opportunities in the immediate family. Thus, impoverished parent–child interactions may worsen even further when so many "substitutes" for interaction are becoming available, such as movies, television, radio, and tape players.

Returning to the second category of reasons for lack of mediated learning experience—namely, the child's characteristics—conditions such as hyperactivity, hypoactivity, sensorial deficits, and emotional and social maladjustment may militate against the parents' attempts to mediate. These conditions can create large barriers between the child and his parents, making good mediating experiences very difficult to achieve. Such conditions require a change in the intensity and/or form of mediational interaction. The initiator, first of all, needs to ensure that the child has actually received the intended mediational interaction. Unless this is verified, very little effect can be expected. By varying mediational interaction, the parent will be able to ensure that it is received and integrated into the child's cognitive system. Then small changes can be introduced. For instance, a hyperactive child, by virtue of his difficulty in attending to a task or a tendency to overattend to irrelevant things, may benefit very little from exposure to direct experiences and to regular forms of mediation. He is mediationally deprived because of his lack of orienting and attending, lack of active searching, lack of selectivity. If we are able to overcome these barriers by producing types of mediation that, by their appeal, by their frequency, and by the meaning with which the mediator endows them, are strong enough to penetrate the barriers produced by the child's condition, his capacity to learn will become increased substantially. Indeed, we have seen some hyperactive individuals reach high levels of functioning through the judicious use of MLE, although some of their hyperactive behavior may persist throughout life (see Figure 16 for additional insights concerning causative factors).

Joseph illustrates how a lack of effective mediation can impair development. All of the professionals involved with him—the neurosurgeon who operated to stop his internal brain hemorrhaging (caused by a car accident when he was 8 weeks old), the pediatrician, the speech and language therapist, the physical therapist—all without exception considered it a miracle that he survived at all. Moreover, that he learned to walk, although with a strong limp, and that he learned to say a few words was considered miraculous. All of the professionals reviewing his case were unanimous in forecasting that he would be incapable of any independent life owing to his low level of intelligence (recorded as in the severely retarded range) and his nearly total inability to communicate.

Since the prognosis was so gloomy, the treatment proposed by the group of professionals involved with Joseph emphasized a pas-

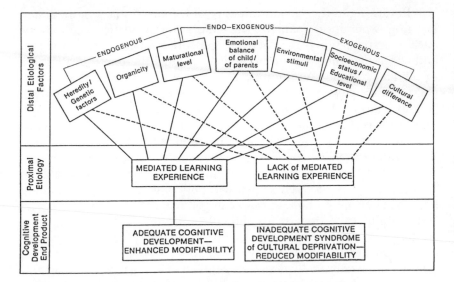

Figure 16. Distal and proximal etiologies.

sive-acceptant approach. One of the authors attempted to persuade his parents to take a more active modificational approach but was not successful. Joseph was placed in a highly regarded residential setting for people with mental retardation, one that practiced passive acceptance, that is, provided residents with comfort and acceptance of the *status quo* as a prime goal. The stress of learning new things was considered undesirable since it made him uncomfortable. The results of this passive-acceptant approach proved to be a self-fulfilling prophecy of the professionals' gloomy prognosis: long-term cognitive stagnation.

When he was brought to us at the age of 12, we assessed Joseph's functioning employing the learning potential assessment device (LPAD). Discovering a capacity for change, we established a positive set of goals for him. After a year of intensive work, during which instrumental enrichment (IE) was used, Joseph started to benefit from his interactions not only with teachers mediating to him but also directly from the environment. Given this progress, Joseph was placed in a foster family, where he had other children to interact with. In the beginning he paid very little attention to what they were saying or doing; his passivity and fleeting attention didn't allow him to benefit from the wealth of stimulation. Only after having been exposed systematically to mediational focusing through the instrumental enrichment program (Organization of Dots, Analytic Perception, Comparative Behavior; see Chapter 12) did he learn to invest his energies in a way that made him able to decode printed symbols and finally to begin to read. The development of a more intelligible and rich language, which accompanied his growing reading ability, affected him greatly. For example, he began to engage in social interactions with the other children in his foster family and, later, with peers.

Today, Joseph is able to benefit from integration in his own family. His mother previously had not been able to deal with him because of her mourning over his condition, which created a total emotional detachment. She left him to the care of nurses and other caregivers. By changing the prognosis and outlook, the mother is ready to reach a stage of bonding and attachment to the child she had previously given up.

We have also had success in helping the hypoactive child—the flaccid-toned, inactive, apathetic child, who does not "claim his rights for attention"—whose passivity sometimes produces a tendency in his parents to abandon their mediation attempts. If mediation attempts cease, a hypoactive child's physical needs will be attended to faithfully; that is, he will be cleaned, fed, and held, but very little attention may be given beyond meeting these basic needs.

The case of Marsha is relevant here. Marsha was referred to us at the age of 23—a beautiful young woman, with an empty look in her eyes, who did not look into the eyes of others. Marsha had great difficulties in reading and writing. Her academic deficiencies led some professionals to assume that she had a very low IQ. Indeed, she had only one topic of conversation, childish comic books, which she talked about incessantly. Her speech was verbose but devoid of meaning. Understandably, nobody wanted to interact with her unless absolutely necessary. She displayed poor reality control, which we thought was due to deficient cognitive functions, which, in turn, made her thinking illogical. For example, she would link concepts that were absolutely unrelated to each other and yet she appeared to consider the construction as normal. When examined, using the learning potential assessment device, she proved to be highly modifiable. Indeed, her ability to engage in higher mental processing, such as solving analogy problems correctly, was achieved relatively easily. Marsha was then offered a full instrumental enrichment (IE) program with the goal of correcting her deficient cognitive functions. We invested many months in mediation with her, and slowly she learned to put information together correctly. For example, she learned to use several interrelated sources of information in making a decision, to inhibit her impulsivity, to formulate verbally the problem to which she was exposed, and then to produce a logical response. After three years of intervention, Marsha became a good thinker and showed strong signs of social and occupational adaptation. Eventually, she learned to be successful in her work at a clothing boutique and became a capable wife and mother.

Why had Marsha exhibited retarded performance for so many years? Seldom can one pinpoint a specific isolated event that might have triggered retarded performance. Possibly her foster parents (she was placed in a foster home as a baby) did not mediate to her sufficiently. Marsha had been a very good, though placid, baby who demanded little from her foster parents. They realized this themselves when they compared Marsha's temperament with that of a girl they adopted, who was extremely demanding. Her foster mother recalls interactions with Marsha as being restricted to meeting basic needs, to which she attended with meticulous care. She loved the child, but since Marsha neither required her presence by crying nor showed animation when approached, the foster mother interacted with her more or less on a demand basis.

The hypoactive child may have a reduced need for stimulation so that in order to attract his attention, one needs to increase the level of intensity in a mediational interaction to match the heightened threshold for activation. A mother brought her 12-month-old child with Down syndrome to us, complaining that her daughter was not responsive to her; that is, she did not turn her eyes toward her when she spoke. The mother expressed the fear that her daughter might be autistic. The author asked the mother to interact with her daughter. Placing the child on the floor, she did not bend down to talk to her but, standing upright, quite a distance from the child, spoke in a soft, very low voice. The child did not respond but continued to stare at the ceiling. The author asked the mother to speak more loudly, but her efforts were very limited, and the child still did not respond. When the author shouted toward the child, she tensed and immediately turned her eyes toward the author as he continued to talk loudly; then she began to cry. The author guessed that the child might have impaired hearing, due perhaps to a type of middle ear effusion that is quite common in children with Down syndrome. This was the case, and the problem was treated with medication. At the same time, the mother learned not only to use a louder voice to interact with her daughter but also to position herself to communicate with her more effectively. Their interactions improved rapidly. The mother's initial approach, which consisted of explaining the disability of the child as being linked to her chromosomal condition, had changed. She had learned to bypass the barriers.

The classic illustration of a barrier to mediated learning experience is found in the autistic child who, because of his emotional detachment and lack of eye contact, is virtually inaccessible to MLE. A child who does not share another's gaze, does not interact, relates to fragments of the human being with whom he is in contact—hands, legs, nose—rather than the whole figure, is cut off from mediation. Interestingly, the autistic child is usually not limited in his direct interaction with objects; in many cases, he interacts quite efficiently, even precociously, with them. This "selective" motivation makes it very difficult to penetrate his socialization inaccessibility. The effectiveness of mediated learning experience in the case of autism will depend strongly on the extent to which the mediator is able to promote a state of dependency in the child that will turn the mediational process into an interaction between partners. If this happens, then we may see a degree of modifiability that is usually not expected from children with autism. Clara's case will illustrate what we mean.

Clara was referred to us at the age of 8 months. Her mother brought Clara and her normal twin brother, John, along in order to demonstrate the great differences in the functioning of the two. It was indeed these differences that caused the mother to notice Clara's early developmental deficiency. The mother, with her sharp instincts and insights, felt that Clara did not respond as did John to her presence, her smile, or her advances to pick her up. After careful neurological and developmental examinations, her doctor began to see that Clara displayed classic autistic traits. For example, she demonstrated an early precocious interest in objects such as a piece of string, which she would jiggle endlessly in front of her eyes. As the two children grew, their development diverged. John, an outgoing child, became more demanding of the attention of his mother and of other adults. Clara was much less interested in people and, in many cases, resisted attempts made by her parents and others to attract her attention, to pick her up, to hug her, preferring to "interact" with her pieces of string.

Attempts were made to help Clara's mother strengthen her mediated learning interaction, but these were not successful. We suggested many different ways to attract her child's gaze, to impose eye
contact, to make the child follow her, to teach her to imitate. The
mother claimed that she had tried everything but nothing worked. It
was clear that Clara's mother's interaction with her daughter, as contrasted with that with her son, was almost completely blocked by
Clara's lack of responsiveness. Then we enlisted her father's cooperation. Clara's father was a jovial man who did not hesitate to lovingly
"impose" his presence on Clara even when she fought against it. He
"made" her imitate him; he "made" her babble; he even "made" her
smile. His insistence broke through the barriers of Clara's detachment, resulting ultimately in a meaningful relationship between
them. Later, we enlisted Clara's grandmother's help. Her grandmother was even more outgoing than Clara's father, exhibiting a
powerful ability to secure a response from the child. Clara's grandmother was so successful at interacting with her granddaughter that
Clara was moved to her grandmother's home to live.

An educator trained in MLE worked with Clara for a two-year
period. Progress made by Clara, especially in the language area, increased her mother's readiness to interact with her. Today Clara is
integrated into a regular school, attends a class for students with
slight learning disabilities, and is an outgoing, cooperative teenager.
Here and there, certain residuals of her bizarre behaviors appear, but
she controls them quickly now. She is a great help to her grandmother at a time the grandmother needs help. What might have
happened if everyone had yielded to Clara's early tendency to avoid
and even reject social interaction?

What about helping autistic adolescents and young adults? Can
they be helped by MLE? Even though age may increase resistance to
change, maturity has its advantages too. The individual's greater experience, insight, and motivation, which are not always present in
childhood, may be well developed in adulthood.

Such was the situation with Ben. When he was referred for assessment, we were told that he did not need a diagnostic workup
since his condition had been diagnosed as autism during early infancy. Work with Ben was frustrating. He was cooperative and disci-
plined but acted like a robot, his performance never varying. When
hugged, he would keep his hands hanging beside his stiffened body,

giving us the impression of hugging a mannequin. He had learned to articulate words, but we could not communicate with him since his speech was totally echolalic (repeating the words and/or tone of voice just heard). For a long period after his referral his verbal interaction was limited to the faithful repetition of what he heard from his conversing partner: "What did you eat this morning?" was echoed back, "What did you eat this morning?" followed by disengagement, which would last many minutes. The conversing partner, losing patience, would then give the correct answer (which was also echoed) and then usually give up on the "conversation." Ben never used a word referring to a feeling of joy, sadness, distress, or other emotion. When asked to mimic how we look when we are afraid, anxious, joyful, curious, angry, or happy, he used one expression, which consisted of protruding his mouth, closing his eyes almost completely, and pulling his hair. It was hard to think that something inside him might be affected by the instrumental enrichment program. But his teachers continued to be hopeful that changes would occur not only in his capacity to cope with the tasks but also in the affective tone with which the work was done. The great difficulty in communication continued for many years. At one point, though, when we did an assessment, we were able to elicit a number of behaviors that pointed to some weak points in the "Jericho walls" behind which he had been hiding in his own world of fantasy.

Eventually, he began to react to the encouragement and verbal reinforcement he had been offered, showing departures from his echolalic behavior. For example, he laughed after he understood one of the cartoons in instrumental enrichment. The MLE to which he reacted best was that which he received during group activities. Increasingly, he took advantage of opportunities to display his newly learned language: He read and wrote Hebrew much more fluently, though slowly; he learned to sing and enjoyed doing so, once even requesting on his own initiative to sing a song. When he began to initiate social interactions, he was placed in a class where he learned Hebrew along with normal adult immigrants. His teachers, guided by us, encouraged him to become involved in the activities of his classmates, who listened to his questions and responded to them. In addition, one-to-one activity therapy was begun in order to intensify his capacity to establish more meaningful relationships. Through activity therapy he started to project feelings after they were displayed and modeled by his therapist. His successful mastery of IE tasks made him progressively more able to use relational modes of thinking, and this opened the way for increased verbal interactions.

The illness and death of his therapist became a source of many new but very painful feelings for Ben. His therapist suffered a long illness, during which she continued to work with Ben, until a few weeks before her death. The therapist, herself a lonely person, shared with Ben her anxiety and pain, enabling him to experience compassion. Following her death, Ben participated at the burial, experiencing feelings of loss and grief for the first time.

Ben left us for his home after five years of work at the institute. A handsome young man, he is currently living with his mother, who acknowledges him to be a great comfort (her husband died a few years ago). He works as billing manager in a small advertising agency and is taking a course in typing and computer use. His speech has become quite fluent and spontaneous, and he volunteers information and answers questions immediately with only occasional echolalic residuals. Through intensive study and practice he has become proficient in playing the guitar. (The author must admit that neither did he believe that this type of accomplishment would be possible nor did he encourage Ben's enormous investment in it.) Recently, Ben gave a number of performances, including in his repertoire classical pieces requiring a high level of competence in reading the scores and fingering technique. Despite some slips, he showed skill in compositions requiring complex movements. He seeks contact with former caregivers and enjoys peers, phoning them weekly to share his achievements. Ben looks forward to marrying (he has been dating but his mother thought—somewhat justifiably—that his girlfriend functioned too far below his own level). His aspirations continue to grow, which is probably the most important factor in his metamorphosis. During our last meeting he kept asking me, half rhetorically, half asserting, "Am I not changed?" "And how!" was my answer.

Ben's case is not to be considered as the ultimate statement about the use of MLE with adolescent and adult autistic or autisticlike persons. Even though there are about 15 cases with which we have been successful, we have had little experience and even less success with totally nonverbal persons with autism. A second and more serious limitation is our present state of understanding of the process that made our mediated learning experience successful. Was it the personalized emotional interactions with the mediators that broke through?

Was it the IE program? Was it the intensive and planned exposure to group life and the amplified mediational opportunities orchestrated there? It is very probable that a combination of all these, and other elements as well, had a synergistic effect. But definitive answers to these questions will require a systematic longitudinal approach to experimentation, data gathering, and interpretation of findings. Additionally, a methodology adequate for the study of the differential effects MLE may have on the great diversity of autistic persons will have to be developed. However, there can be no doubt that the modifiability of individuals who display many types of retarded and disturbed performance can be accomplished through mediated learning coupled with living in a modifying environment.

Another type of child who is often deprived of MLE and, consequently, may display reduced modifiability is, paradoxically, the gifted child. Some gifted children tend to reject any attempts made by the mediator to interpose himself between them and a given experience. Sometimes at an early age this child says, "Let me do it myself," and is unwilling to slow his pace and the intensity with which he interacts with books, building blocks, and other objects in order to let the mediator demonstrate how something works. His rapid processing of information renders him impatient and unwilling to wait until the mediator has conveyed a direction, even if the mediation would be helpful in the long run. Sometimes the parent or teacher of a gifted child may consider any attempt to mediate to the gifted child as futile, saying: "He already knows how to do that. He understands it better than I do and doesn't need any help from me. Each time I try to help he has a temper tantrum." In many instances, both parent and child feel that interfering with the child's "natural" way of interacting with the environment may hamper rather than promote the child's functioning. And in certain instances this may, indeed, be true. However, when one considers the effect of lack of mediated learning experience on other areas of the gifted individual's functioning, especially at later stages and higher levels, one can hypothesize that the lack of mediated learning experience will have a negative effect. In fact, the increase we have observed in the number of gifted underachievers might be explained, at least in part, by parents' or teachers' unwillingness to mediate, to interpose themselves judiciously between the gifted child and the sources of stimulation to which he is exposed. Indeed, if mediated learning isn't provided, gifted children may invest themselves too quickly and too narrowly, limiting their later ability by prematurely focusing all of their attention and energy on specialized areas. All of this must be handled delicately so as not to interrupt their "blazing" interest in a worthwhile endeavor. But a balance must be struck between the child's need to pursue knowledge and the child's (and society's) need to develop an acculturated, as well as competent, human being.

One of the great advantages of using MLE for instructing parents of children with retarded performance is that the parent is not asked to replace his own behavior, which has been culturally determined or produced by his individual preference or style, with a "canned" program. The practice of "coercing" parents to replace their own style of interaction behavior with the interactive patterns of the "successful" parent may have very negative effects. After having tried very hard to give up their own style, their own familiar way of behaving, they may return to what they were used to doing, but with strong guilt feelings. In certain cases they may give up their own interaction styles if they are described as inadequate and inefficient, and, not being able to do what is suggested to them, create a learning vacuum, that is, substantially reduce the amount and quality of interaction with their children.

In contrast, MLE instructors recommend that parents use familiar, preferred interactions that can be used to handle content with which the parents are familiar and that belong to their usual stylistic repertoire. The quality of interaction will then become much more acceptable to them and also will affect their child much more strongly in terms of his structural cognitive modifiability.

CHAPTER 7

Debby

Les chromosomes n'ont pas le dernier mot.
(Chromosomes don't have the last word.)
Le Monde de l'Education, 1983[1]

Debby, a young girl who has Down syndrome, is 18 years old. She is sensitive, motivated, and preparing diligently for employment as a kindergarten teacher's aide; her story touches on all of the instructional techniques advocated in this book. Moreover, it illustrates how Debby's parents mediated her learning experiences, employing an active modificational approach with warmth, tenaciousness, and, when necessary, "tough love."

A day after Debby's birth, feeling that something was wrong with her baby, her mother asked the doctor if everything was normal and was told that the baby was healthy but had a serious chromosomal disorder, called Down syndrome. Naturally, both parents were extremely disturbed to learn this bad news, especially after the hospital staff suggested an immediate placement outside of the family so as not to disrupt the lives of the other four children. After a daylong, seesaw series of deliberations between the parents, and after professional consultation, a decision was made by her parents to take Debby home and try to raise her as they were raising their other children. To begin this normalization process, a name was given to her at the synagogue—as is the Jewish custom—and her birth was celebrated with the entire family, as had been done when their other children were born. The decision to take Debby home was a very difficult one, but the parents, especially Debby's mother, felt that it was the only way for them to avoid guilt feelings on their part and expressions of pity on the part of others.

About two weeks later, a pediatrician, an expert in the field of developmental impairments and mental retardation, was consulted. He reconfirmed that the child had Down syndrome and was in good health, except for pronounced hypotony (poor muscle tone). When her parents inquired about the child's long-range developmental possibilities, he said: "Your daughter is a retarded child; this is unchangeable. No matter what you do for her, she will not attain very much developmentally. So, don't even try to put her in a kindergarten with normal children. In fact, she will have to spend all her life in special facilities. And, if you try to put her with normal children, it will not only be useless but will also become a continuous source of frustration, both to her and to you." This was a turning point for Debby's father, who remembers saying to his wife, "Let us help this child just talk and walk; we shall show what can be done with such a child!"

To be fair to the doctor, his prognosis was probably a routine warning meant to dissipate illusions as to the future of a child with Down syndrome. But its effect was to make the parents more determined than ever to do all they could to promote Debby's development. Without delay and guided by an institute psychologist (one of the authors), they began a process of systematic intervention geared toward maximizing Debby's abilities, focused mainly on the stimulation of her social, physical, and communication skills.

Debby's poor muscle tone was a serious obstacle to intervention efforts. It hampered her experiencing the environment. Even when objects were close to her, her limited ability to reach them added to her disability. In order to overcome these difficulties, her mother interacted actively with Debby, first by introducing herself as a major source of stimulation and then by encouraging the entire family to join her in these interaction sessions. Hours and hours were spent in trying to capture the eye of the child by varying their facial expressions and vocalizations and by placing colorful objects in her bedroom and around the home.

At this stage, Debby was lying inertly, "communicating" only with her eyes. Slowly, as strong emotional ties developed between mother and child, smiling and other forms of reacting emerged. At first her reactions were sporadic, but gradually, with the persistence of her mother's attention, she developed more stable patterns of reaction, ultimately showing distress whenever the stimulation of the mother or of other family members was not available.

The stimulating atmosphere created by Debby's parents fostered the development of the other children too. In fact, the family became a mutually supportive entity in promoting Debby's educational and social development. This mutuality considerably increased the possibilities of intervention and introduced another important element in the mediational process: variety in the nature of the stimulation sources and mediational agents. Thus, her environment became ever richer and more demanding, requiring Debby to adapt, and readapt, to diverse stimulation.

Particular attention was directed toward motivating her to interact with such objects as balls and colorful, noise-producing toys. Activities involving these objects were goal-directed and verbally described to Debby by the members of the family as they were performed. Thus, she learned a great deal by imitation and through developing sharing behavior. Special attention was paid not only to the visual sense but also to all the other sensory modalities. Sounds were modeled and solicited for reproduction; various objects were presented, along with requests for her to touch and to supply verbal labels for the objects; she was put in a sitting position by using physical or human support, so that she could view her world more easily and efficiently. She was carried into new places constantly, involving her in all kinds of human and environmental interactions. Through all of this, she learned to effectively communicate her desires and intentions long before developing intelligible verbal language.

Her physical and movement abilities developed very slowly. Behaviors such as turning from one side to the other, sitting, crawling, walking, jumping, climbing stairs, all appeared relatively late in her life, even when compared with the average developmental rate of other children with Down syndrome. Thus, intensive physical therapy was begun early in an attempt to promote her large- and small-muscle-related abilities. Through imitation, tongue mobility was encouraged, as were vocalizations. In fact, through the mediation of another person describing her movements as she made them, she learned the importance of speech as a valuable communication instrument and developed a sound basis for further language activities. Clearly, mediated learning was occurring.

The first two years of life were the most difficult but also the most exciting for Debby's parents, who started the intensive intervention program on the basis of a challenge but who had to face expressions of discouragement from many people, especially from professionals.

But they were encouraged by Debby's progress, beginning to see the fruits of their mediational investment. The socialization ability of their child gave them particular hope.

The development of speech continued to be very delayed. And, as is the case with many children with Down syndrome, Debby had a protruding tongue, which hampered her in chewing food and in vocalizing intelligible sounds. It also aggravated her drooling problem.

Although Debby's verbal communication skills were very limited at this stage (intelligible speech started to appear only at the age of 3½ to 4 years), she understood verbal cues. Moreover, nonverbal interactions became frequent and intensive. Imitation—based upon interactions with normal models of behavior—proved to be a major vehicle for learning and reinforcement. Her highly developed nonverbal language served as strong encouragement for her mother and other members of the family as they learned to understand her intentions and expressions of pleasure and distress, desires as expressed by postures, gestures, and movements. Eventually, expressive language emerged, and reciprocal interactions became possible and even pleasurable.

At the age of 4, despite the fact that she was not yet fully toilet-trained, Debby was placed in a private nursery school with normal children who were about 3 years of age, so that she would be more comparable with them in a variety of functional areas. The regular nursery school was preferred because of parental conviction that it was important to provide normal patterns of behavior for her imitation. Her parents felt that the earlier integration processes were activated, the greater would be the chances for good social and educational development in the future.

One of the most significant factors in Debby's development was religious and cultural tradition. Both the home and the kindergarten were of a religious orientation, so that mutually reinforcing activities were possible. The transmission of religious culture not only affected her development of a strong value system but also meaningfully affected her social/cognitive functioning. Religious events such as the Sabbath and holidays became important factors around which daily life was organized. Passover, for instance, was associated with spring, and Hanukkah with the beginning of winter. Sabbath meals, with their rituals, special foods, and family customs, became highly significant to the process of Debby's education. In fact, a great many activities during the week were centered around the Sabbath and the preparations for it. Sabbath songs were rehearsed frequently, days were labeled and counted in relation to the coming Sabbath, and daily events were highlighted, ordered, and interpreted according to their proximity and relation with this special day. Gradually, she became capable of anticipating the closeness of the Sabbath by observing the preparatory activities of her mother. The expectation of the Sabbath introduced a dimension by which a relation was created between events experienced in the past, observed in the present, and looked toward in the future. The fact that both of her important educational frameworks, the family and the nursery school, were consistent in their basic orientation amplified the impact of these elements on the development of her cognitive and social life.

A close-knit extended family became a powerful source for her continuing development. Each relative was asked to identify him/herself by name when approaching Debby and to clarify the nature of the family relationship (uncle, cousin). In this way, family relationships became, at a very early stage in her life, a useful domain for mediation of social and cognitive functioning. Astonishingly, Debby learned these rather complex relationships rapidly, and at the age of 5½, she showed a good grasp of the extended family system. For example, she could determine easily the mutual relationship between uncle and niece. In fact, continuous encouragement to define relationships and to adapt to them became an important source for activating her thinking abilities.

Around the age of 6, Debby was ready to change her environment, that is, to begin kindergarten. Naturally, her parents wanted her to be in a kindergarten with normal children. But, despite the favorable referral report written by her nursery school teacher, Debby's parents faced strong opposition to her being integrated within the regular kindergarten in their neighborhood school. Municipal authorities, the psychologist, and the kindergarten teacher all objected vehemently to her absorption, stating that it would be harmful to both her and the other children. Moreover, the majority of the parents of the normal kindergarten children expressed strong antagonism to the idea of integration, not wishing to expose their children to an "abnormal" child. This strong resistance became a serious problem for Debby's parents, who feared that all their work to create normalized conditions for their child was about to be cast aside.

When everything was about to be lost, her father asked for a meeting with the parents of the kindergarten children. After a long and frustrating evening of deliberations the father said: "Listen, dear friends, today I'm here in front of you trying to do my very best for my child. Nobody can guarantee that tomorrow or the day after one of you will not be in a similar situation. . . ." As with a wave of a magic wand, resistance crumbled, and Debby was accepted into the regular kindergarten.

During the school year, further progress was made in a variety of areas. Special investment was made to further Debby's language development. Despite the difficulties of pronouncing words, which became more and more problematic, she was encouraged continuously to use verbal language as a prime vehicle for communication and not to yield to her articulation difficulties and avoid speaking. The other children in the kindergarten were guided by the teacher to react to Debby with patience, both when talking and listening to her. With the help of an assistant teacher, she became involved in, and proficient in, most activities of the kindergarten.

As a result of her proficiency, particularly the ability she showed in interactions with other children, strong social links developed with her normal peers as well as with their parents. While visiting the kindergarten, parents learned to like Debby and, consequently, encouraged their children to interact with her even after school and in their own homes and courtyards. Many of her peers came regularly to Debby's home to play with her. These activities became important ingredients in the educational process and in her acquiring normal social behavior.

The kindergarten period was a highly profitable time for Debby, owing to the coordinated efforts of the family and the kindergarten teacher, who received intensive guidance in how to mediate learning experiences.

For example, Debby was persistently questioned so as to raise her need to describe what she was experiencing; she was encouraged to elaborate in order to increase her understanding of the origins of events and their purpose; she was rewarded consistently for every little success to enhance her feeling of competence. Continuous questioning and the other efforts invested in fostering her abilities caused the development of an inquiring mind and a feeling of self-confidence. The more her language skills developed, the more varied and meaningful became her cognitive activities and her social relations. In addition, play, both individually and in a group, was encouraged in order to enhance her motivation for being involved with peers in social and academic activities.

In order to facilitate her development during kindergarten, and especially to prepare her for entering public school at a later time, Debby was given a special tutorial program. Three times a week she studied with a special teacher. Starting with basic skills, such as matching and discriminating between objects and then comparing and describing their functions, the teacher led her, step by step, to increasingly higher levels of functioning. Care was taken to encourage her to use acquired skills to the point of mastery, gradually giving her the skills needed for beginning reading. At this point, letters were introduced, matched with and distinguished from others, and labeled in connection with words beginning with the letters.

During this time, Debby learned to concentrate her attention on school activities, which she repeated on her own at home. She often played the teacher, showing organizational capacities and tact in guiding her siblings, friends, and even adults in fulfilling different roles that she had learned at school. The tutorial teacher worked with Debby for about five years, contributing significantly to both her scholastic and social development.

Functional independence became a major educational objective during the kindergarten period. Decisions concerning Debby's current abilities and future prospects were discussed with her, in an attempt to involve her actively in shaping her own life. These activities were, of course, adjusted to her level of functioning and world of interests. Nevertheless, it was a continuous struggle not to "leave the child to her own fate," or to simply make all decisions for her.

Throughout these early years of schooling, Debby was educated according to the principles of MLE (see Chapter 5). The three basic characteristics of MLE, namely, intentionality, transcendence, and meaning, became the main features of others', particularly adults', interactions with her. Moreover, the mediators acted according to principles of the learning potential assessment device model (see Chapter 11), assessing to what degree mediation was successful and what could be done to overcome difficulties that emerged, so as to enhance proficiency. Experiences of success and failure in attaining objectives were communicated to the parents, who became central figures in guiding and directing other mediators.

Entering first grade was another critical point in Debby's development. An intensive search was conducted by her parents to find a regular school in which classes were not too large and achievement requirements were not too high. The atmosphere of the school and the personality of the teacher were of special interest in this search. Fortunately, such a school was found, but a trying advocacy process began all over again: to persuade the municipal authorities, the psychologist, the school principal, and the first-grade teacher to accept Debby. However, compared with the difficulties encountered earlier concerning her absorption in the kindergarten, it was much easier now to persuade the decision-makers of the appropriateness of placement in a regular first-grade class, owing to the extremely favorable recommendation conveyed by Debby's kindergarten teacher. The benefits of the early struggle for integration had become instrumental in creating later opportunities for normalized experiences.

The process of functional reading acquisition, which is a major concern for all first-grade teachers, was far from being a smooth one for Debby. It required the concerted efforts of the classroom teacher, a tutor, parents, siblings, and many others, while, at the same time, an attempt was made to avoid the development of antagonistic feelings that would possibly turn her against reading and academic work altogether.

Reading was taught in the synthetic, or phonetic, method—namely, starting with the sounds and names of letters and then moving quickly to forming words. This position was adopted after consultation with reading experts who felt that this method had a good chance for success because of its being anchored in the learning opportunities that had been emphasized during Debby's early education.

At this stage Debby also began a long-term instrumental enrichment (IE) program (see Chapter 12). Although the IE instruments available at that time were not adequate for her age or level of functioning, mediation was geared toward teaching basic cognitive prerequisites considered to be of absolute necessity to thinking and academic activities. Comparative and discriminatory mastery were at the core of these activities. The materials used for these purposes were highly varied, mostly in visual-tactile form, such as Organization of Dots and Orientation in Space (see Chapter 12).

Writing was a very problematic area of learning for Debby. Owing to her hypotonicity (weak muscle tone), she had severe difficulties in using a pencil in initiating and tracing lines. Therefore, writing had to be postponed until her neuromuscular skills developed to the point where coordinated pencil use was possible. It took more than a year before writing was introduced and about three years beyond that until her writing became readable. During this period, much effort was expended in teaching her to copy a written text and to follow visually her own production while tracking it in the text to be copied.

Unfortunately, just as Debby's progress was beginning to accelerate, her school became a special education facility. Although her parents resisted the idea of changing her environment again, they felt that she would not continue to progress adequately if placed only with children who had disabilities. Hence, another school serving a normal population was found and Debby was accepted into it. Owing to her difficulties in reading, and in order to further her social development, her parents were advised, and agreed, to place her in the regular first grade for a second year. As it turned out, this decision proved beneficial. For the first time in her life she had abilities superior to those of her classmates, and sometimes she was able to help her peers with their reading problems. In order to further enhance this positive experience, her remedial teacher was asked to prepare Debby for the lessons a day in advance of their delivery. This became a regular and highly effective procedure.

The most difficult academic subject for Debby was arithmetic. Over the years, intensive efforts were invested in teaching her basic arithmetic skills, but with little success. She did succeed in acquiring the understanding of numbers, including the notion of zero, and counting of objects was mastered quite early. But her main difficulty was in operating with numbers flexibly. Fortunately, in fifth grade, she learned to use a calculator and quickly became adept at using it, including understanding what was necessary to solve the simple arithmetic problems that had baffled her before.

Beginning with the sixth grade, Debby started a regular, more intensive IE program, which was implemented by a schoolteacher during resource room activities. In addition, both a private remedial teacher and Debby's elder sister taught her IE almost daily. Even at this stage, not all of the IE instruments were accessible to her, but additional instruments were gradually and regularly introduced. She was very interested in these activities, which proved helpful from both a cognitive and a motivational point of view. Her insight and logical thinking abilities improved substantially, as did her verbal interaction skills.

At the same time, she was assessed with the learning potential assessment device (LPAD; see Chapter 11), revealing a high level of modifiability and learning potential. This assessment was extremely helpful in guiding her parents and teachers as to how and where to invest their efforts during teaching activities. Special attention continued to be paid to language. For instance, teaching was geared toward definition of terms and the learning of synonyms and antonyms. This mediational process transformed each interaction into an occasion for teaching language without coercion, embedding it in daily events and in the child's fields of interest.

Throughout her elementary school experience, social relationships with classmates were an extremely important and highly constructive element in her development. In this regard, in order to help her with specific problems, student tutoring was introduced both in the classroom and in the schoolyard. For example, at one point, a girl from a higher class took her under her wing to help her to participate with peers more fully. Relationships with the other children became warm and supportive, and she developed strong ties with a number of them. On the rare occasions when Debby was absent from school for health or other reasons, her friends took care to bring the daily homework to her or to phone her in order to chat with her. Thus, the school became for Debby, as well as for her parents, a very supportive frame of reference for intellectual and social development. On one occasion when she was playing in the courtyard with her friends, her father dropped by to visit the school. On seeing him, all of the children ran over to tell him that that day Debby was called to the blackboard by her teacher to write the answer to a problem and wrote the answer correctly and without any assistance. Her success was a pleasurable experience for the entire class and a meaningful event for her and her parents.

In the upper three public school grades, Debby's instructional program intensified and became compartmentalized, involving a series of different teachers for different subjects. At first, Debby experienced some difficulties with this change, owing to her tendency to develop strong personal ties with each of her teachers. However, the supportive attitude of the teaching staff and the special attention she received from all of them helped her to overcome this difficulty. After a few months she adjusted well to the new conditions, and her school life went on smoothly.

As Debby matured, she showed continuing tenacity in trying to overcome her learning difficulties. For example, because of her poor muscle tone and problems with dynamic balance, she had difficulties in jumping. One day she came to her father, asking him to buy her a jump rope. When she got it, she went into the courtyard and began, on her own initiative, to train herself to use it. It was important for her because this was a frequently used game in which (at that time) she could only participate partially, i.e., holding and turning the rope. It took her days and days of practice, but finally she managed to master this complicated motor behavior. Thereafter, her participation in jump rope games became regular. Self-learning initiative became a salient feature of her personality.

The tenacity of both Debby and her mother was important for both of them. For example, when Debby was 7 years old, her mother tried to enroll her in a regular ballet class. When the teacher saw Debby she refused to let her into her class, giving various "reasons" for her refusal. The disappointment of the child was very strong, and she exerted pressure upon her mother to continue her efforts. After many discussions with the teacher, Debby's mother succeeded in persuading her to accept the child on a trial basis for a period of three months. Debby integrated rapidly with the group and was successful in learning to dance quite well despite her physical limitations. In fact, she appeared at the recital of her class at the end of the year. To the delight of the audience, Debby prompted her classmates, indicating the part they were to perform when they missed their cues. She continued her ballet lessons until the age of 14, when she and her parents left the country on a sabbatical leave.

At the end of the fifth grade, Debby enrolled in the local youth group along with most of her school peers. This became a new area of adjustment for her because she had to cope with a completely different socialization framework, based mainly upon voluntary discipline and personal involvement in a variety of highly organized activities. Prior to her enrollment, Debby's parents invited all the counselors of the group to their house, explaining the nature of Debby's condition, her learning difficulties, and the importance of their contribution to her immediate well-being and future development. The reactions of the counselors were extremely positive; she was integrated and supported by all of them. The fact that at the same time some of the other girls of her class joined the same youth group facilitated the absorption process, and Debby interacted smoothly with all the new members of the group. Tutoring was used again as a supportive device, especially in the first stages. Gradually this became unnecessary, and her integration was genuine and highly beneficial for her as well as for the entire group.

When Debby was 12, a Bat-Mitzvah ceremony was organized in her parents' home. More than a hundred people, family and friends, attended the festive event. Debby's parents had suggested to her that they postpone the ceremony by a year or two, but she insisted on holding it at the regular time. Following her father's greetings to the guests, Debby gave a speech that she had written herself, delivering it with charm and self-confidence, uninhibited by the crowd. There were many tears in the audience that evening, and Debby was rewarded afterwards with a standing ovation.

About a year later, Debby became the first child with Down syndrome in Israel to undergo reconstructive plastic surgery (a procedure described in Chapter 10). A variety of physical stigmata were considerably alleviated by the operation, including her protruding tongue, which appeared to be the origin of a number of impairments such as drooling, nose-running, hoarseness of the voice, and inarticulate speech. When first invited to the hospital to discuss the possibility of surgery, she listened carefully, and after leaving the consultation room she ran immediately to the mirror, looked at herself, and exclaimed, "What is wrong with me? Why do I need an operation?" She was reassured by her parents that nothing was wrong with her and that surgery would not be done without her consent. All of the relevant details were communicated to her. For several days she asked questions persistently, repeating them frequently and expressing great excitement mixed with deep concern. Finally, she came to her mother and said, "I'm going to have this operation. I am a girl, and the more beautiful I am, the easier it will be for me to marry." It was she herself who placed the goal of surgery into an adult-oriented perspective. After she made her decision, there was no more questioning. In fact, on many occasions she provided important support to her parents about the upcoming surgery, alleviating their fears and anxieties.

The reconstructive plastic surgery project included 11 children and was implemented over a three-day period. Her parents preferred that Debby not be operated on during the first day. Without discussing this matter with her parents, when the surgeon invited her, together with all the other children, for a final checkup, Debby said to him, "I would like to be the first to be operated on by you." Astonished, the surgeon asked her why she wanted to be first. She replied, "If I am first, l will have a good chance to be home for Sabbath and not be here in the hospital." And so it was. She was operated on first and went home for Sabbath (see Figure 17).

A year after the operation, Debby and her parents went to Canada for a year on a sabbatical leave. Debby was integrated into a special class within a regular school, where she learned, within one year, to read, write, and speak English. She continues to this day to correspond in English with some of her friends in Canada, and her writing is clear and well-ordered—except when she writes in a hurry.

At her graduation from public school, the Israeli parent organization for children with Down syndrome awarded a prize to her school and the youth movement group for their contribution to Debby's education. In front of an audience of more than 300 people, she stood and read a self-prepared speech of thanks to her teachers, counselors, and friends.

Debby's achievements would not have occurred if her parents had accepted the physician's pessimistic expectations that were voiced shortly after her birth. Her parents' strong belief in Debby's modifiability and in their own capacity to become effective mediators led to her achievements in childhood and adolescence.

Today, as a young adult, Debby is attending a vocational school

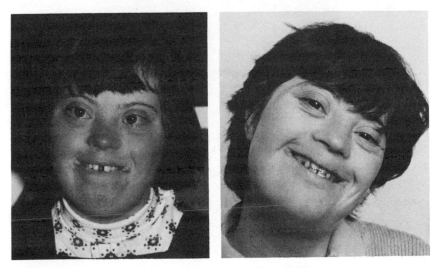

Figure 17. Debby: Pre- and post-RPS.

program where she is preparing for employment as an assistant kindergarten teacher. Moreover, she is a contributing member of her community, participating in a number of its activities, and has friendly relationships with several of its members, especially within the synagogue setting and its social activities.

Not all children with Down syndrome will grow up to be as capable as Debby. But the case of Debby shows us that children with Down syndrome should not be "written off" as being invariably low-functioning and unmodifiable. The pessimistic prophecy of the physician after the first two weeks of Debby's life proved to be totally unjustified. What happened to Debby was attributable to her and her parents' strong belief that intensive intervention would ultimately be rewarding. Through tenacious perseverance, advocacy, and systematic interventions, "chromosomes did not have the last word."

The case of Debby is not unique. Rather, it serves as an illustration of how investment can often be transformed into a highly rewarding experience. In order to highlight this point, we would like to introduce two more children with Down syndrome, Tami and Jason, both of whom had intensive intervention during their early lives (see Figure 18).

Figure 18. Tami and Jason.

Tami received extensive parent–child interaction beginning when she was a baby. From the first day of her schooling she attended regular classes with normal peers. During schooling years, her parents continued to support her and to provide experiences of their own. Last year we received the following letter from Tami's father:

I am sending you a report on Tami's achievements this year. As you know, she is now 10 years old and in the fourth grade.

Last year she repeated third grade in an effort to consolidate the skills that she would need for higher grades. She is also more comfortable socially with younger children. I think the outcome was excellent. She is doing well in fourth grade as I will explain further. She has retained the excellent self-image which sustains her when the going gets a little difficult.

Fourth grade is a difficult one in the United States. It is the first year where students are expected to pick up considerable information from reading, rather than orally. It is a skill which Tami still finds difficult, but I was encouraged to find out that the problems she was having were not atypical for fourth graders.

She is working quite hard to do well this year. She brings home homework almost every day, which we work on with her. As before, pure skills tasks like spelling and arithmetic seem to come quite easily. I am delighted that she seems to understand the mathematical concepts presented to her. She does quite well on mathematical word problems, knows when it is appropriate to add, when to multiply, etc. Of course, the multiplication tables are completely mastered. She also does well in skills used in social studies which include reading ordinary graphs and bar charts, and reading maps including finding latitude and longitude.

She has more difficulty with grammar. She hears and speaks grammatical English, and knows intuitively what is the correct form of sentences. But picking out the noun phrases and the verb phrases, identifying adjectives and adverbs, etc., is more difficult.

More difficult subjects are science and social studies, where the ideas are presented in paragraph form. She can sometimes read a whole page, and not understand the point of what she has just read. The social studies book teaches reading as well; for example by introducing new words in a context which makes their meaning clear, rather than by formally offering definitions. But we have found that she does understand the ideas if we take the time to explain them to her. And then she is able to answer all sorts of questions which illustrate that she really does understand. I am particularly gratified that her recent test scores in social studies and science are quite good.

She has always had an excellent memory. That is very useful for science and social studies as they are presented. She has no trouble memorizing definitions of technical terms. We have to probe to make sure that she understands the meaning of what she has just said. The memory is not particularly short term. She remembers events of several months ago with great clarity. One thing which continually surprises me is that she is able to remember the page number of her homework assignments in several different subjects at the same time.

She has also developed much more fully the ability to recall in the sense of sorting through what she knows. She will frequently reply to a question by pausing, as if to search her memory for the answer. One can almost hear her saying to herself, "Just a minute, let me think" [the motto of the IE program].

Reading is her worst skill. She has great difficulty in reading a story, and telling us the main idea or episode. She often concentrates on a specific incident which may or may not be essential to the story. On the other hand, given a specific question, she can read several pages to find the answer.

Her writing skills also are poor. She writes (and reads) cursive script, but the letters are still not well formed and not neatly arranged. She has much trouble with creative writing, where she is to make something up. Even her letters to her very dear sisters are stilted and sterile.

Socially, I think she is a delight. She is very sensitive to other people, and empathizes very easily and maturely with others. Friends are her greatest joy. We wish she had more, although she does not complain. She certainly prefers the company of younger children where she can take the lead, rather than the company of her peers where she is usually a follower. From what we can tell, the children in school are quite supportive as long as they themselves are not threatened. She often needs help with getting to the next class on time, with getting her books together at the end of the day, with getting dressed quickly after gym class. Classmates occasionally come over to play on the weekends, and invite her to play and to birthday parties. We do find that her classmates have much different interests like clothes, rock music singers, and boys. Tami is oblivious to these.

She has learned to use her charm to manipulate people and situations. I myself am often the victim. But she is also adept at getting others to do favors for her, as you yourself know.

She has a wonderful disposition. She is usually in a very good mood, and enjoys all sorts of activities. Her favorite is playing with friends. She goes to school willingly. She persists undaunted in trying to arrange opportunities to play with friends even when it is clear to us that they are reluctant to come over.

She goes to Hebrew school twice a week in the afternoons and on Sundays, for a total of 7 hours/week. She does very well. Reading Hebrew came very easily. Her memory helps her to remember lots of words. She switches very comfortably between Hebrew and English. She likes the holidays and their preparation. She particularly likes singing Hebrew songs, and going to synagogue. She is a full-fledged member of the Junior Congregation at our synagogue. A few weeks ago, they led the Friday night service for the adults. Tami had a part to read on her own. She practiced it at home, and did very well. I asked her afterwards if she had been nervous. She said she had been a little "embarrassed," and preferred to look down into her book than up at the people looking at her.

Starting this fall, she has been taking Instrumental Enrichment twice a week with a private tutor. He comes to the house after school, for half an hour each time. They have been working on the Organization of Dots, and on some organizational skills like a calendar. He has repeatedly emphasized the importance of being organized and planning ahead. He gave her tasks to do, like keeping a notebook with all homework assignments. She is actually quite organized. She knows exactly what her school schedule is, which days she is to come home and which days to go straight to Hebrew school, what time her favorite TV shows are on, and on which channel. It is hard for me to assess how effective the IE has been, but she is doing so well that we will not change anything. (Reproduced without editing)

Jason is a 13½-year-old boy with Down syndrome living in the United States. He was raised by his parents, who involved him in a variety of intervention programs, mostly in classes for learning-disabled children. In addition, he received a good deal of parent–child interaction.

Recently, Jason was referred by his parents to the institute for assessment and guidance. We have just received the following letter from Jason's mother:

> Charles and I are still glowing from the warmth and intensity of our remarkable visit to Jerusalem. Besides having been a fascinating and spiritually enriching experience, we are overwhelmed at the significance the trip had for Jason and his future.
>
> In the past, we have been delighted when Jason's school placement put him in classes designated for children with learning disabilities, rather than in classes which were designated as "educable mentally retarded." We were always made to feel that he was getting the maximum stimulation and education possible to fulfill his (considerable) potential.
>
> The class he has been attending most recently is called a "Language Learning class," 7th grade, in a normal middle school (junior high). He is in with six other children of the same age (13–14), all of whom are diagnosed as having some kind of learning disability. For the first time in his educational experience in public school, there is another child with Down syndrome in his class. The class has one teacher and three aides, making it almost a 2 to 1 ratio! He receives speech therapy as a related service, three times a week as well as Adaptive Physical Education.
>
> The class is self-contained—except for integration into regular school functions like lunch, recess, and school assemblies.
>
> In reading, Jason's decoding has always been extraordinarily good—but his comprehension of what he has read still gives him quite a bit of difficulty. He loves playing complicated word games, spelling words backwards, doing crossword puzzles, and performing scenes he has

learned from musical shows. But his ability to answer "content questions" has been quite limited.

In math, he is doing multiplication with regrouping (for example: 4769×35) and is beginning to learn division and fractions. He enjoys math and does well in it. His teacher is a very practical young woman who is helping the students learn many practical life skills, such as money managing, meal preparation, budgeting, etc. They also encourage creativity in areas such as writing and art. Jason seems to be well accepted and liked by his classmates and, all in all, we have been pleased with his progress and his positive attitude this year.

Unfortunately, in order to get this enlightened class placement for him, he has to be transported by bus about 40 minutes from our home. This has made after-school socialization almost impossible. When school is over, he must get back on the bus and come home while all of his classmates live in the location of the school. Needless to say, when he returns to our community, nobody knows him—since he is not attending the local school. Our home is quite isolated, with very few neighbors—so the end result is very inadequate opportunities for socialization and recreation.

The local towns have made an attempt to form a "special education recreation program"—but since the population is small and very diverse, he often finds himself in a recreation program with a wide range of ages and a very wide spectrum of functioning levels. It is much less than optimal!

We are still in a state of absolute astonishment at the wonders you were able to accomplish with Jason in the short time we were in Jerusalem. We saw capability for growth, development, and understanding that we never dreamed possible! I am feeling sorry and remiss that we did not discover and embark upon the Instrumental Enrichment/MLE program long ago! In the short time since our introduction to the language and concepts of IE, we have found it much easier to introduce new ideas and explain concepts we might not have thought him capable of comprehending in the past. It's amazing! You may be sure that he will begin a full program of IE as soon as we can set it up.

Even more gratifying is to hear him spontaneously use the phraseology and techniques he has learned in order to help him understand something or solve a problem. I loved it when he was visiting the Western Wall in the Old City and announced, matter-of-factly, "Look! It's all made of parallel lines!"

His other new key phrase is: "Well, Mom, that may be similar, but it's not identical!"

The other day we were discussing various ways a doctor could get information about what is bothering a patient. Jason suggested that the doctor could ask the patient, "What is hurting you?" When I asked him what the doctor would do if the patient was a baby and couldn't answer the question, he said, "The doctor could ask the parents." Then I asked him, "What if the parents weren't there? Then what could the doctor do?" He smiled and said, "Ask the nurse to do a Systematic Search—to find the parents!"

Jason's ability to pick up information and retain it has always been remarkable. We have never doubted his recall of an event or incident in his life. But his reaction to the challenge of new frontiers of thinking, of conceptualizing, of real reasoning—has been frightening to him. He has recently started to resist reading new books that are more age-appropriate, which he has a harder time following and understanding. He tends to retreat to materials with which he is very, very familiar: old books (often embarrassingly babyish), old videotapes of movies he has seen dozens of times already, etc.

Until our visit to Jerusalem, we were afraid that perhaps his ability to process this new, more advanced, level of material was simply "beyond him," just more than he could handle without great psychological stress. We now feel that it is more a matter of how the material is presented to him, how he is prepared for it, and the tools and strategies he is able to bring to the tasks! We are now looking forward to the challenge of helping him to advance in these very important areas.

From the beginning of our experience with Jason, when doctors told us to expect NOTHING, every accomplishment has been a triumph, a source of tremendous joy and pride. I feel that we are on the threshold of a whole new era with Jason, where the accomplishments will continue to thrill and gratify us—and will further insure a full and rich life for him!

We will always be grateful to you for helping us to recognize that the marvelous heights of accomplishment that Jason has already achieved are actually more like "foothills"—and that wonderfully new peaks of endeavor and satisfaction lie ahead! We are so excited! (Reproduced without editing)

Tami, Jason, and Debby, radiant and warm when you speak with them, have had the good fortune to live in an environment and a family that have been powerful mediators and active modifiers, making the best of their condition of Down syndrome.

Yet neither Tami nor Debby was born with the best prospects among children with Down syndrome. A pronounced hypotonicity delayed their development. Their speech was not intelligible. However, as can be seen from the description and letters, they reached a high level of cognitive functioning.

Jason, whose performance as an actor (in "Fall Guy") and proficiency as a student have been largely determined by the persistent and steady mediational interaction between him and his parents, has recently shown, during dynamic assessment, how much more modifiable he is than even his most optimistic parents believed him to be.

The effects of the modifying environments into which these three children were born are visible not only in their plasticity, capacity to learn, and achievement orientation, but also in the quality of their socialization ability.

They represent a sample of what could be done, if not for all, at least for some (perhaps many) children with Down syndrome by an active modification approach, persistent mediation, and instrumental enrichment. The three families exemplify the message "Don't accept the child with Down syndrome as he is but, because you love him, modify him and enhance the quality of his life (and your own as well)."

CHAPTER 8

Early Education for Children with Down Syndrome and Their Parents

Arny awoke to the touch of his wife Helen's hand pressing gently on his shoulder. It was 4:00 a.m. Helen, fully dressed, even to her wool hat pulled down over her ears, was standing beside their bed whispering, "Arny, honey, wake up, it's time to go; the pains are fifteen minutes apart." He dressed rapidly, having rehearsed in his mind everything he would do when the time arrived. However, now that the moment had come, he felt unprepared as he stumbled into his trousers and ran to the garage. "Why do babies always come so early in the morning?" he asked himself as he started the car. Helen, with a small suitcase in hand, slipped into the seat beside him and turned to him with a special glow on her face that he had never seen before. When she looked into his eyes, something passed between them that is as ageless as the universe and as close to heaven as a husband and wife are allowed to ascend while on earth—the dream of beginning a whole new life. In their dream their child would be a fine golfer (they were both avid amateur golf players), attend college (both of them had), and become a successful businessman (Arny had received an M.B.A.).

Five hours and 17 minutes later, Dr. Samuels, their obstetrician, dashed Arny and Helen's dream, putting a wound in each of their hearts that would close over eventually but never heal completely. Finding Arny in the waiting room finishing his eighth cup of coffee, Dr. Samuels congratulated him on becoming the father of a baby boy. He then told him gently that, while he could not be absolutely certain, his new son seemed to have a chromosomal condition called

Pnina Klein is a contributing author to this chapter.

129

Down syndrome,* sometimes known by the outdated term *mongolism.* He told Arny that he had ordered a test to make certain of the diagnosis.

Arny only vaguely remembers the things that happened after receiving that news. He remembers vividly, though, how warm his wife's hands felt as he stood beside her hospital bed holding them to his weeping face.

When Arny and Helen's dream of having a normal child was shattered, they jumped to the conclusion that there was nothing they could do to help their child with Down syndrome lead a productive life. Fortunately for them, and for Thomas, their son (and for other husbands and wives in the future who will have a child with Down syndrome), Arny and Helen were *wrong;* there was a *great deal* that they could do for Thomas.

Actually, the first thing that Arny and Helen needed to do was obtain accurate information about the condition of Down syndrome since there is so much misunderstanding about it. For over 100 years, people with Down syndrome have often been portrayed as uneducable, nearly completely dependent on others, and sometimes even less than fully human. This misunderstanding is tragic since people with Down syndrome have considerable potential, particularly if they are nurtured with the kind of intervention and mediation described in this book.

When the report of the blood test that Dr. Samuels ordered came back from the laboratory, he sat down with Helen and Arny to tell them that the test showed clearly that Thomas had Down syndrome. Fortunately, Dr. Samuels was prepared to respond to the flood of questions that he knew from experience would come (and *needed* to come). The questions, and answers, under these circumstances usually take the following form:

Question 1: "What is Down syndrome? What causes it? Whose fault is it? Could it have been prevented? How can you, our doctor, be certain that our child has it? Will it happen again?" ("Is it a random universe? Will all of my children have birth defects?")

Answer: Down syndrome is a chromosomal disorder. Children with the condition have an extra chromosome in their cells, the result of faulty cell division in the egg or sperm before conception, or the

---

*"Syndrome" means a cluster of specific symptoms. "Down" is the name of the physician credited with describing Down syndrome.

result of an error in cell division occurring shortly after the ovum is fertilized and begins to divide.

Chromosomes are chemical strands appearing somewhat like complex "zippers," with each "tooth" of the zipper representing a gene, a coded portion of the whole zipper. Each gene carries a different piece of information and is a complex chemical structure in its own right. While chromosomes can be seen through powerful microscopic magnification, genes are too small to be seen even with the most powerful microscopes.

Each form of life has its own genetic code and special set of chromosomes, which differs from life form to life form in terms of chromosome size, shape, number per cell, and other characteristics. The typical human being has 46 chromosomes, while people with Down syndrome have 1 extra chromosome. How does this happen? In humans, the mother and father ordinarily contribute 23 chromosomes each at conception, creating the normal complement of 46 per cell. Sometimes, however, the chromosomes, from father or mother, do not "unzip" properly, do not divide in half as they should before conception, and 1 extra chromosome is carried into the new cells that become an embryo. This is called chromosomal nondisjunction, or failure to disjoin. Hence, embryonic cells, and eventually all cells in the baby, will have 47 chromosomes instead of the typical 46.

Each chromosome has different characteristics, such as differences in size, shape, and combination of various genes. Down syndrome occurs when certain, identifiable chromosomes (those designated as number 21, using a charting system) stick together, creating a tripleting of chromosomes rather than the normal pairing (see Figure 19).

If a tripleting had occurred in some other pair of chromosomes— for example, the pair designated as number 13 on the chart—the child would have a specific syndrome but not Down syndrome.

Unfortunately, medical researchers have not discovered why the error in cell division occurs, although scientists know that it can be of either maternal or paternal* origin and is correlated with the aging of either parent, with the clearest correlation related to maternal age. Other than that, it seems to occur by chance (except in some rare instances in which one parent may be a carrier for the condition, that

---

*In at least 25% of live births of babies with Down syndrome, the father can be identified as contributing the extra chromosome.

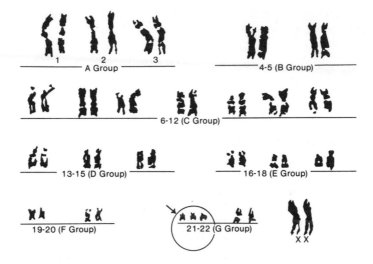

Figure 19. Chart of chromosomes (karotype) of a female with Down syndrome. (The arrow shows the extra chromosome at the number 21 position, as circled on the chart. Drawing based on photo of karotype in a pamphlet, *Down Syndrome*, published by the National Down Syndrome Congress).

is, a carrier for the translocation form of Down syndrome. If a husband or a wife has a relative with Down syndrome, the couple may want to seek professional genetic counseling before having children to find out whether either is a carrier for the translocation type of Down syndrome). Thus, other than seeking genetic counseling, scientists know nothing that the wife or husband could have done to prevent Down syndrome, short of preventing conception itself.

Down syndrome occurs in approximately 1 out of 1000 live births* during a woman's prime childbearing years (usually the mid-20s) and in about 1 out of 40 live births after a woman reaches the age of 45 years. Hence, while it is important for women in their later years of fertility to know that their chances of having a child with Down syndrome increase with each year after their mid-20s, the chances are not 1 : 1 even in their late 40s or early 50s.

Running laboratory tests on a sample of a child's blood shows whether the child has Down syndrome. To do this test, the sample is

*Four out of five fetuses with Down syndrome are aborted spontaneously.

cultured under special laboratory conditions to enable the cells to divide. At the point of cell division, cells are killed, treated with chemicals to make certain features of the chromosomes stand out, and photographed under conditions of high magnification so the chromosomes can be arranged in accord with the charting system. Nondisjunction is responsible for about 95% of Down syndrome cases. In the other 5% of cases the extra chromosome is not floating free, so to speak, but is attached to another chromosome. This is the rare condition called translocation, mentioned earlier. In other equally rare circumstances, a child will have a type of Down syndrome called mosaicism. Mosaicism means that some but not all of the cells in the body contain an extra chromosome. Children with the mosaic form of Down syndrome seem to be less affected on the average in terms of their functioning, as compared with children with the more common form of the syndrome, but there appears to be little or no relation between the percentage of normal cells and the child's functioning ability. At this time scientists do not know what causes chromosomal nondisjunction, translocation, and mosaicism, but they are convinced that this mystery of abnormal chromosome division will be solved before the turn of the century.

New parents should know that the extra chromosome producing Down syndrome is a perfectly *normal* number 21 chromosome, which comes directly from the mother or the father. In other words, it is not a chromosome from "somewhere else or someone else," nor is it a defective, "bad," or unhealthy chromosome. Also of importance for them to know is that, because the two parents personally contributed the chromosome material, their new child with Down syndrome will resemble them and other members of their family. Their child, as distinctive as every human being is, will also be uniquely theirs.

Clues that a child might have Down syndrome are often obvious during an infant's first days of life. Noticing that a baby has a slightly "Oriental" appearance (which spawned the term *mongolism*, an erroneous racial association since true Oriental people and people with Down syndrome show clear facial dissimilarities), hospital personnel will examine the child to see if certain physical characteristics that often, though not always, accompany the syndrome are present. For example, they will look to see if the child has almond-shaped eyes with a fold of skin at each inner corner, a flat nasal bridge and flattened cheeks, short ears, "floppiness" of muscle tone (hypotonia), inward-turned, shortened, little fingers, abundant neck skin, absence of Moro's reflex—a reflex appearing in a normal baby when body support is carefully and suddenly withdrawn, whereupon the baby's muscles tighten. None of these signs, or even clusters of signs taken together, can definitely confirm a diagnosis of Down syndrome, however, since no child who has this syndrome will show all of the signs (there are more than 50 of them), and any single so-called cardinal sign observed in confirmed cases of Down syndrome can also be found in nonhandicapped children. Confirmation comes *only* through examining the chromosomes of a child suspected of having the condition.

Question 2: "How serious is this problem?" ("Is there any hope that my child will even respond to me when I play with her?")

Answer: While there are several types of chromosomal conditions that are far more devastating to a child's development than Down syndrome, the condition is certainly not to be taken lightly.

Table 2, completed by a group of researchers,[1] should prove helpful to new parents as they attempt to judge what type of physical, social, and language development to expect at a particular age.

As the table shows, young children with Down syndrome tend to be delayed in every area of development as compared with normal children. However, notice that there is a great deal of variation among individual children with the condition. In other words, their developmental prospects are highly individualistic, just like those of normal children. Furthermore, research findings gathered over the last 20 years show that children with Down syndrome, particularly those who have received early education, often function at the educable level in school, have productive hobbies, are contributing members of their families, and are well received in their communities. Indeed, their stereotyped portrayal as *in*educable, *un*skilled, and *un*productive is *un*realistic and *un*fortunate. Yet even recent textbooks sometimes mistakenly portray them as low-functioning and with little vitality. For example, a well-known psychologist[2] portrays children with Down syndrome as follows:

> Some children with Down's syndrome learn to speak a little and to master simple chores. In most cases, however, they cannot speak or can utter just a few hoarse sounds, and they seldom learn more than elementary self-care. These children tend to be affectionate and docile compared to other retarded children. Because of their numerous physical deficiencies, their health is poor; many die before reaching adolescence. (p. 370)

TABLE 2. Language, Muscular, and Self-Care Development in Children
with Down Syndrome as Compared with Normal Children[a]

	Average age normal child does it (months)	Average age child with Down syndrome does it (months)	Range in which child with Down syndrome does it (months)
Language ability			
Says "mama" and/or "dada"	10	24	12–40
Obeys simple commands	18	41	26–60
Combines 2 or 3 words spontaneously	21	42	24–69
Utters 3-word sentences	24	46	30–60
Physical ability			
Rolls over	5	6	1–6
Sits unsupported for 1 minute	8	11	6–30
Creeps	10	17	8–34
Pulls self to standing position	10	18	12–30
Stands at rail	11	17	9–36
Stands alone momentarily	14	22	12–44
Walks with support	13	22	11–48
Walks unsupported	15	25	15–50
Walks upstairs unsupported	18–24	38	26–48
Walks downstairs unsupported	24–30	42	32–52
Self-care ability			
Feeds self in part	9	24	9–42
Drinks from cup or glass unassisted	21	30	18–48
Feeds self "fully"	18	35	18–58
Dresses (simple garment)	24	44	22–86
Dresses self except for tying shoes, buttoning	36	66	36–102
Toilet training begun	36	66	36–102
Bladder training begun	18	24	12–40
Bowel control	24	38	15–50
Washes hands and face unassisted	42	56	39–86
Brushes teeth unaided	48	58	48–69

[a]Figures have been rounded as they were taken from the data of Fishler, Share, and Koch,[1] and
some of the abilities in their data have been omitted here.

In the area of intellectual ability, expectations are frequently in particularly serious error. Thus, while most school-age children with Down syndrome will have moderate, not severe, intellectual impairments, their classmates, their teachers, and sometimes even their parents often underestimate their potential. That is very unfortunate because people with Down syndrome are today achieving success in areas of education, vocation, and self-sufficiency, especially if they received long-term active modification of a high quality. Hence, there is considerable cause for optimism, even though the condition will not "go away," which leads us to our next question.

Question 3: "Is there a cure for Down syndrome?" ("Oh, how I want to find a miracle cure so that my baby can become normal.")

Answer: Children who have 47 chromosomes in their cells at birth will have that number in their cells for their entire lives. What is more, if one were somehow able to miraculously remove the extra 21st chromosome from each cell, the manifestations of Down syndrome would not disappear because they were laid down in the early stages of embryonic development. Nonetheless, while it is not possible to prevent Down syndrome in a primary way, we can actively pursue ways to maximize whatever developmental abilities the child has through active modification efforts.

A fourth question, one that parents may not ask out loud at the time of their child's birth, is this:

Question 4: "Will our new child live very long? And will our child have a life worth living?" ("Will he be able to contribute anything of value to society?")

Answer: Fifty years ago, children with Down syndrome seldom reached adolescence. Major causes of death were heart disease and infection. With advances in medical knowledge, the advent of antibiotics, and improved care for heart defects, including cardiac surgery, the outlook has changed dramatically. There is still an appreciable risk of death in the early years, especially for children with a serious heart defect, but after that point is past, a child with Down syndrome will often live into adulthood.

Regarding the question of a life worth living, new parents of a child with Down syndrome often have glaring misconceptions about the condition, stemming from outdated, distorted statements in books and magazines, many of which imply that their child will be grossly abnormal. For example, depressing expressions such as "mongolian type of idiocy,"[3] "unfinished children,"[4] and "monster"[5] have appeared throughout the past 100 years in reference to Down syndrome. In at least two cases, their status as human beings has even been called into question: In 1927, one author[6] suggested that the condition of Down syndrome represented a regression to a nonhuman species, i.e., to an orangutan. In 1968, another author,[7] attempting to comfort a bereaved parent who after an emotional struggle had concluded that he must institutionalize his child with Down syndrome, wrote: "People in the B_____s [the parents' name] situation have no reason to feel guilty about putting a Down's syndrome baby away, whether it's 'put away' in the sense of hidden in a sanitarium or in a more responsible lethal sense. It is sad, yes. Dreadful. But it carries no guilt. True guilt arises only from an offense against a person, and a *Down's is not a person*" (pp. 59–64, italics added).

Sooner or later parents will need to deal with their feelings at the deepest, and perhaps most troubling, levels of thought. Part of this process is mourning the loss of the normal child that they had dreamed of having. Some parents may even feel that God is punishing them with a child with Down syndrome because of some sin they have committed; they should stop to consider that even the most religious and loving parents can have a child with Down syndrome. As deep feelings are bared—a process that often takes considerable time, and often the assistance of someone skilled in counseling in matters such as these—parents will also need to receive factual information that will help them to decide whether they will be able to cope successfully with their child's condition.

Short-term coping is, of course, related directly to the question of whether the infant will be taken home from the hospital, put up for adoption, or placed in a residential setting, which leads to the next question.

Question 5: "Should we take our newborn child home? How will he affect the lives of his brother and sister?"

Answer: Occasionally, some new parents appear to be unable to genuinely love their new child with Down syndrome even after the initial shock and depression have passed. To "force" them to raise a child whom they clearly and deeply reject is totally inappropriate; in fact, it is psychologically unhealthy, both for them and for their child. In many cases of "rejection," however, a counselor will observe that parents, while initially reluctant to keep their child at home, may soon be receptive to this possibility once they are educated on how to cope successfully with raising the child on a long-term basis. We believe that parents should keep a child with Down syndrome in his own family if possible, at least during the child's early years of life. Why? Because several studies have shown that children with Down syndrome who are raised at home in their early years do better developmentally, on the average, than those who are placed in a large residential facility.[8,9]

Raising a child with Down syndrome at home is done most effectively when parents consider not only the child's needs but *the total family's needs*. Having a brother or sister who has retarded performance is an experience that most normal children adjust to without too much stress, although they do encounter difficulties from time to time that require special understanding. For example, Margaret Adams, a psychologist, reports that preadolescent and teenage children generally show a fairly high degree of constructive acceptance toward their retarded brother or sister, but often need additional attention and support during this challenging period of adjustment.[10]

The adjustment or maladjustment of brothers and sisters begins with the early reaction of parents. If parents are not showing hostility or are not filled with fear, guilt, and ignorance, the infant with Down syndrome's chances of being accepted by brothers and sisters are good. Once the initial adjustment hurdle is overcome successfully, however, brothers and sisters will be faced with additional problems—some external to the home, such as the unkind words of thoughtless peers. Dr. Adams notes that the pressures on parents in caring for a handicapped child may overwhelm the normal needs of other children in the family. In fact, there is a risk that the development of normal siblings will become blighted by emotional neglect, distorted family roles ("junior mother, junior father"), and significantly reduced social contacts. However, if the whole family pulls together positively and cohesively, both the child with Down syndrome and his entire family will benefit.

We began this chapter with the story of Arny and Helen at the time that their child, Thomas, was born with Down syndrome. When Dr. Samuels, their obstetrician, broke the news to them, their dreams were shattered. Once they began to recover from the initial shock, they began to ask questions similar to the ones we have explored. When Dr. Samuels finished answering their questions, and after Helen and Arny talked over the situation with each other, their parents, their close friends, and other parents of young children with Down syndrome, they reached a turning point: They decided to take Thomas home and make the most of their circumstance. At that critical point, they shifted their attention to asking questions with an orienta tion toward the future, such as Will Thomas need early education services? Will he be able to go to school? Will he have friends? What about work? And how about living outside our home as an adult? Will he be able to handle his sexuality appropriately? What about marriage; is that out of the question? And what will happen to Thomas when we die?

The section that follows addresses their first question, that is, the need for early education services.

EARLY EDUCATION

As researchers, we believe strongly in the importance of early education for children with Down syndrome. We recognize, however, that there is still a great deal to be learned about how to approach early education *most effectively.* In this vein, the eight early education studies for children with Down syndrome we are about to summarize will reveal that a statistically significant change in intelligence, language, or some other developmental area can be brought about with a fair degree of consistency through a variety of intervention methods and programs. But showing statistical differences favoring one type of program over another is *not* the same as showing fully *meaningful* differences—that is, differences that are culturally relevant and important, lasting, and valuable to the person with Down syndrome, to his parents, and to society in general.

To sharpen awareness of how to judge the effectiveness of different programs, one of the authors has employed an acronym (FRIWAFTT) to help university students who are preparing to teach young children with handicaps to appreciate the dilemmas in judging the worth of program outcomes. The acronym serves as a tongue-in-cheek overview of the early education movement in America from the 1960s to the present.

FRIWAFTT stands for the familiar saying "Fools rush in where angels fear to tread." In using the acronym the author hastens to point out that the meaning he is attaching to the word *fool* is that of the personification of Don Quixote, who was brave, loving, and ambitious—qualities to be admired greatly. But, like the endeavors of

Don Quixote, who tilted at windmills, those of many early education encounters, while brave, loving, and ambitious, are colored by considerable naïveté.

The acronym can be divided into three parts, each of which signifies approximately one decade of the early education movement. The first three letters (*FRI*) signify the beginnings of high interest and investment in early education programs, such as Head Start, many of which began during the late 1950s and early 1960s for children from economically poor and stressed families. The *F* stands for *f*eelings of great enthusiasm and optimism that launched the early education movement; *R* stands for large amounts of *r*evenue that were poured into early education projects; *I* stands for *i*gnorance—the kind of well-intended ignorance that is present when a massive educational movement begins without the underpinnings of experience, policy guidelines, and research results to guide its path. For example, if one looks at the rationales offered for some early Head Start programs, one can find justification statements for providing physical-education-type activities based on "evidence" gathered from observing the movement patterns of salamanders that had or had not been anesthesized early in life. This was hardly the kind of finding upon which to build thoughtful, effective early education programs for young children with disabilities, but there wasn't much else on which to build in those days.

Following on the heels of this *FRI* period came the inevitable consequence of a movement that was expected to move too far too fast without a sufficient base of sound information, i.e., the *WAF* period, which stands for *w*aste, *a*bortive attempts, and *f*lashy findings. This part of the history, occurring in the late 1960s and 1970s, was the period when early stimulation programs came into existence (and often disappeared) in the blink of an eye. It was a period when funds were sometimes wasted on exotic gadgets; the period when flash-in-the-pan programs promised great improvements in child intelligence but sometimes gave far too little thought to the essential basics of proper hygiene, safety, and comfort of the children. This was the period of expanding involvement with poor urban minority children, who were not wealthy from an economic perspective but had rich cultural and ethnic backgrounds from which we could have developed stimulating and meaningful activities. Instead, we often ignored their unique and valuable racial and ethnic heritage. It took educators some time to catch up with the fact that the impulse to build a "bigger and better American dream," well intentioned as it was, was not always educationally or socially fruitful, and sometimes was harmful to the individual as well as to the dream.

But educators did catch up with themselves soon after this *WAF* period—or should we say that history caught up with them—as we entered the third decade of the early education movement, the part we're in now, the *TT* period of the 1970s and 1980s, which stands for tightening of funds and tidying up of early education efforts. Today, there is guarded optimism about the effectiveness of early education. The guardedness is based on the movement's need to devote much more attention to establishing *meaningfulness.*

As programming for young children with disabilities such as Down syndrome approaches its fourth decade, we believe that early education will not fade from history simply because educators are unable to teach every child with a handicap in the United States to spell *cat* correctly. Rather, it will fade if educators treat children with handicaps and their families in a meaningless manner, that is, ignoring cultural factors, forcing parents into a rigid schedule, emphasizing bombardment-type activities, ignoring the child's and parents' interaction style preferences and living routines, and violating accepted principles of child development. Such orientations are to be avoided at all costs. Early educators are, after all, entering a very sensitive period of a family's life where an infant with a handicap is developmentally vulnerable and parents' ability to cope successfully is often precarious.

One way to look to improving meaningfulness is to see how important the early interactions are between a child with Down syndrome and his parent or parents, and how interactions can sometimes break down. One author[11] found that babies with Down syndrome tended to be less responsive to, or more disassociated from, their mothers' vocal behavior pattern than were nonhandicapped babies. For instance, the vocal behavior of babies with Down syndrome was more often relatively inconsiderate of their mother's vocal dialogue, i.e., they vocalized simultaneously with the mother, interrupting her "turn" in the dialogue. These inharmonious interactions imposed difficulties on the mother's attempt to engage her infant with Down syndrome in smooth-flowing, give-and-take verbal interactions. A mother may also encounter difficulty nursing her child with Down syndrome owing to his weak sucking response. This difficulty may create self-doubt in the mother and may further impair the feeding interactions.

These findings emphasize, again, the importance of a harmonious flow of caregiver–child interactions. Indeed, the young child and the parents' development could be thought of as a "mutual embrace," three people linked together inextricably, each dependent to a very considerable extent on the others' development for his or her own thriving. This crucial, interdependent linkage between a child's and the parents' development is not often fully appreciated. For example, consider the circumstance of parents with a baby with Down syndrome who, because of difficulties in nursing and a delay in producing a smiling response, may not ignite a desire in his parents to play and take care of him in a socially and intellectually stimulating manner. Two studies[12,13] have looked specifically at the interrelation of affect (e.g., smiling, speaking with a lively intonation) and intellect. In one of the studies, the researchers worked with 14 infants with Down syndrome who were living at home and receiving creative types of social stimulation from their parents. For example, the parents were instructed: "Using a loud deep voice, pronounce 'boom, boom, boom' at 1-second intervals." "Blow gently at hair for 3 seconds; blow from side across top of baby's head." "Stick out your tongue until baby touches it. (Help your infant to touch your tongue with his or her hand if necessary.) Quickly pull tongue back in as soon as baby touches it."[12]

Results showed that infants with Down syndrome laughed in response to these activities in the same order as did nonhandicapped infants, although their achievement in this behavior was delayed by several months. Infants with Down syndrome, like the nonhandicapped infants, laughed first at physically intrusive items and only later at items calling for greater intellectual sophistication. In fact, intellectual development, assessed by a well-known infant-development test, paralleled and was predicted by the level of the child's affective development. Furthermore, there was striking individual consistency across affective, mental, and motor measures, showing the organized nature of development, even retarded development.

The second study[13] of the relation between social and intellectual variables examined the development of mirror self-recognition in young children with Down syndrome. Fifty-five children with Down syndrome, ranging in age from 15 to 48 months, participated. During the treatment condition, mothers placed their children in front of a mirror for 20 to 30 seconds, carefully observing and recording their children's behaviors on a checklist. Behaviors on the checklist included gazing at the mother's image, affective expressions such as smiling and pouting, communication attempts such as sounds and words, and motor behaviors such as claps and kisses. Of critical experimental concern was the infant's nose-touching response following a hoped-for recognition of a rouge-smeared nose reflected in the mirror. This response was assessed as follows: After children observed their reflections, mothers turned them around and, while pretending to wipe their noses, as they would do if the child had a cold, smeared green rouge onto their noses. Then, children were again shown their images. Mothers were asked to remain quiet and unexpressive throughout the entire procedure.

As these psychologists predicted, children with Down syndrome showed a lag in the development of mirror self-recognition, corresponding to their delayed rate of intellectual development as measured with a popular infant-development test. For example, when the typical 22-month-old nonhandicapped infant's image is altered by rouge, he indicates self-recognition by touching his nose while looking in the mirror. In contrast only a small percentage of children with Down syndrome, those with higher developmental scores, touched their noses by this age. Nevertheless, in general, when developmental age (not just chronological age) was equated, children with Down syndrome showed socialization development parallel to that of nonhandicapped children.

From these two studies it should be clear that two crucial aspects of a child's development called "social" and "intellectual" are really not separate entities but are interrelated. Furthermore, it should be obvious that interactions between parents and a baby play a crucial part in the child's development because the parents are by far the most influential individuals in the child's life during the child's early years, not only stimulating the child's development but sustaining life itself. Hence, establishing good interactions between the baby with Down syndrome and his parents is critical for *all* of them and is a key to unlocking the door to *meaningfulness* that has been a recurring theme in this chapter.

We turn now to the question of the effectiveness of early education in terms of the impact of a particular experimental program on children's development. Results of early-intervention studies gathered recently, through a computerized search of the literature, add considerably to our encouragement about its usefulness, although, echoing this chapter's theme again, much remains to be done to make early education fully meaningful.

In selecting studies from the early-education literature for review here, we used a "quality-control" checklist to judge the studies' strengths and weaknesses, ultimately leading us to select only those able to withstand a scrutiny of their experimental procedures so that we can be reasonably certain that an outcome of a study is not produced by chance.

After screening more then 50 contemporary studies, we judged 8 to have an acceptable level of experimental rigor. In the first of these 8 studies, researchers[14] taught mothers of young (age 12 to 33 months) children with Down syndrome to use behavior modification techniques (for example, systematically rewarding children for accomplishments with words of praise and smiles) to promote language, self-care, and movement abilities. A second group of children with Down syndrome, the nontreatment group, received only general health care counseling. After six months of programming, children in the treatment group showed significant improvement in their language development but not in the other areas.

A second group of researchers,[15] tracking individual behavioral change, showed that early two-word verbalizations, known as pivot-open type words (e.g., "allgone dinner," where *allgone* is the pivot word and *dinner* is the open word), could be taught to two preschool children with Down syndrome who were vocalizing at the one-word stage of language development. Instruction took the form of play in which a teacher, having taught the children several nouns and a verb, dropped an object such as a toy auto into a box and took it out again when the child voiced the right two words. Not only did both children learn to produce two-word pivot-open verbalizations, they generated several of these verbalizations without training later on.

A third group of researchers[16] prepared parents of six young (3 to 5 years) children with Down syndrome to be language trainers. The goal of this program was to increase children's verbalizations in terms of length and complexity. Parents used play, imitation activities, and conversations as stimulation vehicles. Results of the study revealed significant improvements in children's verbalization length and complexity.

In another study,[17] 21 infants with Down syndrome, all under the age of 27 months, were enrolled in a program featuring biweekly, one-hour stimulation sessions focused on speech and movement development, along with directions for parents to follow in promoting these types of accomplishments at home. Results indicated that there were no significant improvements in language or movement abilities in the 21 children who received the program as compared with 16 who did not receive it.

A fifth group of researchers[18] provided a language program to preschool children with Down syndrome that began with verbal requests (e.g., "Bounce the ball on the floor"), progressing to a demonstration of the activity paired with a verbal cue, and ending with verbal directions for actions alone. Results showed significant improvements in the expressive language of children in the treatment group when compared with children in the nontreatment group.

A sixth group of researchers, including one of the authors of this book,[19] provided a program to promote young children's language development through structured play activities delivered through child–parent interactions. Called Project EDGE (expanding developmental growth through education), it served 35 children with Down syndrome, from the time they were newborns up to the age of 5 years (17 in a treatment group and 18 in a nontreatment group), all of whom lived at home. Parents in the treatment group provided structured play lessons that included interactive play with simple objects and toys (such as a brush-comb-mirror set, a doll, crayons, a rubber glove), a step-by-step activity sequence for each object or toy that included a suggested vocabulary list, and photographs of objects and toys intended to promote reading readiness.

At the end of five years of stimulation there were significant differences favoring the experimental group in terms of intellectual and motor development. However, the two groups were highly similar in language development, the project's main curricular emphasis. Hence, results of the study were interpreted as providing general support for the early education of young children with Down syndrome but not for the EDGE curriculum itself.

In a seventh study, experimenters[20] emphasized a broad spectrum of stimulation activities for 16 preschool children with Down syndrome living in a small nursing home in Sweden. In this study, special attention was given to socioemotional and motor stimulation. After 18 months, a treatment group showed significant improvement over a nontreatment group. One year later, the effects of the stimulation had disappeared in the treatment children as a group, but differences among individuals remained, favoring children who had undergone treatment in terms of both speech and movement stimulation.

The final early stimulation study to be included here[21] focused on an approach based on techniques from physical therapy. Twenty children with Down syndrome (10 in a treatment group, 10 in a nontreatment group) received physical therapy based on objectives written for each child, such as "Will maintain prone on elbows, with head at 45° for 12 seconds." Sessions took place in the infants' homes, each session lasting about 40 minutes, and were carried out three times per week for nine months. At the end of that time there were significant differences favoring the children who had undergone treatment, but not in all respects. That is, they did well on individual therapy objectives but not on general measures of cognitive and movement performance.

Summing up,[22] in these eight fairly well done, but not perfect, studies involving young children with Down syndrome, one finds encouraging outcomes. First, it is gratifying to see that seven out of eight of the studies show statistically significant improvements favoring children who were treated over those who were not, although the differences are not always exactly what the experimenters had targeted as their main concerns. Nevertheless, the proportionately large number of positive findings among these studies, which have a relatively high level of rigor, is cause for optimism. Taken together, they show that substantial improvements can be made in the development of children with Down syndrome, using a variety of approaches. Furthermore, when coupled with the findings reported earlier in this chapter that parents of young children with Down syndrome who have received sound early education feel a need (or show a need) for improving their ability to communicate and care for their child, and have greater confidence in their coping abilities in general, the legitimacy of such early education becomes evident.

In closing, it should be noted that the young children with Down syndrome who were in the studies described in this chapter did not receive the type of systematic early MLE developed by Pnina Klein and others (see Chapter 13 and Appendix E). Preliminary findings gathered in Israel show that it is a powerful means of producing and strengthening fruitful, satisfying parent–child interactions, and that parent–child interactions themselves can be described as "rich" or "lean" using MLE attributes in an observational system. It seems very likely that early MLE will produce structural cognitive modifiability in children with Down syndrome, though at this moment the program is too new for us to say anything definitive about this exciting possibility.

CHAPTER 9

Toward Literacy, Social Acceptance, and Community Integration

There seems to be no abatement in the number of "cries for help" that one of the authors receives from parents who are worried about the educational future of their child with Down syndrome. Many echo a common concern: They allege that school personnel who are making placement decisions often have inappropriately low expectations about their child's educational prospects.

Perhaps part of the problem is that some school officials appear to think that children with Down syndrome will, at some point in their elementary school years, simply stop growing developmentally; that is, they will reach a developmental "plateau," so why bother educating them. There is not much information about such a plateau. And even if it is a real phenomenon, it should not lead to giving up on active modification since attaining a decently high educational plateau is certainly preferable to not reaching upward at all. Interestingly, at least one group of researchers,[1] in a recent study of 39 young home-reared children with Down syndrome in Australia, did not find a plateau effect across the preschool period. This finding does not, of course, override a possibility that a developmental plateau may occur later in the school years. But even if a plateau occurred in, for example, IQ during the school years, it would *not* necessarily mean that progress in language, social, recreational, vocational, and other areas would stop during those years.

Perhaps part of the problem of low educational expectations stems from the fact that some regular education personnel are still

sorting out their feelings about integrating children with Down syndrome in schools with nonhandicapped children. The integration
(and mainstreaming) movement is, after all, only 12 years old. Moreover, the sorting-out process may include dealing with feelings about
Down syndrome which they realize are archaic but which continue to
produce nagging vestiges of uncertainty anyhow. Perhaps this
should not be surprising since the person credited with first describing the condition in 1866, Dr. John L. Down, associated the condition
with ethnic degeneracy, using words such as "idiots who arrange
themselves around the Mongolian type."[2] Thus, the syndrome, in
some people's minds, may still carry with it the incorrect notion that
people who have it are bound to have extremely low intelligence
quotients.

A special problem for parents is to convince school officials that a
sizable number of children with Down syndrome should have an
opportunity to attend an educable class, that is, one where appropriate emphasis is given to academics. Indeed, professionals sometimes
assume that children with Down syndrome are always trainable, a
false assumption that persists despite evidence to the contrary. To
illustrate the problem, about 13 years ago a disturbing statement
appeared in *Psychology Today* about the educability potential of children with Down syndrome: "You show me just one mongoloid that
has an educable IQ. . . . I've never seen even one [who is educable] in
my experience with over 800 mongols."[3] When that statement appeared,* we decided that it must not stand unchallenged since one of
the authors and his colleagues were on the brink of completing an
experimental early education project (Project EDGE) for children with
Down syndrome and their families and felt an obligation to give
parents whatever appropriate advocacy support could be mustered as
their children entered school. Therefore, a computerized search of the
literature, spanning the years 1967 through 1975, was begun. We
expected to find numerous examples of educability in the articles that
were uncovered. What we found, instead, was a body of literature that
was in shambles from a scientific standpoint, making it difficult to
refute directly the pessimistic statement about educability that had
appeared in *Psychology Today*. To illustrate how flawed the reports
were (and still are in many cases), in the 105 studies that were un-

---

*In September 1987, *Psychology Today* did an excellent feature article on Down syndrome that provided a corrective update on educability expectations.

covered and contained data pertinent to educability, information on a number of basic variables was often omitted, including confirmation of diagnosis through an analysis of the child's chromosomes; sex; type of residence (home or institution); and basis on which people were selected for the study.

Regarding just the area of sex of participants, in 63 of the 105 studies sex was not reported at all. Researchers who ignore individuals' gender as a variable seem to reinforce implicitly the stereotype that all people with Down syndrome are alike, a gross overgeneralization.

Setting aside the procedural limitations of most of the studies we examined, there were 29 studies in the pool of 105 in which at least two conditions were met: (1) Diagnosis was confirmed, and (2) the intellectual measure used was identified. In these 29 studies, there were several people with Down syndrome who had IQs in the educable range (IQ 52 or above on a Stanford-Binet, a well-known intelligence test), not only across individuals with the relatively rare translocation and mosaic forms of the syndrome but in those with the common nondisjunction form as well. At the end of the article that summarized this search of the literature,[4] we bolstered our argument for the tenability of educability by highlighting results of a five-year early education study that had just been concluded, Project EDGE (which was described briefly in Chapter 8). Children in Project EDGE were assessed on a number of measures at the time they concluded project involvement, that is, when they reached 5 years of age. The 35 children (17 treatment, 18 nontreatment), all of whom had the non-disjunction form of Down syndrome, resided in their own homes in the Chicago and Minneapolis-St. Paul areas. Looking at the IQs of the treatment group at age 5, we found that 11 of 17 children in the treatment group had scores in the educable range. Furthermore, while children in the treatment group had, on the average, significantly higher IQs than did nontreatment group children at the end of the project, 50% of the children in the control group also had scores in the educable range. Thus, at the time of school entry, parents who have reared their children at home, providing them with a variety of early stimulation activities, have every right to feel that their child with Down syndrome has about a 50/50 chance (which are pretty good odds compared with past pessimistic forecasts) of doing well in a class for students designated as educable. They should not allow their child to be placed in a class for students designated as trainable until a thorough assessment is done with a variety of assessment tools, including, if possible, a form of the LPAD.

Focusing on the educability issue from another vantage point, academic achievement, Project EDGE children in the treatment group (control group data not yet available) have now been in public schools for several years past the termination of their experimental early education program and are now about 14 years of age on the average. Two years ago we conducted a follow-up study. Of particular interest is the finding that 11 of the 15 children are reading with comprehension at or above the second-grade level, although their IQs have diminished over time. To us, one of the acid tests for advancing the argument for educability in behalf of people with Down syndrome is to be able to show evidence of their attaining a reasonable level of reading comprehension during their public school years. Most of the EDGE children in the treatment group have met that test. Furthermore, the majority of them are currently in educable classes or in regular/educable class combinations and are doing well in them. Thus, the majority of EDGE children in the treatment group, now barely past the midpoint of their public school education, are well on their way to becoming reasonably literate, that is, able to read large portions of many consumer documents. It is well to keep in mind, however, that the children in the EDGE treatment group have been through an intensive early education program; hence, they do not represent the accomplishment level of all children with Down syndrome. Nonetheless, to offset an argument that EDGE treatment children's accomplishments are just reflective of "hothousing," other studies have also shown positive growth in academic development in children with Down syndrome when systematic instruction has been applied.[5,6]

Educability is, of course, more than acquiring ability in academics; it is also improving one's capabilities to socialize effectively. School-age children with Down syndrome may not be inclined toward socialization activities that place demands on them for physicial abilities. Movement, an important part of physical development and an ability that makes the environment more accessible for exploration (and cognitive stimulation), is a problematic area for children with Down syndrome. Often their muscle tone is poor (infants are frequently described as being like "rag dolls" when picked up), leading frequently to delays in such achievements as sitting and walking. Later in life, they tend to have poor balance while in motion, making recreational activities, such as outdoor games, difficult to master in the usual fashion. Often, because they feel fewer rewards from physical activity, they become sedentary, gaining too much weight, making physical activity even less appealing.

To complicate matters further, a child with Down syndrome is often delayed in speech and language development, partially because of muscle tone problems that may adversely affect the orchestration of movements involved in speech production, including respiration, and coordination of the palate, lips, and jaws. Delays in speech and language development can lead to decreased parental expectations, which, in turn, can further inhibit the interaction patterns of parent and child, causing delays in a whole array of developmental areas, including socialization.

Fortunately, some of the speech and language problems of people with Down syndrome can be prevented, or at least remediated to some extent. For example, parents of infants with Down syndrome can learn to alter their language interaction characteristics, learning to expand what their child is able to produce.[7] And the frequent hearing impairments that accompany the condition can often be remediated with a hearing aid (or through medication if due to middle ear infection). Furthermore, dental problems that can limit communication can be minimized or eliminated altogether with fluoride and sealant treatments and through good oral hygiene practices.[8]

Communicative proficiency begins early in life, and its development or underdevelopment has long-term educational implications. For example, smiling is a communicative act involving several facial muscles, and since a baby with Down syndrome often has poor muscle tone that often causes smiling to be delayed, a mother may become disheartened because her baby does not return her smile. Whereupon, she may withdraw from interacting with her baby, creating long-term problems for them both. Fortunately, mothers and fathers can learn to recognize this problem and then can learn to pace their interactions accordingly. In a similar vein, teachers can learn to augment the verbal directions they give a student with Down syndrome, adding modeling and physical prompting to enhance their instructional impact.[9]

Parents of nonhandicapped children *expect* their sons and daughters to grow up to become independent adults; parents of children with Down syndrome *hope* that their offspring will learn to lead at least semiindependent lives as adults.

The life expectancy of adults with Down syndrome has increased substantially in the last 50 years. In 1929, the life expectancy for people with Down syndrome was about 9 years.[10] Now some individuals with Down syndrome survive into their 60s and 70s.[11] With future improvements in medical, nutritional, educational, and social services, this trend toward a longer life can be expected to continue. Hence, parents of a young child with Down syndrome would be wise to prepare themselves for the time when their son or daughter will mature, and probably leave home.

Preparation for leaving home should begin early in every child's life. In this regard, while a preschool child is not expected to learn adult skills such as operating a typewriter, he should be taught good work habits, such as handling his toys with care, so that this positive behavior undergirds his work 20 years later.

Adolescence can be a pivotal time for people with Down syndrome. Learning to inteiact positively and appropriately with peers and to use community facilities independently is especially important to bridging the gap between adolescence and adulthood.

Recreational activities such as Special Olympics are useful in helping people with Down syndrome feel good about their athletic accomplishments and in creating a more positive attitude toward people with Down syndrome. However, they offer relatively little in promoting two skills the child with Down syndrome will need once Special Olympics ends, namely, skill in the independent and functional use of community recreation facilities, and skill in interacting successfully with nonhandicapped peers, as well as with peers who have Down syndrome. To illustrate how these needs can be met through recreation programming, two researchers[12] taught Amy, an adolescent with Down syndrome who had severely retarded performance and was nonverbal, to use a community bowling alley independently. Specifically, Amy was taught to initiate and complete an entire bowling sequence on her own (i.e., secure a bowling lane, obtain shoes, bowl, and pay), and also to order a soft drink and snack from a concession stand in the facility. Eventually, she was also taught how to walk to the bowling alley on her own.

Teaching the full use of the bowling facility was planned by gathering information through a systematic observation of the facility. The observation, called an environmental inventory, led to the construction of a task analysis, a "recipe" of sorts, which included several environmental adaptations to help Amy to overcome, or avoid, problematic aspects of using the bowling alley environment independently. For example, since Amy had virtually no expressive language, she was taught to use a small card on which printed phrases appeared (i.e., "my shoe size is a woman's 7") to inform the attendant of her bowling needs.

The judgment of appropriate ball weight and finger hole size was simplified by determining that she had sufficient strength to use the heaviest ball available in the bowling alley. Thereafter, the ball's weight was ignored and she was taught to select a ball into which her fingers could be easily inserted and removed regardless of its weight.

Another obstacle involved producing the standard number of steps needed to approach the foul line with the customary coordinated side arm movement of the ball as it is released. This complex skill posed a problem for Amy, who has difficulties with dynamic balance and coordinated movement, as do many people with Down syndrome. To overcome this obstacle she was taught to use a simplified style of bowling involving walking up to the foul line without swinging the ball, then engaging the full side arm swing and ball release at the foul line. Although this is not the most popular style, it is used by some nonhandicapped bowlers, and it helped avoid the difficulty of teaching her the full approach style.

Training sessions occurred twice each week for an hour and a half to two hours per session. To prepare for a session, the adult instructor would check to see which step of the task analysis was to be used in beginning the instruction, based on Amy's prior achievement.

To initiate a training trial, the instructor gave a verbal cue (e.g., "Amy, go to the bowling shoe desk"), rewarding an appropriate response, if one occurred, with praise. If the appropriate response did not occur, or the response was incorrect, the instructor repeated the verbal cue and demonstrated the desired behavior. If the response was still not produced or was incorrect, the verbal cue was again repeated and Amy was physically helped through the desired behavior. Her instructor kept track of correct and incorrect responses by noting them directly on a task analysis checklist.

Amy acquired the three sets of skills (bowling, purchasing a drink, and use of a vending machine) in 30, 10, and 18 instructional sessions, respectively. At this rate, an instructor could train an individual with abilities similar to Amy's in the combined set of skills needed for the complete, independent use of a bowling center in just

6 weeks, using three sessions per week, if the three sets of skills were introduced concurrently.

Findings of this study show clearly that age-appropriate skills and enjoyable tasks can be promoted through task analysis and other techniques. Not explored in the study, however, is the possibility that nonhandicapped people might enjoy being friends with people who have Down syndrome.

A few years ago one of the authors and his associates also designed a study utilizing a community recreational bowling facility.[13] The purpose of the study was to explore the effects of structuring (orchestrating) social interactions between nonhandicapped adolescents and adolescents with Down syndrome who were same-age peers, through a technique called cooperative goal structuring.[14] To achieve this purpose, interaction occurrences across three social interaction conditions (cooperative, competitive, and individualistic) were compared. Participants were 30 adolescents from three different public schools in urban Minneapolis, 12 of whom had Down syndrome; the other 18 were nonhandicapped students. These 30 students (18 girls and 12 boys) were assigned randomly to one of the three conditions so that 6 nonhandicapped students and 4 students with Down syndrome were in each group, and so that there were equal numbers of boys and girls in each condition.

In the cooperative condition, students were preinstructed to maximize their group bowling score to meet a common goal (improvement by 50 pins as a group) and were encouraged to interact as friends, i.e., to offer each other encouragement (e.g., "Go get em!"), reinforcement (e.g., "Great!"), and assistance (e.g., help in handling a ball). In the competitive condition, students were preinstructed to maximize their own score so as to outperform everyone else. They were told that their purpose was to bowl the best score—to beat everybody. In the individualistic condition, students were preinstructed to increase their own scores by 10 pins, to concentrate on improving their own score, and not to worry about other bowlers' scores. Basic bowling instruction, identical for all three conditions, was given equally in all conditions throughout the eight-week study.

Using a frame-by-frame recording sheet, observers categorized all understandable verbal interactions of each bowler with any or all of the other bowlers in the group on a continuous basis. Results showed that the number of positive heterogeneous interactions (people with Down syndrome talking pleasantly to nonhandicapped people or vice versa) in the cooperative condition was significantly higher than in either the competitive or individualistic conditions. In fact, in the cooperative group, students received more positive interactions both in terms of interactions with similar peers (homogeneous) and across nonsimilar peers (heterogeneous).

With regard to the effects of cooperative interactions on attitude, nonhandicapped students' ratings of students with Down syndrome were significantly higher in the cooperative condition than were nonhandicapped students' ratings in either the competitive or the individualistic condition.

Shifting to the accomplishments of adolescents with Down syndrome from the EDGE project mentioned earlier, they are quite well-rounded in terms of their recreational interests and activities, such as sports and hobbies.

Recently, a questionnaire was sent to EDGE parents of children in the treatment group at the time those children were around 11 years of age. Results of a portion of that survey, which focused on participation in sports, recreation, and leisure activities, are shown in Table 3. As can be seen, these youngsters are quite active and show a variety of important accomplishments.

During adolescence, an individual with Down syndrome not only should learn to socialize and use community facilities, such as recreation centers, but also should be prepared for the working and independent living parts of adult life in a community. Fortunately, in many locales there are group homes or apartments that are, or can be made, suitable for long-term independent or semiindependent living for adults with disabilities.

The mother of a man with Down syndrome experienced mixed emotions when Brad, 25 years old, expressed a desire to move into a residence for adults.[15] Although his mother wanted to offer her son the "dignity of risk," to help him to grow and develop as an adult in an adult situation, she had many fears about encouraging him. For instance, she feared that people might think she was "putting her child away." She worried that she might be ruining family togetherness and that Brad would miss the comfort of his home and family. His mother admitted that she was not prepared to accept that her need to be needed was being undermined. On the other hand, she recognized that it is normal for children to move away at some point.

Fortunately, Brad's family had begun early to train him for independence. As a youngster, Brad learned, for instance, to operate the

TABLE 3. EDGE (Expanding Developmental Growth through Education) Children's Social/Leisure Activity Development at around the Age of 11 years[a]

Child	Participation in outdoor activities	Hobbies	Participation in organized activities	Interest in the arts
A	Swimming, skiing, basketball, running	Computer graphics, painting and drawing, listening to music	Brownie, member of school basketball and softball team	Had lessons in piano, violin, dance
B	Water play, riding on a snowmobile	Avid wrestling fan and other TV watching	Scouts, outings with a social club for retarded citizens	Enjoys social dancing
C	Biking	Latch-hook rug making	Softball team in community, Special Olympics	Member of choir
D	Jogging, swimming	Art, woodworking	Bowling league	Plays guitar and harmonica, loves art
E	Swimming	Collects baseball and football cards, loves to read the sports page of newspaper	Participates in school wrestling, floor hockey, Special Olympics, took golf and swimming lessons at YMCA	Listens to music
F	Swimming and camping	Reading and listening to music	Softball team at school, Special Olympics	Listens to music
G	Softball, sliding, skiing (but doesn't like outdoor activities very much)	Creative crafts, Legos	Special Olympics, Christian Social Club	Loves to draw and to do things in crafts, loves to listen to music

TABLE 3. (*Continued*)

Child	Participation in outdoor activities	Hobbies	Participation in organized activities	Interest in the arts
H	Skiing, skating, jogging, camping	Listening to music, taking care of small children, typing	Special Olympics, Camp Fire Girls, ushering at children's theater	Loves piano lessons, loves to write stories
I	Skiing, softball, camping, bicycling	Bowling, reading, video games	Special Olympics, Boy Scouts, YMCA	Loves to draw and dance
J	Camping, swimming, biking, roller skating	None	Variety of activities through Community Service Agency	Listens to music
K	Camping, bicycling, swimming	Listening to music	4-H, Special Olympics	Listens to music
L	Swimming, fishing, miniature golf	Listening to music, cooking	Participates in Total Teens, a group for games and socializing	Likes to dance and paint, enrolled in ballet class
M	Fishing, camping, biking, skiing, baseball, basketball, lawn games, riding motorcycles	Weight lifting and exercising	Adapted Recreational Services, a social group for adults with handicaps; weight lifting and body building	Enjoys listening to music

*a*Results of questionnaires sent to parents of children in the experimental group.

family's washing machine, prepare his own lunches, get his clothes ready for the next day, and make purchases at the local grocery store. This training was a major factor in his successful adjustment.

But what about the problems of early senility about which we have heard so much? Ten years ago, the prognosis looked gloomy. For example, three authors[16] wrote, "In Down's syndrome, the reward for survival beyond age 40 is presenile dementia," and another[17] said, "It is . . . generally known that the person with Down's syndrome has really no true adult life. In the twenties, signs of premature aging are observed." Currently, however, the prognosis is considerably brighter. First of all, it has not been demonstrated that *all* individuals with Down syndrome exhibit symptoms of early senility. Second, it cannot be assumed that deterioration of behavior in adulthood is related only to physical factors. Environmental factors, such as institutional placement, inadequate nutrition, and a lack of physical exercise, meaningful work, and environmental stimulation, account for some of the observed downturn in their development later in life.

Life at 40 holds greater rewards than senile dementia for H., a middle-aged man with Down syndrome. H. has not exhibited behavioral symptoms of premature senility. On the contrary, he lives a vital life and continues to develop new interests, involving himself in adult education activities and piano lessons. A paragraph[18] from a description of H. (who was 45 years old at the time) highlights his accomplishments:

> For many years, H. has held two part-time jobs, one in the morning and one in the afternoon; he has a savings account of almost $14,000. He is well known and well liked in the community, and moves about freely. He is a happy fellow, interested in what is going on, likes to be well-dressed, and has a good sense of humor. He is very reliable (for instance, in taking telephone messages for his parents), and is careful to be on time for his work. He is very much attached to his family and likes living at home; he attends church and an adult Sunday School class and goes regularly to social club for retarded adults.

H. may have set the pace for other adults with Down syndrome, many of whom will survive to a later age and who will benefit greatly from a challenging and stimulating environment.

An area of special concern for parents of adolescents or young adults with Down syndrome is sexuality. What little mention there is of sexuality is usually related to masturbation. Opportunities to engage in wise, age-appropriate, and meaningful heterosexual activities are often unavailable to adults with Down syndrome; or, if they are available, they may not be taken advantage of fully.

Unwanted pregnancy is probably parents' greatest fear, although medical literature indicates that "the male with Down's syndrome rarely assumes the [sexual] status of a male adult,"[18] and that males have not been known to father children.[19]

For young women with Down syndrome, menstruation may pose some dilemmas for them and their parents. If a young woman with Down syndrome shows mildly retarded performance, she is very likely to be able to learn how to take care of herself independently during menstruation. A young woman with severely retarded performance may find menstruation a frightening experience. With the onset of menstruation also comes the possibility of pregnancy. Females with Down syndrome have conceived, though infrequently, and have a relatively high probability (50/50) of giving birth to a child with Down syndrome. The best moral training at home cannot assure that, away from home, a young woman with Down syndrome may not be taken advantage of or, because of her intellectual limitations, may use poor judgment. Many parents ask for contraceptive advice for their daughters, some request sterilization, and others ask for a hysterectomy.

With respect to sexuality, we believe that human sexual intercourse necessitates responsible behavior. The responsibilities conventionally observed in marriage, for example, a legal covenant (and frequently a religious one as well), offer a stronger foundation for a sexual relationship than intercourse outside of marriage.

Society is providing an increasing number of opportunities for adults with Down syndrome to marry and live with a modicum of assistance. This is a positive move since the need for love, intimacy, and companionship is not restricted to nonhandicapped people. Furthermore, since the "exercise of successful marriage" does not have an enviable record of success among nonhandicapped people, those adults with Down syndrome who are capable of understanding the privileges *and* responsibilities that attend marriage might do at least as well in matrimony as nonhandicapped people; perhaps they might even do better.

Independent adult living demands an array of competencies. An innovative program of continuing education for adults with disabilities is offered at the State University of New York's Brockport campus.[20] A non-credit course, Basic Skills in Independent Living, is supported by state taxes, service organizations, and a modest registration fee of $10. The program seeks to provide experiences in using skills in public settings and includes course work in human sexuality, swimming, bowling, judo, pizza making, and public safety. A person involved in the course introduces us to C. and M., both of whom are 22 years old, through an excerpt from an anecdotal record:

> It has been hard for C. to develop age-appropriate behaviors, but his college student volunteers were not interested in his tantrums. M.'s volunteers quickly learned that M. was adept at avoiding anything new and a master at manipulating situations to her advantage. Both of these young people have grown and matured in this college setting and their parents have been quick to capitalize on their more adult behavior. M. has become a sports fan and watches any gymnastic special she can find on TV—a change from her beloved "soaps." C. has learned that he can no longer jump blindly into the pool. He has learned to deal with his own strength and size. He recognizes the responsibility of being in a group of people who are not going to give him special consideration because he is retarded.

Although there are almost no statistics available on the rates of employment of adults with Down syndrome, it is well known that many are capable of responsible employment. We contend that there are jobs that *more* adults with Down syndrome would be able to perform with proper training because some perform them *now*. For instance, in 1978, K., a 19-year-old woman with Down syndrome, was a librarian in a school for mentally retarded children.[21] J., a man in his early 20s with Down syndrome, operated the addressograph and mimeograph machines in the office where he worked. He also "goes to the post office and the bank, prepares the morning and afternoon coffee, and is a helpful and trustworthy worker."[18] D., a 23-year-old man with Down syndrome, worked for a firm that manufactures contact lenses, where he earned $2.90 an hour for maintenance work.[22] D. also mowed lawns with a $2,400.00 tractor he purchased out of his own savings and, on weekends, voluntarily cleaned the fire station, for which he was officially cited as "Honorary Minnetonka Fireman." S., a 31-year-old man with Down syndrome, was employed successfully as a grounds maintenance worker with a state planning commission.[23]

Marc Gold[24] has initiated some highly creative work relating to the vocational training of people with retarded performance. Taking issue with the position that people with Down syndrome are capable of performing only tasks that require little training, skill, or attention, he contended that we need to revise our expectations about the kinds of jobs they can perform, especially when they are trained systematically. Gold's point is illustrated in an investigation he conducted that focused on the capabilities of 64 moderately and severely retarded adolescents from sheltered workshops who were trained to assemble bicycle brakes using form, or form plus color, as cues. Following training, the adolescents (about 40% of whom had Down syndrome, according to Gold) were required to assemble the complex 24-piece brakes, exactly as they came from the factory. After intensive training employing behavior modification techniques, 63 of the 64 adolescents exhibited 100% correct assembly on six out of eight consecutive trials. A year later, 53 of the 64 assembled the same 24-piece training brake, demonstrating that many had retained their skills. Although Gold did not wish to emphasize the classification of his subjects, he did compare performances of the people with Down syndrome with the others and found no significant performance differences. Gold's investigation illustrates the high potential of systematic training for the improvement of employment opportunities.

Not only is job success related to how well we train people with Down syndrome for employment, it is also related to *where* the training is provided. Up to the mid-1970s, the "flow-through" model was the standard of vocational services in the United States. Using this model, the young adult with Down syndrome is placed into sheltered employment to acquire skills that are presumed to be prerequisites for competitive employment. Those who demonstrate increasing competence are supposed to "flow," that is, advance to better and better employment opportunities. In reality, however, individuals with handicaps, especially with serious handicaps, are usually placed at the bottom levels of the continuum,[25] where less than 3% ever advance to competitive employment.[26] Hence, in the mid-1970s, several innovative demonstration projects[27,28] began to show impressive outcomes by circumventing the flow-through model completely, proceeding directly to training at the site of competitive employment. By circumventing sheltered employment, moving directly to successful nonsheltered vocational placement, these demonstrations provided convincing evidence that a lack of productivity can be more a function of the program than of the individual.[29]

Competitive employment programs offered on the community job site provide additional benefits, such as increased social skills by participants,[30] more individualized program options,[29] reduced program costs,[31] and positive influences on both staff and consumer morale.[31]

One of the prime techniques for making on-site community vocational placement viable is the utilization of "supported employment,"[32] which combines an emphasis on the full range of normal job benefits with provisions for ongoing support at the work site for those for whom competitive employment is unlikely.[33] Some of the provisions that can be made to support the person with a disability in competitive employment are to provide special devices that allow the person to accommodate to regular job tasks and working routines in a "nontypical" manner, and modifying a standard job task for partial participation and/or nonstandard completion. Providing a "vocational partner," a peer who is accomplished in a job and who will assist the person with Down syndrome to master the job, after which the partner will gradually reduce direct training involvement until the individual with Down syndrome is able to function capably on his own, can be very helpful too.

Shifting our attention from vocational training, we shall see how recreational training can play a strong role in promoting living successfully in the community as an adult.

Earlier in this chapter we described how Amy, a teenager with Down syndrome, learned to use a bowling alley independently. And we presented research findings showing that teenagers with Down syndrome and normal same-age peers can be brought together for fruitful social interactions during recreational bowling. Both of these descriptions illustrate how preparation for adult community integration should begin during adolescence. But what about people with Down syndrome who do not have transition experiences in adolescence or who do not have a sufficient number of them to make the preparation "stick"? Leisure education can still be taught effectively in adulthood for people with Down syndrome. Indeed, it is important to introduce instruction properly regardless of age since participating in games, drawing, playing a musical instrument, bowling, camping, and other recreational activities bring personal pleasure, offer pleasant interactions with others, promote mental health and physical fitness and often serve as an important catalyst in intellectual development.

Two authors[34] recently completed a study in which two adults with Down syndrome (one 27 and the other 29 years of age), both of whom had relatively low IQs, were taught to use independently a community recreation center near the group home in which they resided. Neither of the men had ever set foot in the recreation center, even though it was located only six blocks from their group home.

Objectives of the study were to teach the two men, C. and L., to walk together independently to the recreation center, to select and effectively use an age-appropriate game in the center, to retain the new skills, and to generalize the skills they learned to another community recreation center in the city.

Prior to the program, an environmental survey was conducted to identify the skills needed for an adult to participate independently at the center. On the basis of the survey, three activity plans were constructed, involving going independently to the recreation center, borrowing fooseball (a fast-paced table game) equipment, playing the game appropriately and returning the equipment afterward, and returning independently to their group home.

Both C. and L. had socialization problems and had a very limited repertoire of age-appropriate recreational abilities. For example, on the way to their first visit to the community recreation center, when the instructor offered the verbal cue "Use the recreation center," to see what they could do before training, C. and L. proceeded to a nearby tot lot and began to play on the animal swings and with toys designed for preschoolers.

Training began using cues, rewards, and corrections when errors occurred. For example, a verbal cue was given (i.e., "C., release the fooseball onto the table"), followed by social reinforcement by the instructor (e.g., pat on the back, verbal praise) for a correct response. Within a 20-week period, all three recreational skills were mastered by both of the men.

Regarding the maintenance of skills at the recreation center, seven months after the training ended, a retention probe was arranged; that is, no modeling, physical prompting, or social reinforcement was offered. Across the three skill areas, 95 to 100% of the steps were achieved independently by both men. Furthermore, when introduced to an unfamiliar recreation center across town, both men were able to function independently and competently, showing nearly 100% performance in the new environment.

One of the most recent programs for social and vocational integration of persons with Down syndrome has been developed and activated at the institute's Hasbro Paradigmatic Clinic for the person with Down syndrome in Jerusalem. Currently accommodating 12 people, this program has as its goal to prepare persons with Down syndrome to become capable of assisting other persons, such as physically handicapped aged persons.

The program includes training in areas such as communication, physical assistance, human development, personal security, first aid, instrumental enrichment, and physical education. Independent living topics, such as homemaking and shopping, enhance the students' abilities to cope with a great variety of situations, both as caregivers and as efficient socially integrated persons. The duration of the preparatory program is approximately one year, taking into consideration the variety of skills to be taught and the need to consolidate newly acquired knowledge by offering practical tryout experience under supervision and guidance.

This program is a concentrated effort to create a meaningful and modifying environment for the person with Down syndrome and to answer a pressing societal need. Transforming the individual from a dependent person into a care provider who contributes to the well-being of society is a radical change in the usual life of a person with Down syndrome. It not only should enhance the social involvement of persons with Down syndrome but also could significantly reduce their own level of dependency.

If successful, the program should help modify public opinion and influence social policies toward people with handicaps in general and persons with Down syndrome in particular.

The inception of this program was met with enthusiasm from prospective students and their parents. Moreover, directors of hospitals, day care facilities, and hostels for the aged have expressed readiness to be active contributors to its success. Even though it is in its initial stage, indications are that the quality of help offered by the person with Down syndrome to people who are aged and/or severely handicapped is very good and deeply appreciated. Bonds seem already to have been produced between caregivers with Down syndrome and the recipients of their help.

From many points of view, this program can be considered "revolutionary," reflecting a strong belief in the power of intervention to induce and then foster modifiability in both the person with Down syndrome and people with whom he interacts. A person with Down syndrome, when provided with appropriate active modification, can become an individual who makes a valuable contribution to his family, school, place of employment, and society as a whole.

CHAPTER 10

Reconstructive Plastic Surgery
An Extreme Form of Active Modification

Down syndrome reveals itself in distinctive facial features that make the condition so recognizable that even people who know nothing about it technically can recognize it. Such ready recognition often creates continuing discomfort for parents who have children with Down syndrome when they are out in public together. Wherever they go, the threat of stares, behind-the-hand whispers, and unkind comments shadow them. Some parents adapt to this threat eventually and do not curtail their social activities. Others, however, withdraw to the safety of predictable environments—their home, local church, and neighborhood shop—hoping with all their hearts that some day soon labels such as "mongoloid" will drop out of society's vocabulary forever. Happily, looking across the history of society's attitudes toward people with disabilities shows that remarkable progress has been made toward accepting and integrating people with disabilities. However, studying that same historical record also suggests that it would be "Pollyannish" to assume that labeling and stereotyping die rapidly or easily. Therefore, active modification efforts must be mounted on all fronts, including the biomedical front. Until reconstructive plastic surgery (RPS) became available, few professionals thought of physically changing the characteristic facial features of Down syndrome. Now that it is available and used with increasing frequency, parents and professionals tend to divide themselves into two camps regarding its use. One camp opposes it on grounds that it may "unmask" a child with Down syndrome who might need the protection afforded by the syndrome's high recognizability, saying that society, not the child with Down syndrome, needs to change. Those favoring it argue that since nonhandicapped

Yael Mintzker is a contributing author to this chapter.

169

people have access to RPS, why not let people with Down syndrome have access to it also? They contend that society is glacially slow to change, and that the person with Down syndrome who aspires to attain social integration cannot wait until society becomes sufficiently accommodative.

This is just a small introduction to the issues surrounding RPS, issues that are hotly debated and involve fundamental moral, ethical, and individual rights and religious questions that may also stir up old taboos.[1,2] We will return to these issues at the end of this chapter, but let us now look at what is involved in the procedure itself and what its effects have been so far.

In the last 10 years, more than 600 children and adults with Down syndrome have undergone RPS in a number of countries. Most of the surgery has taken place in Germany, Great Britain, and Israel, but there are increasing numbers of operations occurring in the United States, Canada, Australia, and other countries. The rationale and medical procedures involved in this type of surgery have been described by several professionals.[3–8] Similarly, the psychological aspects of RPS have been reviewed several times.[9–13] According to proponents of RPS, the procedure is intended to attain goals of both a cosmetic and a functional nature. The term *cosmetic* in the RPS context has to be understood differently from its more common connotation because the ultimate objective of the surgery is *not* to make the person beautiful by aesthetic standards. Nor does it seek to make the person look completely normal. The main purpose of the surgery is to reduce the saliency of the characteristic physical stigmata of Down syndrome that make the condition so easily identifiable and "categorizable."

For functional purposes, RPS should be looked at from a perspective that focuses on its broad meaning in fostering social acceptance and, ultimately, social integration. Reducing the protruding tongue, for instance, can be important not only for aesthetic reasons but also for a variety of functional reasons, such as facilitating the intake of liquid and solid food, or for possibly enabling better speech articulation, though there are no conclusive data to support this latter goal as yet.

Surgically, RPS often involves one or more of the following procedures:

1. Removal of a wedge-shaped portion of the tongue's tip (partial glossectomy).
2. Reduction of the epicanthal folds (folds of skin at the margins

of the eyes) through raising the nasal bridge with a silicone insert or a portion of cartilage taken from another part of the patient's body. (This insert also tends to eliminate the commonly observed almond shaping of the eyes.) In certain cases, though, the epicanthal folds require direct surgery.

3. Straightening the oblique lid axes of the eyes.
4. Augmentation of the receding chin and/or raising abnormally flat cheeks with inserts of silicone or cartilage.
5. Repair of hanging lower lips.
6. Correcting dysplasia of the ears in terms of both position and size.
7. Widening of the nostrils to facilitate breathing.
8. Removing fat from the upper neck and lower half of the face (see Figure 20).

The surgery itself is generally not complicated, usually lasting about an hour or less if silicone implants are used, depending on the number of physical stigmata to be corrected. (With bone and cartilage implants it takes more time.) Postsurgery recovery is of a relatively short duration, usually requiring a few days of hospitalization, and healing is generally rapid except for the tongue, which requires about four to six weeks for complete healing. During this period, except for the first two or three days, eating and speaking are not hampered too much.

RPS is an extreme manifestation of the active modification approach. This attempt to pull the person with Down syndrome "out of the corner" is, without question, intrusive intervention, one meant to

Figure 20. Sites of reconstructive plastic surgery (RPS), a schematic drawing.

significantly affect the lives of both the individual with Down syndrome and his family. Hence, weighing the pros and cons of using such an intervention requires serious attention as to its possible implications.

The advocates of RPS have been animated by a strong desire to provide more normalized life conditions for the person with Down syndrome. The difficulties that persons with Down syndrome encounter when they try to enter normalized, or even quasi-normalized, environments are well known. The fact that the ability of a person with Down syndrome may exceed that needed in a school or job setting is often overshadowed by the distinctive physical characteristics of the condition and the inappropriately low mental functioning expectations held by employers and others toward people with this condition.

Furthermore, owing to the conspicuousness of the physical stigmata associated with Down syndrome, the syndrome is often easily detectable. But in counterdistinction to less obvious (and, often, less stigmatizing) conditions, in this specific case early detection does not always lead to positive, active modification. In fact, the stereotypes associated with this condition, perpetuated across many generations, lead almost invariably to feelings of pessimism and helplessness on the part of the parents. These feelings may culminate in one of the following basic attitudes:

Rejection. Experiencing strong feelings of helplessness and frustration, parents may try to detach themselves from the problem by rejecting their child so as to protect themselves and other family members from the effects of his condition. Occasionally, parents may place their child in a residential facility or foster home. Although such placements do not necessarily reflect an attitude of rejection, the child himself, as well as his siblings, often consider it an expression of such an attitude. Rejection may also manifest itself in cases where the child is kept at home but is neglected or even abused. A very reduced level of investment in the child's modification may also be the product of a rejective attitude.

Reaction Formation. This is a well-known defense mechanism by which individuals try to cope with their anxiety feelings provoked by inner conflicts. Often it expresses itself in unconditioned love and overprotection. Such an attitude, instead of enhancing a child's development of autonomy and competence, creates and maintains dependency, impairing the well-being of both the individual and his family.

Overcompensating Acceptance. This attitude is expressed in perceiving the child's condition as one in which there is nothing to be done: "My child is a beautiful child, a capable child; everything is just fine with him. Don't touch him and don't teach him; he will make it. He is an angel." Such an overcompensating distortion of reality immobilizes the parents, possibly leading them to do no more than provide love and affection in generalized massive doses. Although love and affection are critical ingredients of adequate child rearing, if they hamper intervention, the effect may be to preclude the child's further development and even reduce his current level of functioning. Tragically, when overcompensating acceptance occurs, parents set themselves up for an emotional upheaval when the reality of their child's disabilities breaks through the fragile defensive barrier they have created.

These three attitudes are basically counterproductive to the development of the child, significantly reducing his (and his parents') ability to cope with the environment. As already mentioned, people with Down syndrome, having a condition that is easily detectable, are often consigned to a separate "class" to which others react with preconceived attitudes, usually without trying to learn about the individual "behind the face." Rather, it is often the case that the external appearance of the person with Down syndrome, with all its negative associations deeply anchored in misperceptions and folklore, strongly influences social and educational practices, as the following episode will illustrate.

A chemical researcher taking a leave of absence from his company had been invited to become a visiting researcher at a university in Boston. Inquiring about educational facilities for his son, Craig, a 14-year-old with Down syndrome, the father was referred to an agency responsible for special education programs in the Boston area. Craig, who had always attended a regular school and interacted primarily with normal peers, seemed to be well suited for integration in a regular school rather than a special segregated one. Craig's parents submitted their schooling application, accompanied by a report from their son's teacher detailing the child's ability to function ably in a school program with normal children, along with records of his achievements and difficulties in various scholastic areas. The reply they provided said, in essence, that, according to the details presented in their application and the report of his teacher, their son would ordinarily be integrated in one of their regular school programs. However, because he had the physical characteristics of Down syndrome, regretfully, they would be unable to accept him in an integrated program. Obviously, Craig's physical appearance (and associated stereotypes), not his intellectual and social abilities, determined his possibility of being integrated into a regular education program.

Another case further highlights the importance of external appearance to social and educational integration.

Fran, a 14-year-old youngster with Down syndrome, was referred to the institute by her parents, who were deeply concerned about her future. Fran was about to finish the seventh grade in a special school for children classified as educable mentally retarded (EMR). This educational achievement was somewhat unusual according to the prevailing educational expectations of that period, which almost universally favored placement of students with Down syndrome with students classified as trainable mentally retarded (TMR). Despite the fact that Fran mastered reading, writing, and many other scholastic skills and had an amiable personality, she was referred by the psychologist of her municipality for placement in a sheltered work program for young adults with severe intellectual disabilities. Her parents were keenly aware of their daughter's intellectual accomplishments, her high level of motivation, and her desire to continue her studies and to live among normal peers. Consequently, they were distressed by the psychologist's recommendation, which was accompanied by a psychological report showing Fran's IQ of 68. (Her verbal IQ was even higher, reaching 78.) Her parents contended that the assessment did not reflect their child's potential and referred her to the institute for a reevaluation. A dynamic assessment, using the learning potential assessment device, was begun. Its results showed that the parents' impressions were well founded. Fran showed a good capacity for learning, being able to learn and integrate problem-solving processes and to generalize from them to new problems that required similar problem-solving behaviors. Her learning difficulties were mainly due to an oversensitivity to conditions of frustration, resulting in feelings of extreme incompetence. Hence, she tended to react defiantly to each hint that she needed help, possibly because she had difficulty admitting that she might be weak in certain areas of performance. Her behavior reflected a persistent and exhaustive fight against feelings of insecurity.

Following the LPAD and an analysis of its findings, it was recommended that Fran be placed in a regular seventh-grade class for environmentally disadvantaged children. This environment was chosen in order to offer her a chance to become involved in normalized curriculum activities and to interact with students modeling normal behaviors.

After an extensive search for an appropriate educational program, followed by a long campaign to permit her to be admitted, Fran was accepted in a regular school. During a two-year period, she developed substantially, functioning close to normal scholastic expectations in a variety of areas. However, she experienced socialization difficulties, becoming highly argumentative with parents, teachers, and peers. Fortunately, this was interpreted as reflecting a normal developmental trend of adolescence and increasing self-assertion, which had been strengthened by interactions with her normal peers.

After she finished elementary school, Fran's parents and the institute staff felt that she should remain in a regular school so that she could continue to be with students of her own age and an environment with both tolerance for her problems and encouragement for her self-assertion. A "live-in" setting was eventually recommended, one in which she would be able to interact with disadvantaged adolescents who were undergoing a preparatory program for integration into regular high schools.[14]

When institute psychologists considered Fran ready for regular high school, her parents and the institute staff were confronted with the true consequences of Fran's appearance. All efforts to enroll her in a regular school were in vain. Despite continuing persistence, Fran was rejected even by programs that were serving students functioning at lower levels of intelligence than Fran manifested. The apparent reason for rejection was, essentially, that accepting a child with the characteristic appearance of Down syndrome into their school would stigmatize the school and its entire student population. As a result, Fran became extremely conscious of her appearance, which, in turn, affected her social behavior considerably. She would retreat into a corner so as not to be observed eating, being ashamed of her protruding tongue, a feeling that only increased when her entire mouth area became covered with remnants of the food she was eating.

According to conversations held with the principals and staff of the regular schools, children in regular classes strongly opposed enrolling a child with Down syndrome, fearing that their classes would get a "reputation" and they themselves would be stigmatized as "retardates." Principals also said that parents of nondisabled, albeit low-functioning, children were opposed to such an integration, threatening to remove their children from the school if it occurred. These reactions were encountered repeatedly as parents and staff continued to negotiate with educational facilities, deepening the feelings of disappointment and frustration for everyone, especially Fran herself. Eventually, Fran's functioning began to deteriorate rapidly, magnifying feelings of despair in both Fran and her parents, who feared that all their years of intensive investment might come to naught.

These two cases show clearly that educational, social, vocational, and community living opportunities are strongly influenced by the physical appearance of the individual. Related to this point, Aviad[15] found that more individuals are classified as mentally retarded during their school years than are so classified as adults. Many "disappear" into regular life as adults, despite the fact that they were classified as mentally retarded in their school years. However, the fate of people with Down syndrome is different because of their external appearance. Society does not permit them to "fade into adulthood." Consequently, normalization is extremely difficult, even when the individual's level of functioning would justify community integration and productive employment.

RPS has the potential to be a powerful catalyst in normalizing the appearance of people with Down syndrome and increasing their possibilities for leading a more normal life. With all of its inherent difficulties, RPS may, in some cases, not be too great a price to pay for acceptance and integration into regular society.

In considering RPS seriously, parents should be informed fully as to its risks, likely benefits, inherent difficulties, and expected outcomes. Moreover, parents must be prepared for the ongoing need for active modification, such as speech and language therapy, in order to actualize the possibilities opened up by surgery. In no case should RPS be considered a kind of "magic wand" that will, by itself, solve all problems. RPS, in and of itself, is not meant to improve mental functioning but must be accompanied by other short-term and long-term educational interventions. RPS is only the beginning of a long and very challenging road, one that will require continuous investment in order to materialize new options that have been opened up by the surgery. At the same time, it should be emphasized that parents of children with Down syndrome, and society in general, have the right and duty to act to create normalizing conditions for persons with Down syndrome. This may or may not involve performing RPS.

Speech and language achievement illustrates the importance of combined and continuous intervention. Reducing the size of the tongue does not necessarily improve the person's vocal intelligibility. Rather, intensive speech and language therapy is required in order to activate and maximize the effect of the surgery. Reducing the size of the tongue may, however, render this and other interventions more possible and efficient. Frequently, speech therapists working with persons who have Down syndrome invest their efforts almost exclusively in language development (e.g., vocabulary, syntax) rather than in the improvement of articulation. This is often justified by therapists as being attributable to the difficulties caused by the protruding tongue, which impedes articulatory therapy. Thus, shortening the tongue may positively affect the readiness of the speech therapist to work with a person with Down syndrome in a way similar to working with normal-functioning children who show speech production difficulties. Additionally, conversations with normal children provide appropriate speech and language models and, hence, are a necessary intervention to increase the possible effects of tongue reduction.

Experience has shown that often parents do not wish to enter into any daring endeavor with their Down syndrome child because they do not want to disrupt his real or imagined "happiness." There is no doubt that happiness is a highly desired goal for every person. But parents must realize that an oversheltered life is not the way to achieve real happiness because it does not lead to true adaptation or self-fulfillment—not for them, not for their child.

Putting ourselves in the position of parents facing the need to decide about RPS, we pose here a series of questions that are often heard during interactions with parents who face an RPS decision, and offer some responses to them as well.

Why not change society instead of altering my child's appearance? There is no doubt about the desirability of investing efforts in changing negative public attitudes and social policies that inhibit and even harm people with Down syndrome. Such support is already germinating in many countries and has produced some significant successes. But changing society is an extremely lengthy process, one that may take decades or even generations. Furthermore, even when laws and/or social policies are changed, there is still a very long way to go until such laws or policies significantly affect the attitudes of the general public. A child with Down syndrome has little time to wait for such changes and cannot always depend upon their outcomes. Something concrete and meaningful must be done *while* society gradually adjusts to a new orientation toward people with retarded performance. Opening avenues for integration must always be a combined endeavor of intensive, active social and educational efforts to modify the individual and his level of functioning as well as intensive efforts to modify society. Both types of interventional processes are vital in order to maximize integrational options.

Is it ethical to intervene and change God's creation? This question was asked by a 24-year-old man with Down syndrome to whom plastic surgery was suggested. He said, "If God made me like this, why should I be changed?" The plastic surgeon, who was knowledgeable in Judaic studies, answered him with a saying based on a citation from the Holy Bible: "God created the world, but the process of creation should always be continued." His answer had a significant impact on the final, affirmative decision of this young man. Interestingly, such questions arise very rarely when RPS is requested by normal individuals, even when it is performed solely for aesthetic purposes.

The advocates of RPS feel that interventions that create conditions for significant improvements in the individual's life are desirable and legitimate. Parents have not only the right but the duty to do all they can to improve the life conditions of their offspring. In the case of persons with Down syndrome, who are either incapable of taking (or unlikely to take) such initiatives on their own, it is perhaps even more imperative that family and social agents play a meaningful role in this decision.

Will the operation, in and of itself, improve my child's cognitive and mental functioning? The answer to this question is no. RPS has no direct effect upon the mental functioning of the individual, although mental ability may be positively affected indirectly by RPS by creating better conditions for social interaction. These include a lessening of

negative self-consciousness and possibly opening up more normalized educational opportunities where higher levels of mental activity are necessary in order to cope with mainstream environments.
The ultimate effect of RPS will be determined by the nature and
intensity of the social efforts and educational investments that are
extended to maximize new expectations and new options.

*What role should the child play in the decision-making process concern-
ing the surgery?* The child with Down syndrome has essentially the
same rights and prerogatives as any other child. Naturally, the decision-making process will have to be adjusted to the age of the child at
the time of intervention and to his or her general level of functioning.
Even with normal-functioning children there are certain situations in
which parents have to decide on their own about interventions. Such
decisions are made according to what parents consider as being best
for their child. In all cases where child involvement is possible, in
both the preparatory and postsurgery stages, such involvement is
highly desirable and usually very helpful.

What dangers are involved in RPS? RPS always requires general
anesthesia, which, on the basis of statistical probabilities, presents
some danger to any patient, normal or handicapped. However,
among the 600 children and adults with Down syndrome who underwent surgery in Israel, Germany, and other countries, there have
been no reports of any fatality or any serious negative outcome associated with anesthetics. Special care should be taken—as in any surgical intervention—to ensure the general health of the patient. It is
ultimately up to the physician to decide if a particular individual may
or may not undergo surgery from a medical point of view.

Will surgery on the tongue negatively affect speech? From our experience, the answer to this question is no. On the contrary, speech
abilities might be affected positively by making the person more accessible to systematic speech therapy and, if mainstreamed, to normal speech models. Similarly, other functions related to the mouth
cavity may be positively affected. For instance, the process of taking
in food and retaining it in the mouth until it is swallowed may be
improved significantly. Drooling is often reported to diminish or to
disappear altogether, as reported by parents whose children had

tongue-reduction surgery. In fact, follow-up data collected at the institute show that this is one of the most predictable positive outcomes of RPS.[16]

Do physical effects of the surgical intervention persist over time? As far as we know, when silicone implants have been used, only in a few cases were new implants needed. Fewer problems of this sort seem to occur when flesh and bone transplants are used. Sometimes when introduced early in life, cheek or chin implants may have to be redone after adolescence in order to adjust to the new general maturity of the person and to the developmental changes that have occurred. When necessary, such surgical adjustments take relatively little time and do not present any particular difficulty.

What is the most appropriate age to perform RPS? RPS can be performed at almost any age. Advanced age is not an impediment to the implementation of surgery, and children have been operated upon as young as 3 years of age. Technically, RPS is possible (and sometimes performed) earlier than age 3. Some professionals believe that it may be advisable to perform surgery at the prekindergarten age in order to offer the child better possibilities for integration at the beginning of his schooling. This opinion is not shared by all. The prekindergarten age is considered by some professionals as too early a stage for RPS because of the traumatic nature of the surgery, and they advise waiting until early adolescence or even young adulthood. (There is ongoing research by Mintzker, at the institute, as to the differential effects of speech therapy upon children who have and have not undergone tongue reduction at an early age.)

After the operation, does the patient experience considerable pain? As in any surgery, there is pain and discomfort following the operation. According to our experience with patients, as well as reports of parents, generally, pain does not exceed what a person can support with standard medications. After a few days, pain disappears almost completely in most cases. Naturally, individual differences occur that are partly related to the person's level of tolerance to pain. The implants themselves usually do not cause pain or inconvenience and are very well supported by the patients.

Is the child frightened by the thought of surgery? If so, how should he be prepared for it? The reaction of the child to the surgical intervention is, in great measure, contingent upon the way he is prepared for the event. Extensive preparation is *imperative,* and wherever it has been done properly, no negative aftereffects have been reported. The child, as well as his parents, should be informed *fully* of the goals of the surgery, its procedures, and the inconveniences attached to it, as well as its implications for their life afterward. All information should be shared fully with the candidate for surgery in order to avoid unrealistically high expectations or a disproportionate amount of anxiety. It is advisable that parents facing this decision meet with parents of children who have undergone surgery. It is also important that parents, teachers, siblings, and peers be actively and continuously involved in this process. At the hospital, parents should assist the paramedical staff in their daily treatment, encouraging and comforting their child. Such an event may also become a good occasion for a family "celebration" in which the child who received surgery may be the "hero." Teachers and peers can play a significant role in creating and maintaining a warm and encouraging atmosphere during the preparatory and postsurgery period, emphasizing the positive changes that have occurred in the child's appearance and talking about future activities.

Do we not cause damage to the child by raising unrealistic expectations in him? This question arises frequently among both parents and professionals who consider that raising "unrealistic" expectations may become a source of frustration for the child. But which is more damaging: to raise higher expectancies and to struggle for their materialization, or to maintain low expectations and perpetuate nonadaptation and "happy" dependency? Not to struggle because of fear of failure leads to the passive acceptance of the condition as an immutable characteristic of the child. What is realistic for a child is determined to a great extent by our own goal settings, by the efforts we make in both planning and implementing interventions, by our continuous "dissatisfaction" with the stage of development already reached, by a persistent struggle to continue the process of growth and development, by meaningfully involving the child in the process of his own development. RPS should be viewed from this perspective, that is, as one significant way (certainly not the only one) to facilitate the attainment of higher goals, something that will be viewed positively by parents, by the person with Down syndrome, and by society at large.

Won't we raise unrealistic expectations as to marriage (and parenting)? Marriage should not be excluded, *a priori,* from the array of legitimate alternatives available to people with Down syndrome. Naturally, there are many issues and practical concerns to be considered before taking steps in this direction, but marrying should not necessarily be viewed as unrealistic. In fact, entertaining the goal of marriage may itself play an important role in generating adult developmental progress in a person with Down syndrome. In some cases, marrying and establishing a household, even when requiring continuous assistance, may increase significantly the chances of avoiding institutionalization, or living in social isolation. Mothers and fathers of children with Down syndrome can play a very important role in educating their daughters and sons to be reasonably skilled in activities that pertain to becoming a wife or husband.

The above is not meant to minimize the difficulties inherent in acquiring skills involved in marriage. It is our contention that marriage (and parenting, even if possible only for a very small percentage of people who have Down syndrome) should not be excluded altogether from the life goals of people with Down syndrome.

RPS can play a positive role in such goal setting by making the achievement of marriage more possible. In fact, from a sheer socialization point of view, prospects for marriages are greatly reduced for persons with a large protruding tongue, or those who drool persistently. But if these problems can be eliminated or reduced substantially through RPS, marriage might at least become more feasible for people who have Down syndrome.

Are there any scientific data concerning the effects of the surgery? Owing to the fact that RPS is a relatively new method of intervention for people with Down syndrome, "hard data" are still limited. Some follow-up data are available, but most of them relate to aspects of the surgery and are somewhat subjective because of the fact that the main sources of data are parents who are, naturally, highly invested in their child's current and future success. Keeping these limitations in mind, let us take a look at some recent findings.

In a study done by institute members[16] involving more than 50 parents whose children with Down syndrome underwent RPS, about 72% of the parents expressed ratings of satisfaction ranging from "high satisfaction" to "satisfaction" with its overall outcome. Another 24% reported the results of the surgery to be "fair," and 3.5% of the parents expressed "general dissatisfaction" with its outcome. When the parents of children who received surgery were asked if they would recommend RPS to their best friends, 84% of them answered yes, 13% said that they would agree to such a recommendation but with some reservations, and 3% said no. Hence, from parents' perspectives, the general level of satisfaction was relatively high.

In the aforementioned study, parents were also asked to react specifically to particular outcomes of RPS. Every child requires a somewhat different kind and degree of intervention because physical stigmata are differentially expressed in individuals with Down syndrome. Ratings reflecting perceptions of "great improvement" were reported by parents as follows:

Tongue shortening	94%
Correction of slanted eyes	87%
Silicon implants: nose bridge, cheeks, chin	80%

One of the parents reported that the tongue operation had a detrimental effect, and two reported a detrimental effect in relation to the eye slant correction. Parents reported also that surgery caused significant positive changes in the general facial appearance of their children, albeit not always to the desired extent, and that residuals of physical stigmata persisted, as expected, after the surgery. No differences were found in the outcomes of the surgery in relation to the child's sex or age at the time of the operation. Taken together, these findings reflect a relatively high level of parental satisfaction with outcomes of the surgery.

One of the most important objectives of RPS is to improve a number of functions pertaining to the areas of activity associated with the mouth, such as eating behavior, and speech. These areas, if improved meaningfully, may significantly affect parental and educator goal setting, enabling the expansion of the child's areas of activity and his social possibilities. The institute's data on parental perceptions of improvement showed that 60 to 80% of the parents reported slight to considerable improvement in eating ability and in a variety of mouth-related areas, such as drooling reduction (72%), mouth closure (70%), fewer sores around the mouth (68%), and breathing through the nose (71%). In addition, parents also perceived improvements in a variety of respiratory functions, such as less breathing with open mouth, cessation of snoring, and reduction of runny noses, although the percentage of parents reporting improvements in these areas were lower, running from about 40% to more than 70%. The most dramatic results had to do with reactions to the tongue-reduction surgery, where 90% of the parents reported that protrusion of the tongue disappeared completely. (Similar results were obtained when teachers were asked about their impressions concerning the effects of the tongue surgery.)

With regard to parents' perceptions of postsurgery changes in their child's speech, significant improvement was reported in intelligibility (66%) and articulation (55%). Children's confidence in speaking was also reported to be considerably improved (54%). Perceived reduction of stuttering was around 40%, and reduction of hoarseness of the voice was shown as approximately 30%.

Intelligibility, articulation, and other speech characteristics are interconnected codeterminants of the accessibility of the individual to interpersonal communications, becoming prime factors in the development of the child's social interaction capabilities. As already stated, these improvements require substantiation through more objectively gathered information, as well as assessment of the duration of effects over time.

Are there any data available from nonparental sources? In another study done at the institute,[17] more than 250 boys and girls, seventh- and eighth-graders (ages 12–14), were exposed to a series of pictures showing faces (front and profile) of children with Down syndrome before and after surgical intervention. They rated each picture on the following four dimensions: *beautiful–ugly, intelligent–stupid, good–bad,* and *pleasant–unpleasant to be friends with.* On these four dimensions, postsurgery photos were rated significantly more positively than the presurgery ones. A most interesting finding of the study refers to the relation between the perception of physical appearance and of intelligence. Correlations between the two variables were around .65, showing that physical appearance is quite strongly correlated with the perception of whether a person is perceived to be intelligent or not.

RPS may be considered to be a form of intervention strongly

reflecting an active modificational approach. This is due to the fact that it involves the use of surgery under general anesthesia and may be perceived as being of a traumatic nature both physically and psychologically. It is an attempt to change a most essential characteristic of the individual's physiognomy that is most recognizable as the persona, namely, the face. Thus, embarking on the RPS path of intervention should not be considered a minor decision. This is reflected by the strong emotional reactions among both parents and professionals when discussing this topic.

Recently, one of the authors of this book, who takes a conservative stance on the use of RPS (who hereafter will be referred to as author C, standing for conservative view) was approached by a friend whose child with Down syndrome was about to enter junior high school. The child, Gregory, was developing very well but wished to shed the label associated with his condition. His father wanted to know if Gregory was a good candidate for RPS. At that point author C had to sort out his feelings, which included sharing his reservations with the other authors of this book who take a more advocating stance toward its use. The essence of that "debate" is presented here for the instruction of parents who might be considering RPS.

For author C, the fundamental issues revolve around two interrelated questions: (1) Which person with Down syndrome should (or should not) be a candidate for RPS? (2) How much caution should be observed in pursuing it, considering the serious nature of the surgery and the type and amount of evidence currently available about its effectiveness? Author C believes strongly that interventions requiring the most of children and/or their parents, and also involving substantial risk, should be approached with the most caution. Does author C think that *any* person with Down syndrome is a likely candidate for RPS? Yes, but, at least for the present, he would see the following three conditions as necessary prerequisites for deciding to consider it strongly:

1. That the person with Down syndrome has internalized and currently expressed a devalued label (e.g., "retard," "mongoloid," "dumb") about himself.
2. That the person with Down syndrome has sufficient cognitive ability, or convincingly documented cognitive potential, so

that the reduction of his identifiability as a person with Down syndrome will not put him in a position of repeated potential failure. This might happen because people who don't know him will not be able to recognize him as having a condition usually associated with retarded performance and may expect him to perform acts that are well above his capabilities. In other words, the facial characteristics of Down syndrome, if removed surgically, may be a serious loss to a person who is not cognitively capable of meeting normal, or even near-normal, expectations, putting him in the unenviable position of facing skill expectations that he cannot meet.

3. That the parents have the "right" motives for involving their child in RPS, that is, a desire to maximize his abilities to live as normally and fully as possible, not the motive to "sacrifice" themselves for the child with Down syndrome or the motive to make their child into an "unachievable achiever." If parents choose to drain themselves totally in terms of time, energy, and emotional reserves, even risking the loss of a positive relationship with a spouse and other children, that motive is commendable. But "martyrdom" of this sort is neither necessary nor practical, considering that a husband and a wife have responsibilities to each other and to their other children, as well as to their child with Down syndrome. Even parents with the most altruistic motives have limits as to what burdens they can assume without devastating themselves, their children, or each other—and, in the end, ironically, possibly even rejecting their child with Down syndrome.

Are there any situations where all of these conditions have been met? Gregory and his parents met all three conditions. About two years ago his parents decided, at Gregory's initiative, that RPS was appropriate. Gregory was about to enter a regular junior high school and said one day that he did not like to look like a "retard." His father and mother, loving and intelligent people, listened carefully and compassionately to their son and led him through many introspective discussions in order to surface his motives, for him as well as for them to see. Gregory was reading with enjoyment and comprehension at the third-grade level, an excellent accomplishment for an 11-year-old child with Down syndrome. He had been in an integrated public elementary school for several years where he was in a special class for educable children part of the day and mainstreamed in a regular class for the other part of the day.

After many months of preparation, Gregory had RPS. He is doing well now, though it is too early to tell if his speech and language have improved significantly, even though his parents are convinced that it is beginning to improve. He receives speech therapy on a regular basis. Currently, he looks a bit more normal, though he and his parents still "see Gregory" when he and they look in the mirror together. Furthermore, Greg continues to be recognizable as a person with Down syndrome even though the distinctiveness of the facial features of the condition have been slightly reduced. Gregory's parents say that they are pleased that they went through with RPS, though they would not want ever to go through anything like it again. (They remember vividly seeing their son being rolled toward the operating room and suddenly confessing to each other that they were having feelings that they never expected, exclaiming together, "My God, what are we doing?")

RPS for Gregory included tongue reduction as well as altering the shape of his eyes and the contour of his nasal bridge, cheeks, and chin with transplants of tissues and bone from other parts of his body.

In the opinion of author C, Gregory's case met all three of the conditions outlined at the beginning of this discussion. Thus, weighing the potential benefits against the likely deficits, he was able to encourage Greg and his parents to think seriously about having RPS.

But what about the lack of hard data in support of the effectiveness of the procedure? Even in Gregory's case, the benefits expected were not clearly apparent or assured. Indeed, as already noted, there are few "hard" data about the effectiveness of RPS, that is, findings that have been gathered under reasonably rigorous scientific conditions, are objective, and have been interpreted by people who have no personal investment in the surgery's outcome. The one study[18] that has looked at the effects of tongue reduction on a rigorous experimental basis showed no benefits accruing to the group receiving surgery, even six months after the operation. In this study, tongue-reduction surgery was performed on 18 children with Down syndrome (9 males, 9 females, ages 5 to 19 years). Possible changes in articulation were evaluated pre- and postoperatively and during a five-month follow-up. No differences in articulation abilities were found in the surgery group, as compared with the nonsurgery group, either right after the surgery or at a six-month follow-up. Additionally, parents' ratings of perceived speech improvement were not significantly different in the two groups. It is important to point out, however, that people who had the operation did not receive any additional speech and language therapy after surgery. *All authors of this book are in strong agreement that surgery alone is not a sufficient intervention! It must be followed by various forms of active modification, including speech therapy.*

The other two authors who participated in writing this chapter take exception to the position of author C on a number of points. During their relatively extensive experience in Israel, no physically traumatic or psychologically devastating outcomes were reported for either the children receiving the surgery or their parents. Naturally, parents expressed anxiety, but intensive careful preparation and supportive counseling before, during, and after the operation ameliorated those feelings considerably. The most intensive anxiety feelings were expressed by the first group of parents whose 11 children were operated on. Anxiety feelings were doubtlessly increased by the fact that no such operations had ever been performed in Israel and by the fact that there was a limited amount of information available about its application. Later, parents of children who had to decide on RPS did not have to cope with so much uncertainty, and, consequently, their anxiety feelings were considerably reduced.

Concerning the preconditions formulated by author C, the other authors react as follows:

First, while they agree that not every person with Down syndrome should undergo RPS, they contend that the ultimate decision should be based upon different premises from those suggested by author C. They argue that the main determinants in the process of decision making have to be anchored in the needs of the child himself and the goals to be attained rather than in the self-awareness of the child as to his condition, his level of intellectual functioning (which is in many cases an outcome of a lack of systematic and well-planned intervention), or even parental motivation or financial circumstances. This is not to say that such factors ought not to be considered at all. On the contrary, when necessary, efforts should be invested in order to overcome such difficulties, and surgery can possibly play a highly significant role in mobilizing efforts to do so.

Second, the other authors suggest that surgery should be performed—whenever possible—on a "preventive" basis, trying to avoid having the child experience rejection from family members, educators, and others. They note that the feelings of inadequacy of the people with Down syndrome have rarely led to autonomous initiative toward introducing meaningful changes in their own life conditions. Rather, their feelings of inadequacy lead to a fatalistic self-perception, overcompliance, or resentment stemming from passive acceptance of their condition. The frequently observed low level of initiative (sometimes termed "docility"), which often characterizes people with Down syndrome who have not received an active-modificational approach, leads to a perpetuation of passive acceptance and even rejection by society.

The concern of author C for loss of identity as an individual with Down syndrome following RPS is not substantiated by the data accumulated until now in Israel. To the other authors, the problem of the person with Down syndrome is rather the opposite one: Owing to his specific facial characteristics, such a person may lack an individual identity. He is mainly perceived as a member of a well-defined group called Down syndrome rather than as an individual possessing unique characteristics. The group features outweigh by far the essential uniqueness of the individual, and the external appearance overshadows his own particular appearance. This global perception, although based upon and referring to physical characteristics, also influences the way his mental prospects and abilities are perceived. RPS could play a positive role in the opposite direction, helping to ensure that the individual's self-identity will not be lost, and may even become more clearly pronounced. In fact, on the basis of parents' reports following surgery, children seem to be more recognizable as members of their family and not just as members of the Down syndrome group.

As to the concern raised by author C about maintaining the person's identity as an individual with Down syndrome in order not to raise unwarranted expectancies, it seems to the other authors of this chapter that such a position may be detrimental to the development of the individual with Down syndrome. The outcome of such an approach might be adherence to passive acceptance, which leads, among other things, to placement in a sheltered environment rather than to investing efforts in adjusting the individual to normalized life conditions.

As to author C's concerns about the family's well-being, the other authors ask: Would a similar concern be voiced in the case of a child with a terminal illness such as leukemia? Wouldn't parents do everything to ameliorate their child's condition, even when hope is minimal? Wouldn't parents want to be able to say that they did all they could to alleviate the medical problems of their child? The other authors claim that not having RPS could result in general neglect, since it is well known that visual and hearing deficiencies, orthodontia problems, speech inadequacies, and postural and motor maladaptations are treated less often and/or less aggressively with children who have Down syndrome than with normal siblings or peers.

Finally, regarding author C's concern about the lack of hard data involving the effectiveness of RPS, this is a serious consideration. It will take some time to collect enough data in a systematic way to address the effectiveness question. Meanwhile, parents' and peers' positive perceptions related to the effects of the surgery are highly encouraging. In certain cases, RPS may become a catalyst that can help parents and others to adhere to active-modificational rather than to passive-acceptant approaches. This phenomenon appeared to occur with parents who, following RPS, became much more active in, for example, their search for methods and conditions aiming to integrate their children in normal settings.

In summarizing, *all* of the authors are in agreement that RPS is a legitimate intervention for some people with Down syndrome. The authors are not in agreement with respect to how actively RPS should be pursued, how often and to whom it should be applied, and the degree of confidence parents and professionals can have concerning its effectiveness. They are all in *total* agreement that RPS will *not* be effective without implementing complementary modificational approaches, such as speech therapy, following RPS. And, of course, all of them agree that RPS is only one of many interventions that should be considered as a form of active modification.

In the chapters that follow, we see how the principles of active modification and mediated learning can be applied in meeting important contemporary educational challenges.

CHAPTER 11

The Learning Potential
Assessment Device

In this chapter, and subsequent ones, we will deal with the applied systems derived from the theory of structural cognitive modifiability, the theory of mediated learning experience, and the active modification approach. In the first part of the book we attempted to answer two major questions that stem from the issue of cognitive redevelopment and the enhancement of intelligent behavior. The first question was: "Is modification important in the cognitive area?" In answering, we described the essential role of cognition in the adaptation of the individual, particularly its meaning for the person whose retarded performance limits him to a marginal place in society. Indeed, we contended that cognitive processes are a *vital* part of the individual's personality and overall competence. The second question was: "Is cognitive modification possible?" In answering, we showed, both by individual case histories and through group studies, that not only is structural cognitive modifiability possible, it is a *unique* characteristic of human beings. Therefore, it needs to be kept foremost in thought when choosing educational interventions. This led us to advocate an active-modificational approach, rather than a passive-acceptant approach, using all means feasible to modify the individual's cognitive functioning.

Now we will try to answer a third major question, one that follows naturally from the first two: "If cognitive modification is indeed important and possible, *how* can it be done?" How shall one go about actually modifying the cognitive structures of an individual with retarded performance, doing it in a way that will allow him to modify himself? The answer to this question certainly does not reside in a single approach. There are several approaches and theories stressing a belief in the modifiability of the individual.[1-4] These, too, are the products of a belief that modifiability is both necessary and possible. Many of these approaches are, however, oriented mainly toward the normal functioning individual. Few address the whole range of cognitive dysfunctioning. Furthermore, many of the programs based on these approaches deal with the content of cognitive processes, be it specific skills, units of information, or mental operations. Few are geared toward the establishment of the prerequisites of thinking.

Educational applications based on the theory of structural cognitive modifiability take form in (1) the learning potential assessment device, (2) the instrumental enrichment program, and (3) the shaping of modifying environments. These three applied systems form a whole, oriented and activated by a theory, converging toward the same goal: to modify the individual.

Modifying the individual begins with the use of the learning potential assessment device (LPAD), a dynamic assessment approach designed to evaluate the individual's capacity to become affected structurally by both formal and informal opportunities for learning. Then, the process of modifiability continues with the instrumental enrichment (IE) program, whose goal is to increase and develop the capacity for learning, making IE a "learning-to-learn" program. Ultimately, the process ends (though, if successful, it never really ends) by shaping the environment of the individual so that the increased capacity to learn will be enhanced by modifying environmental conditions, creating a synergism, an educational "chain reaction."

In describing the three applied systems, we will begin by introducing the case history of J. The LPAD, IE, and a modifying environment, working together, changed J.'s life in a dramatic manner.

J. was referred to one of the authors for placement within the framework of Youth Aliyah, an organization charged with the ingathering of Jewish children. (At that time, one of the authors was the director of Youth Aliyah's psychological services, responsible for the intake and placement of children with developmental problems.)

The government authorities dealing with J.'s case claimed that they had made great efforts to place him, but without success. Because he was an individual displaying severe intellectual deficits and wayward asocial behavior, a residential setting for people with retarded performance would not accept him owing to his "pathological" behavior, and a hospital would not admit him owing to his severe mental retardation. The referral to the institute came as a last attempt to solve the problem of placement.

J. was only one among thousands of cases presenting policymakers and educators in the new and developing Israel with the same dilemma: how to handle immigrant children who were categorized as mentally defective. In the 1950s the author had already confronted this dilemma many times when dealing with children from North Africa on their way to Israel, and even earlier when working as a youth leader and teacher of young children and adolescents who had survived the Holocaust. It was during these periods that the author developed his approach to retarded performance, deciding to use a dynamic approach to evaluate the individual's propensity for, and readiness to, change rather than focusing on what he was able to do as measured by static psychological tests. Indeed, as a result of this change in assessment procedure, thousands of children and adolescents were helped to become integrated among normal individuals. They proved the legitimacy of the optimistic prognosis of "modifiability" in ways that were as convincing as the research results that were to follow.[5,6] But would we be able to do the same for J.? The social worker referring him to us was familiar with our work with children from Youth Aliyah and sincerely hoped that we would be successful.

When first seen, J. was a small, forlorn, dull-appearing, shy child, showing total lack of interest in everything but the piece of cake that was on the table in front of him. Looking at it with coveting eyes, as if it were the gold of the pharaohs, he seemed to be hungry not only for cake but for warmth; but he did not dare ask for the latter. Repeated experiences of rejection did not permit him to ask for anything. In his village he was notorious for stealing from the marketplace and from homes, showing more of this activity than any other of his peers. But, despite his length of experience, he didn't anticipate the inevitable outcome: being caught by the angry victim, beaten up, brought to the police, and released soon after. (What else could one do with this child whom no residential setting, even one for delinquent children, would accept?) Or didn't he care about what would happen to him? It is impossible to know what went on in his mind. Thirteen years old at the time of his referral to the institute, J. didn't seem to be interested in being helped, and this passive resistance disarmed even the most earnest and skilled educator. When during the LPAD administration he was asked to draw a human figure, he hastily drew a "blob" and looked happy with his production (especially with the "cowboy hat" he placed on the creature's head). He showed no feeling of insufficiency, supposedly considering this drawn figure as the crown of his creativity. His lack of self-criticism and many other signs of retarded performance made us consider the possibilities of modifiability to be rather limited.

When we started to mediate the drawing of an articulated human body to him—showing him that between the head and the trunk there is a neck, that the arms do not come out directly from the head but rather from the shoulders, that the eyes are not below the mouth (as he had drawn them), and that the nose is between the eyes and not, as he drew them, on one side of the face—he listened carefully. But, when asked to draw a human body again, he drew the same blob, as if this image represented the internalized reality of his own body image. In order to change his drawing, we drew a figure in front of him, accompanying our rendition with the verbal description of the parts we were drawing, and their location. But, again when asked to draw a figure, he returned to his old blob for a third time, as if this were his fortified residence, which he would not give up: "This is what I do, whether you like it or not." The same resistance to change repeated itself in many other assessed areas.

At this point, we decided to concentrate our efforts on teaching him the prerequisites of thinking about lines and shapes. Thus, we taught him to compare shapes and lines with those he drew using four simple geometrical figures—square, triangle, circle, and diamond. When we saw the difficulties he experienced in producing a proper square and, even more, a diamond, we went back a step and taught him to draw individual vertical and horizontal lines and then to link them into a square, and to draw diagonal lines and link them into a diamond. At times we had to take his hand and guide it. Particular difficulties presented themselves in the drawing of a diamond. He couldn't reverse the relations between the lines with his pencil, and each time he had to do so he tended to continue with the line in the same direction (see Figure 21). But in the course of this mediational interaction, J. became more curious and cooperative. The mediator/examiner, confronted with the difficulties J. showed in imitating, looked for other ways to mediate his learning.

The deficient functions that interfered most were impulsivity on both input and output processes (i.e., when gathering information as

Figure 21. J.'s diamond drawing.

well as when responding to it); lack of spatial orientation (up and down, left and right); lack of systematic search (how could one be systematic in looking for something that had not really been seen in the first place?); and lack of use of two or more sources of information. (Perhaps he did not combine the act of stealing with its outcome. Being caught and beaten was not, in his thinking, a necessary and unavoidable outcome of the act: "What's bad about stealing? Nothing except the bad people who, for some obscure reason, catch me and punish me.")

J.'s assessment continued for about three weeks. At first, he did not attend for more than 20 minutes without starting to stretch, yawn, and quit, but with continuous efforts and increased success on his part, his interest accelerated dramatically, to the extent that, eventually, the examiner had to call each session to a halt. The changes in J.'s competence, which began at a very slow pace, became more and more pronounced. For instance, as we already mentioned, when mediation began in drawing a square or a diamond, guidance of his hand was often required. But by the end of the LPAD assessment, all we needed to do was to give J. verbal instructions and he was able to draw these shapes by himself, relying on his stored information gathered through previous acquisitions. Soon, he became able to solve analogy problems and to deal with the symbolic processes needed for reading.

Equipped with these data, we started again to look around for placement possibilities. Unhappily, the staff of prospective settings remained unconvinced that J. would be a good candidate. J.'s being a wayward, abandoned, and delinquent child made many of them reluctant to accept him. Unable to find a suitable placement, we decided to place him in one of our own educational facilities, which accepted any child, no matter how severe his condition. We chose a combined foster home and group care program, where children lived in the houses of members of an agricultural cooperative but functioned for the greater part of the day as a group in a special school and in extracurricular activities.

Once placed there, J. proved to be a model student. He learned to read proficiently in a very short time. In fact, his appetite for reading was such that it earned him the name of "the professor." He used to walk in the streets of the village with his book open, reading. He also became active in the religious community of the village and an accepted member of the Israeli Youth Movement.

Three years after his placement in this special environment oriented toward modifying the cognitive structure of its students, J. was able to enter a regular vocational high school. Following his successful integration in the vocational high school, he was placed in an academically oriented regular high school. Before placing him in the academically oriented high school, we provided private tutoring in mathematics, physics, and chemistry. His private tutor claimed that he had seldom found a learner as efficient as J. An intensive IE program was offered to him throughout this period in support of his academic curriculum. Placed in the 11th grade of the academically oriented program, he proved to be an excellent student.

Shortly thereafter, however, he dropped out of school without warning, and it was only after many efforts to trace him that we discovered that the reason for his abrupt departure was that his mother was dying. He had decided to abandon everything in order to be of help to her in her last days. He also took over the responsibility for his hospitalized sister, as well as for an older brother who had been placed in a home designated as one for the severely retarded.

We respected his decision, asking him only to keep in contact with us in case he needed help. J. did need help, asking for our assistance to take his sister out of the hospital in spite of her serious learning problems. Insistent that his sister be helped as much as he, J. was instrumental in having his sister placed in an environment similar to the one in which he had been helped. Furthermore, he moved his severely retarded brother into an apartment, which J. took over after his mother's death, making it their new home. Today, J. is a probation officer, is successfully married, and promises to finish high school and to continue his academic education, hoping to become a teacher some day. In his town he is known as the "social worker" for the deep concern he shows for wayward children.

J. serves as a powerful illustration of the role of dynamic assessment in unraveling the potential of the individual to be modified. LPAD revealed his modifiability, the IE program increased his modifiability, and the powerful modifying environments in which J. was placed produced incredible changes.

THE LEARNING POTENTIAL ASSESSMENT DEVICE (LPAD)

As the story of J. shows, the LPAD plays a decisive role in reorienting the educational system toward a more active modificational approach. The LPAD is a method used to evaluate the propensity of the individual to become modified, to study the reasons for his low functioning so as to be able to remedy them, and to pave the way for the development of more efficient levels of functioning. Perhaps the LPAD can be understood most clearly by contrasting it with conventional methods of measuring intelligence. Conventional intellectual measuring devices are static in the sense that the examiner presents the task, observes the behavior of the individual, and ascribes a given value to it, based usually on the performances of a norming group, i.e., others who have taken the test. The underlying assumption of conventional tests is that responses and ascribed values represent the full extent of the examinee's intelligence, his knowledge, his skills, and—to some extent—even his personality and emotional makeup. The conventional approach is static because nothing is done to affect the pattern of answers of the individual. And it is static because its outcomes are considered to be representative of the whole repertoire of the individual's intellectual capacity even though the test covers only a very narrow sample of the individual's cognitive repertoire. Furthermore, the scores (e.g., IQ, Developmental Quotient, Mental Age) become one of two bases (the other being the outcome of an assessment of adaptive behavior) for determining labels (e.g., "profoundly retarded," "severely retarded," "moderately retarded"). A particularly disturbing step occurs when results obtained from a conventional intelligence test become the basis of forecasting an individual's adult functioning. Often, an assumption is made that level of functioning at that time not only is representative of what the individual does on the conventional test, as given by a particular person, at a given hour of the day, under specified conditions of alertness or vigilance, for example, but also is representative and predictive of what the individual will be able to do years later under very different conditions of functioning.

The major theoretical belief generating this static approach is that human intelligence is a "hard-wired" characteristic, leaving little if any room for change, irrespective of the conditions the individual experiences. The LPAD, based on a very strong belief in human modifiability, makes a sharp distinction between the observed level of functioning of the individual and his possibility of becoming modified. His observed level of functioning may be low, as was true of J., who was not able to respond adequately to tasks in which, developmentally, he should have been proficient. But his cognitive functioning was modified. New cognitive structures were produced in him through IE and other appropriate interventions.

A low level of intellectual functioning may occur for many reasons. One may explain a low outcome in a given test by the reluctance of the individual to answer; it may be due to a transient state of fatigue, or to negativism; it may be due to the specific nature of the task, or to the language in which it is presented. To declare the individual incapable of doing well on an intellectual assessment on the sole basis of what he has done when presented with the test in a static manner not only may be misleading but can lead to making decisions that will tragically affect the individual's life forever. Granted, some misdiagnoses can be avoided by the experienced psychologist. And there are those individuals whose incapacity to respond to tasks presented in a static fashion at a given moment genuinely reflects their current repertoire. But this does not mean that they will never be able to expand it!

The LPAD represents a significant shift in assessment, one that changes the practice of testing in four major areas: the structure of the instruments, the nature of the test situation, the orientation to process, and the interpretation of results. The LPAD is a "test-mediate-test" approach. It first tests the examinee without intervention in order to establish the baseline of his current ability to respond. During this part of the LPAD, the examiner observes the behavior of the individual and studies carefully the reasons for his failure and the process by which he responds. In this way, the examiner will determine what might be needed during the second phase—the mediation, that is, the teaching phase. During this second phase, the examiner/mediator will induce changes in the functioning of the individual, changes that will become the object of evaluation during the third phase.

The third phase is a retest in which the individual is again given the series of tasks without mediation. In the third phase, the examiner studies the effects that the mediational intervention has had on the individual's ability to solve new problems. In this way, the extent to which the individual is able to benefit from a focused learning experience and the changes produced by it can be determined. Thus, when J. was unable to produce a human figure, the mediator intervened in a variety of ways, teaching him how to draw by making him aware of the structure of the human body. After the mediation took place, J. was again given the human figure drawing task to see how much better able he was to draw after receiving mediated learning.

A very important note should be inserted here; that is, users of the LPAD do not use the term *measurement*. Therefore, many of the techniques underlying conventional measurement assumptions are not applied. For example, the concept of long-term predictability does not have a place in the dynamic assessment. As a matter of fact, everything is done in order to *undo* the predictive value of the initial assessment by modifying functioning through the mediational process. Thus, when a 12-year-old child with Down syndrome is unable to count when a conventional measurement instrument is used, the conclusion might be that his lack of counting ability points out that he is not able to learn to think abstractly and, therefore, the concept of number is not accessible to him. The dynamic use of the LPAD will challenge this conclusion and will search for the reasons that counting behavior was not acquired and then set out to change these. Changes that are introduced will provide the new basis for evaluating the modifiability of the individual.

When first seen, Sara proved unable to perceive the number of dots that she had to count to construct a geometric figure. She omitted dots, did not explore the whole field, and had only a fragmented view of the things to be counted even when asked to count with the help of her fingers. Her unsystematic way of exploring caused her to re-include some of the objects she had already counted and to miss others. It was necessary to make her invest more in looking at the task, exploring in a more systematic way the things she was supposed to perceive and register. After a few hours of this type of mediation, her capacity to count and to group things changed significantly.

The first change required by the shift from a static to a dynamic approach to assessment consists of a modification of the type of test instruments used. Figure 22 shows how the LPAD is designed. The center of the figure represents a task that will be mediated to the examinee. The concentric circles represent increased levels of complexity and novelty of the tasks given to the examinee after the mediation of the initial task. The surface of the cylinder shows different languages in which a problem can be presented—verbal, pictorial, and numerical. The vertical axis represents different types of operations: logical multiplication, seriation, syllogisms.

As an illustration of its application, we will use the Analogy task, in which the examinee has to choose the appropriate missing figure from a number of distractors (e.g., irrelevant shapes). The examinee

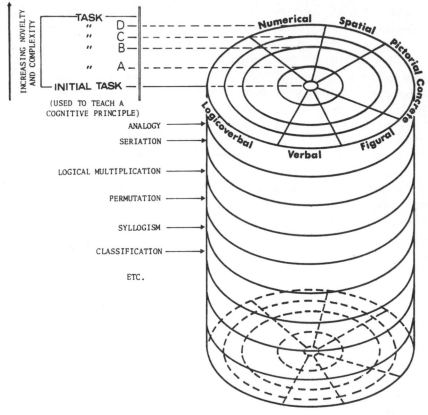

Figure 22. The LPAD model.

first has to find the relation between the two upper figures of the problem and apply it to the lower line (see Figure 23). Practically, the child must discover the relation (similarity and differences) between the circle with lines and the square with lines and then establish the same relation between the circle that is half black and half white with a missing figure. Obviously, the figure that is missing will be a square that is half black and half white.

This task, taken from the LPAD variations of Raven's Progressive Matrices (B-8), an innovative pattern utilization task, poses great difficulties for children with subaverage IQs. This difficulty has led one professional,[7] an ardent defender of the genetic/hereditary view of intelligence, to consider the accomplishment of this particular type of test item as forever inaccessible to those classified as educable mentally retarded. Another professional[8] claims that even training may not help such individuals with mental retardation solve this and other problems requiring abstract thinking.

The LPAD challenges these two views, first by equipping the failing individual with the prerequisites for understanding the problem and learning how to solve it, and then by finding ways to prove what the individual has learned through the process of mediation, making him more efficient in solving problems with the same underlying principle but requiring a "rediscovery" and a reapplication.

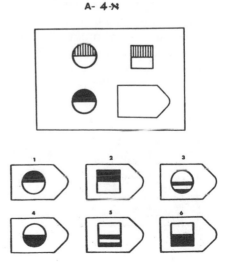

Figure 23. LPAD variations of Raven's Progressive Matrices (B-8).

Thus, we mediate the Analogy task by helping the examinee to understand a transformation: "The circle has been transformed into a square. The vertical lines at the top stay the same. The circle in the second row will be transformed into what? If we do the same thing to the second circle that we did to the first, what will we have here as the missing part? Of course, a square. What will be in it if we no longer have the vertical lines? The same thing as in the circle, black in the upper half and white in the bottom half."

An additional strategy for solving the analogical problem will also be mediated to the person in the form of categorization: "Here in the left column we have the family of circles. What will we have in the right column? The family of squares. So a square is missing. What is the name of the family in the upper row? The family of vertical lines at the top? What will be the name of the family in the bottom row? Yes, the family of half black, half white. So, what are we missing? We are missing the square that is half black, half white."

This process of mediation will not content itself with just offering the solution or training for the test but will create conditions for observing, registering, comparing, and interpreting, which will change the total *structure* of the individual's cognitive functioning. The same is true for other tasks such as the Organization of Dots, where the solution of the problem will be supported by mediating the characteristics of the square and of the triangle, the way in which the square can be found under the adverse conditions of rotations and overlapping, how to attack the problem before proceeding to solve it, how to inhibit impulsivity, how to select certain stimuli so that they will respond to the required standards, and how to find the constancy of the square across changes in its position and its relation to the other figures (see Figure 24).

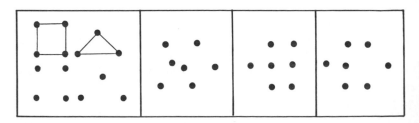

Figure 24. LPAD Organization of Dots.

All the principles of mediated learning experience are applied in the interaction between the examiner and the individual being assessed in order to produce the prerequisites of higher-order thinking. Once this is done, the individual is provided with tasks that represent variations, that is, are progressively different, more novel, more remote from the initial task that served as an object of mediation. The concentric circles on the surface of the LPAD model represent such variations of the initial task that require an adaptation (see Figure 22).

The responses of the individual to these variations will enable the mediator/examiner to answer the following questions: First, to what extent has the individual I am assessing proven to be able to understand and do the initial task? Second, how much investment is required, and what is the nature of the mediation needed in order for him to master this particular task? Third, to what extent was he able, with what he has learned through the mediational process, to solve problems requiring that he adapt the learned elements to a novel task. And finally, what is the preferred way to produce the desired changes in him?

The alternative ways of presenting a task, using a variety of languages of presentation and different types of operations, will enable the examiner to further explore the meaning and extent of the produced change: Will the individual be better able to solve a numerical analogy after he has learned to solve a figural one? Will he be able to learn more rapidly to solve a syllogism after he has learned an analogy?

The battery of tests included in the LPAD was chosen for a number of reasons. First, the tasks must be of sufficient complexity to enable them to be perceived as representing a variety of cognitive functions and not just one particular simple, fragmented type of function. Hence, the reproduction of simple figures is not included. Rather, tasks are used that require planning ahead and looking for systems of reference before drawing.

The tasks also require representational and abstract thinking rather than concrete thinking. We want to "stretch" the individual's functioning to higher levels rather than to "bend down" to what he is able to do now. Thus, tasks chosen require comparative behavior, reasoning, representation, and logical thinking, among others (see Appendix B).

Finally, the tasks chosen will be structured so as to permit the detection of very small changes produced by task exposure and through mediational interaction. It is understood that even the most powerful mediation cannot always produce spectacular changes. But as we set out to assess modifiability, we are interested in "sensitizing" the tasks to enable us to detect even the most rudimentary modifications in the individual's cognitive structure. Hence, we plan to see changes in the way the individual explores the data, in the amount of time he attends to a task, in the way he moves pieces of the task around, in the manner he uses elements of the solution he discovers, and similar activities.

Another area of change required by the shift from the static to the dynamic approach is in the test situation itself. The dynamic assessment (LPAD) situation is radically different from the static psychological testing situation because the examiner is not functioning just as an observer or as a registrar of responses but is *involved actively* in modifying the cognitive structure of the individual. The assessor will not be content in establishing that the individual being assessed does or does not succeed; he will actively shape and mold the responses of the individual through mediation. This will create an assessor's role that can be characterized as that of a dynamic teacher or an active learning guide or mediator, who uses many means to bring about cognitive change. These means will include providing intensive feedback, offering information needed in order to operate more successfully on the next task, and mediating a feeling of competence based on the way he learned to solve the problem after he failed initially. The mediator will also mediate the meaning of success in tasks and will provide the child with insights as to what made him succeed or fail so that he will be able to avoid failure strategies in the future.

Generally, the test situation will not be structured as in conventional testing situations, where it is necessary to keep test procedures uniform in order to compare the results obtained by the person with those of a group of individuals considered similar to him (a norm group). Instead, the examiner will adapt the test situation and its requirements to the particular person, comparing the individual's performance with his own previous performance, not with that of a norm group. Many of the children assessed with the LPAD are transformed by it in terms of their self-image, their feeling of competence, and, particularly, their readiness to engage in exploratory behavior by being given the opportunity to succeed (this they get plenty of, and will get even more of it later in IE activities).

The third difference between conventional measurement of intelligence and the LPAD is the shift of emphasis from product to process. In the LPAD, very little attention is given to the product or to the absolute magnitude of a result. More importance is attached to learning about the process that has brought about a particular product. To achieve this, there are two conceptual tools that are used in the LPAD (as well as in the instrumental enrichment) program.

One conceptual tool is a list of deficient cognitive functions that are likely to be responsible for the failure of the person as well as serving as a set of target functions to be corrected (see Appendix B). Was the child unable to gather the proper data, or did he fail because of his unsystematic way of looking at what he did gather? Did he use two or more sources of information? Was he not precise enough? Did he not compare sufficiently? Could he not find a way to formulate his answers so as to make them acceptable to his partner, the examiner? It makes a great difference to know whether the child failed because of an inadequate input, elaboration, or output process, or a combination of these. Being able to determine the source of his failure enables us to attack its source—the specific dysfunction(s) responsible for the failure. This also enables us to give a differential weight to the error. For example, it makes a difference if the child has not been able to see properly, to think properly, or to express himself properly. One may see children who fail their exams because they do not have the proper means by which to express themselves. They have ideas but no way to articulate them. In order to understand a child's functioning, it is necessary to interpret his successes and errors, correct the errors, and then understand the process that underlies the change that has been produced in his functioning.

A second conceptual tool that enables us to understand the process involved in the functioning of the child is the cognitive map (see Appendix C). Each mental act can be analyzed with the help of a set of dimensions by which its level of difficulty can be determined. The content of the task may be more or less familiar; the language in which the task is presented may pose difficulties; the level of abstraction and complexity may significantly affect the examinee's efficiency. A very important dimension in the cognitive map is the level of efficiency that the task requires in order to enable the individual to master it. There are tasks that require a certain speed or level of precision in order to be mastered. Reading is an example of one such task. If you do not read with enough speed and precision, you will not have a feeling of ease in performing a reading task, and reading will not be mastered. Understanding the process that enables one individual to do certain tasks and not others is of great importance in establishing each person's way of handling tasks and, thus, is important in promoting the individual's learning capacities.

Thus, we see that the LPAD is an attempt not just to assess an individual's intelligence but to derive a set of intellectual goals for him. Goals that are established solely on the basis of conventional testing may be set too low. However, if we establish educational goals based not on what a person can do now but on what we consider that he will be able to do when we offer him the intervention necessary to raise his level of functioning, these goals will be much more meaningful and influential for his future quality of life.

Another difference between the LPAD and a conventional intelligence testing approach is in the interpretation of results. The LPAD does not produce a summary score such as an IQ. Rather, it looks at each type and level of an individual's functioning, considering each in terms of its quality and meaning. Isolated successful responses are not ignored, as is often the case when the results are presented in the form of a global IQ score. In LPAD, a single success, seen even against the backdrop of generally low-level responses, is interpreted as an important indicator of intellectual capacity, one that has to be uncovered by further exploration. It is the instances of *success* of the individual that are the focal point for the analysis of the reasons for success and failure. Indeed, if one looks carefully at the behavior of groups of individuals who are considered to be severely retarded, one can often see instances of adequate behaviors, which, given proper interpretation, indicate that the individual can/could function better than he does if we help him to do so. One professional[9] says that even in the behavior of people with seriously retarded performance, signs of inferential thinking and operational behavior can be found. If these behaviors are correctly interpreted and understood, one can establish goals that are very different from those based on labels. It is not the magnitude of the change but the *quality* and *nature* of the change that are important. Each interpretation of LPAD results takes into consideration the learning *process*.

The learning potential assessment device has been applied successfully with thousands of culturally different or culturally deprived children, people with Down syndrome, and others who have retarded performance. The principles of dynamic assessment embodied in the LPAD can be applied to a broad and diverse set of individuals, provided that one introduces mediational interaction that will then modify their functioning. For example, extensions of the LPAD methods have been developed for use in early education.[10–12] Also, a systems approach in the use of the LPAD has been developed recently by a group of researchers.[13] In this systems approach, an LPAD group-administered assessment is followed by intensive work with educators concerning each individual's performance and the class outcome as a whole. Curricula are shaped according to these findings, and parents are advised about the investment they and their children should make in order to realize individualized cognitive goals.

CHAPTER 12

Instrumental Enrichment

The instrumental enrichment (IE) program is strongly related, both historically and conceptually, to the learning potential assessment device, which provides the framework and set of guidelines for constructing IE intervention techniques. Even though the LPAD is not a prerequisite for the adoption of the IE program, it is of great benefit to have the teacher who is charged with the application of the instrumental enrichment program be exposed to the LPAD. Indeed, the use of the LPAD provides a "minicourse" in mediating learning experience, allowing the IE teacher to experience *in vitro*, either through observing or administering the LPAD, the kinds of changes that can be produced in the cognitive structures of an individual. From its overall vantage point, the LPAD offers the IE teacher a broad-based view of what the interventional program should be and the results that can be expected if the program is applied in an appropriate way.

Instrumental enrichment is a program composed of two major elements: a set of materials—the "instruments"—and an elaborate teaching system based on mediated learning experience. The materials consist of a set of 14 instruments (clusters of exercises) with names faintly descriptive of their specific content, such as Organization of Dots, Orientation in Space, Analytical Perception, Comparisons, and Categorization. (A small sampling from each of the instruments is inserted at appropriate spots throughout this chapter.) Each of the instruments contains a series of paper-and-pencil exercises that are presented, not in the form of a booklet, but page by page. The reason for this pacing in small increments is that the mediator needs to have control over the learning experience elicited by the tasks. The MLE nature of the interaction is evident in its calling for the careful selection of stimuli and the filtering, scheduling, and organizing activity of the mediator. If we gave the student an entire booklet, he would probably scan through it quickly, trying only to satisfy his own curiosity, and would not interact with the individual tasks in a productive way.

The program is initiated, preferably in a classroom situation, which can vary in size from 10 to 30 children, depending on the level of their functioning and the variation in their need for individual mediator interaction. Preference for group teaching (versus individual instruction) stems from our belief that, if the group is properly guided by the teacher/mediator, the diversity of that group can foster divergent thinking and enrich the interactions of participants.

The total program involves about 300 hours of exercises, which can be spread over two years according to the particular rhythm in which the pupils work. For pupils with more retarded performance, it will be necessary to extend either the number of hours of exposure weekly (to 5, 6, or even 7 hours) or the length of the program to three years. This extension will usually be required for children who have Down syndrome, and for those who display serious attentional deficits. For a number of reasons it is highly preferable to have the program taught by increasing the number of weekly hours over a period of two years because in this way the students will be more likely to be exposed to the total program; the risk of partial exposure due to student attrition, teacher mobility, and school dropouts will be minimized. The intensity of the program rather than its length should always be the primary consideration in implementing instrumental enrichment. (At present, the author of instrumental enrichment is preparing a shortened version of IE for classroom application over a period of two years at a rate of three hours weekly.)

In addition to the classroom implementation of IE, it can be offered in individual tutorials, although, as has been pointed out, the socializing and amplifying aspects of interactions in groups will be lacking. Nevertheless, in cases where pupils cannot attend school or attend a school where IE is not offered, or where deficiencies exist that require instruments not available in the classroom, individual tutoring may be indicated. Over the last 20 years, IE programs have been developed for students classified as mentally retarded, deaf, cerebral palsied, autistic, and communicationally and/or motorially disordered. Recently, IE has been introduced to students attending afternoon learning centers for individuals classified as learning-disabled.

The main goal of instrumental enrichment, consonant with the theory of structural cognitive modifiability, is to promote the propensity to learn and to be modified by learning events. Instrumental enrichment does not focus on adding to the repertoire of knowledge of the individual (although this will happen). Rather, the emphasis is on making the student able to learn how to acquire more information and to figure out what to do with it, to make him more efficient in his efforts to acquire new skills, and to make him more able to find adaptive ways to solve problems. This makes instrumental enrichment different from programs that orient their efforts toward the acquisition of specific cognitive skills or adaptive behaviors. The difference is akin to giving someone fish to eat each day, or giving him the necessary equipment, knowledge, and skills to enable him to catch his own fish whenever he needs to or wants to.

How does instrumental enrichment achieve this ambitious goal? The following six instructional subgoals are put to work in shaping the nature of the program and the techniques used in its application:

1. Correcting deficient cognitive functions (see Appendix B).
2. Teaching the verbal tools and operations necessary to master IE tasks.
3. Mediating intrinsic motivation through habit formation.
4. Mediating insight and reflective thinking.
5. Producing task-intrinsic motivation.
6. Mediating a shift of the self-image from that of a passive recipient of information to that of an active generator of information.

The correction of deficient cognitive functions (subgoal 1) is embodied in all of the instruments because of its central importance in modifying an individual's overall learning abilities. Deficient functions should not be considered as defects of the individual or regarded as immutable characteristics of his behavior. Rather, they should be considered as ways of interacting with learning tasks that are, for some reason, inadequate.

For teaching purposes, deficient cognitive functions can be divided into three phases of a mental act: input, elaboration, and output. *Input* is a phase in the behavior of the individual in which information is gathered about the problem to be solved. Information is gathered from both external and internal sources. "When I see four points at equal distances, I will add information stored in myself in order to project into these points the concept of a square." The two sources (internal and external) have to combine in order to recognize, identify, elaborate, and form relations, among other activities.

Deficiencies in input will often be due to inadequate attentional investment, making perception blurred and sweeping. Deficiencies in the input level are reflected in an impulsive, first-come/first-respond, trial-and-error, unsystematic approach. Certain elements of the problem will be given only a very brief look, while others will be focused on too intensively.

Deficiencies may also be partially due to a very limited felt need for precision, or to the fact that the concepts necessary (such as spatial or temporal concepts: up, down, right, left, before, after, same, different) are either missing or not used.

One of the greatest teaching challenges in overcoming input deficiencies occurs when a student does not simultaneously integrate two or more sources of information. He handles them one at a time, rather than combining them and perceiving them as parts of the whole.

Another input difficulty is a student's inability to see an object as constant even when changes occur in some of its attributes. Thus, perceiving a square as constant across rotations in its position is necessary in order to find this square when it is intermingled with other figures. Likewise, the tendency to perceive the square in its usual orientation will make it difficult to see when diagonal lines are run through parts of it. So, specific attributes of the square will have to be taught. Or, when the student is confronted with a triangle-finding task like those included in Organization of Dots (see Figure 25), a focused, concerted investment is required in searching for the triangles that may appear as a part of a square or may be smaller or larger than the one learned originally. It will require thinking to overcome the difficulties involved in detecting triangles in overlapping figures. The student will have to inhibit his impulse to rely on first-perceived/first-respond behavior, and trial-and-error habits will have to be eliminated from his repertoire.

We have observed that many students diagnosed as having attention deficits benefit from prolonged systematic exposure to IE tasks such as Analytic Perception (see Figure 26), where the parts must be separated from the whole and then recombined to create the whole again. These exercises have taught students to invest their attention efforts to the point that they become much better able to

Organization of Dots

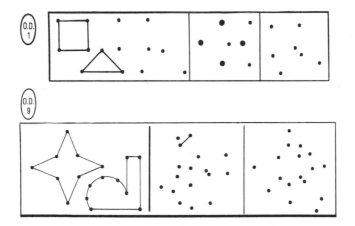

Figure 25. In the Organization of Dots, the student must find shapes in an amorphous, irregular cloud of dots. The task is made more complicated by varying the density of the dots and increasing the complexity of the figures and changing their orientation. Successful completion demands segregation and articulation of the field. Organization of Dots is usually the first instrument taught because of its highly motivating nature.

attend to (and sometimes become proficient in) reading and writing operations as well.

Use of multiple sources of information will be fostered in many of the instruments. Being given a task in the instrument called Instructions (see Figure 27) will of necessity make the individual search for many sources of information, and the same will be true when he deals with Orientation in Space I or II (see Figures 28 and 29). A good illustration of mediating the use of multiple sources of information is present in the Analytic Perception and Categorization tasks (see Figures 26 and 30). Figure 29 instructs the learner to choose a position that is available at the left side of the page, choose the correct drawing from the four human drawings on the upper part of the page, place

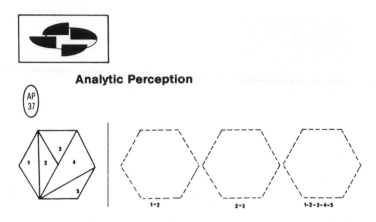

Figure 26. Analytic Perception is designed to correct the blurred, sweeping, and global perception that results in incomplete and imprecise information processing. The student learns that any whole may be divided into parts through structural or operational analysis, that every part is a whole, that there is a relation between these parts, and that there is a possibility of forming new wholes by a recombination of the parts. Finally, students learn that the division of a whole into parts is arbitrary and depends on external criteria, needs, and goals. *Sample direction:* "In each of the following outlines, you are to draw the section that is composed of the parts whose numbers appear beneath the outline. Pay attention. Do not include the lines between the parts you draw."

the chosen figure in the center of the field, go back to the line where the instruction is given to relate it to one of the four objects bordering the field, and finally discover how these two objects relate to each other. The path the child is asked to follow requires him to work systematically, step by step; it does not "tolerate" erratic behavior as is all too often observed in the individual with a learning disability.

In the second phase of the mental act, the *elaboration* phase, information (data) gathered at the input level is worked through—that is, transformed, reduced, encoded, turned into symbols or relations, operated upon, organized, compared, combined. Data become sources of inferences leading to the generation of previously nonexistent information, requiring the child to construct a mental design. Such construction is especially apparent in the Representational Stencil Design (RSD) task (see Figure 31), which requires the student to construct varicolored designs by superimposing at least one stencil on

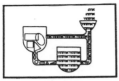

Instructions

(I 40) A diagonal line bisects the_____ parallel to sides #____and____. There are two horizontal lines: one_____ the hexagon and the other is at the bottom of the hexagon.	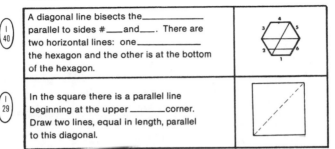
(I 29) In the square there is a parallel line beginning at the upper _____corner. Draw two lines, equal in length, parallel to this diagonal.	

Figure 27. Instructions emphasizes the process of decoding verbal instructions and their translation into a motor act, and the encoding of a motor act into a verbal modality. The tasks counteract impulsivity, encourage planning behavior, reduce ego-centricity, etc. Students learn to look for key words and relations and to clarify any ambiguity by asking appropriate questions.

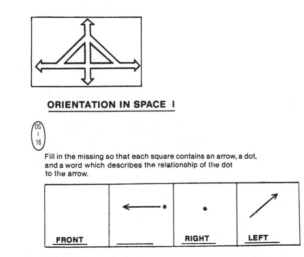

ORIENTATION IN SPACE I

(OS I 16)

Fill in the missing so that each square contains an arrow, a dot, and a word which describes the relationship of the dot to the arrow.

Figure 28. Orientation in Space I seeks to enhance the ability to use concepts and a stable system of reference for describing spatial relationships. Students learn that per-ception of an object or event depends on one's vantage point and that the relation between pairs of objects and/or events shifts with the change in the position of one or both parties to the relationship.

ORIENTATION IN SPACE II

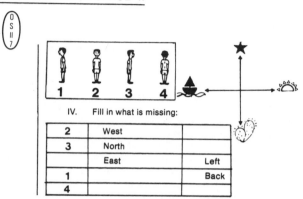

IV. Fill in what is missing:

2	West	
3	North	
	East	Left
1		Back
4		

Figure 29. Orientation in Space II deals with the use of compass points and coordinates. Positions are fixed and constant; they need no referents by which to describe position, location, or orientation. In later tasks, the relative personal system of spatial reference is combined with the absolute universal system.

top of another. The student will have to represent for himself a transformation produced by his mental decisions. "How does placing stencil number 18 on top of stencil number 7 change the appearance of both stencils? Then, how will putting number 6 on top of number 18 affect all three of them?" Such decisions will have to be made in anticipation of the desired designs and will produce in the individual a new way of thinking, one using representational thought.

Confronted with IE tasks such as Family Relations (see Figure 32), a student will have to be able to infer from given information who the members of the family are as indicated by limited descriptions. For instance, "Whose son is Robert, who has a nonmarried sister—as compared with George, whose sisters are all married?" The learner will have to overcome one of the most disabling characteristics of retarded performance, namely, an episodic grasp of reality where the student experiences everything as an isolated event with very little

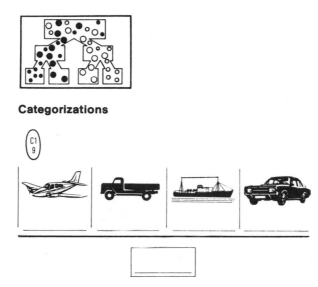

Figure 30. Categorization focuses on the organization of data into superordinate categories on the basis of common unifying principles of classification. The student learns that he or she is the primary determinant in projecting the relationships by which to organize objects and events since it is possible to divide and redivide the same universe according to many different criteria. *Sample direction:* "Label each picture. Choose a general name that describes the four pictures in each row and write it within the space provided beneath the row."

relevance to what preceded it and even less to what will follow.

Thus, seeing an object or seeing something happen to it does not elicit the questions "Has this already happened to me? Was it the same? Was it different? When did I see it? Was it a long time ago?" All these modes of thinking establish relations between the different experiences, comparing, and grouping things together, creating analogies. "Oh, I have already seen it five times. This looks very similar to that other item. This must belong to the same family." Individuals with an episodic grasp of reality do not establish relations between things but rather register them passively. They do not sum up their behavior; they do not group the things they see. Such a passive attitude leaves very little place for active learning, and the individual is not modified by his experience.

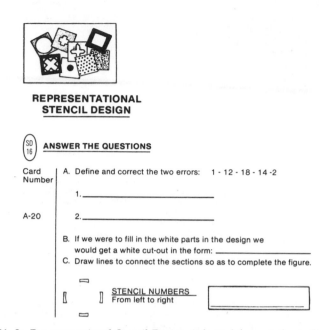

**REPRESENTATIONAL
STENCIL DESIGN**

Figure 31. In Representational Stencil Design (adapted from Arthur's Stencil Design Test, 1930), the student completes a complex sequence of steps involving a purely representational reconstruction of a design. The modeled design is created by the superimposition of separate stencils, differing in color and size and shape of the figures cut out of them. To accomplish the task, the student must analyze the complex design, identify its components, and mentally superimpose the necessary stencils, bearing in mind the nature of the transformation that is occurring.

Instrumental enrichment is designed to teach the individual to constantly project relations between things, relations of identity, similarity, opposition, or incompatibility. He is mobilized to become an active perceiver and organizer of his experience.

Amazingly enough, the elaboration part of the mental act, which is identified as thinking itself, is far easier to change in the individual than the other two phases, input and output. Those who have worked with instrumental enrichment are continually amazed to see the ease with which many children who are supposed not to be able to think abstractly, not to be able to represent anything that is not immediately seen, become able to demonstrate their propensity to learn and become efficient in complex thinking. In fact, changes in

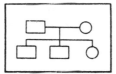

FAMILY RELATIONS

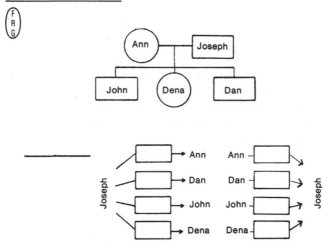

Figure 32. In Family Relations the family is the paradigm for all social institutions, and kinship is the carrier for teaching symmetrical, asymmetrical, and hierarchical relationships. The conservation of identity over transformations is presented through the multiplicity of roles family members can assume. *Sample direction:* "Look at the diagram and write the relationship between Joseph and the members of his family as indicated by direction of the arrow."

this phase of thinking are often the first to be observed in many retarded performers, as compared with the phases of input and output, which require a much greater investment and often a long period of time before they become consolidated, crystallized, and efficient.

The *output* phase of the mental act is where the individual has to emit his response, the product of his elaboration of the data gathered initially. The response must be precise and detailed enough to be understood and accepted. This phase is probably the one that is most responsible for the failure of individuals to solve problems and to adapt themselves to new situations. This is particularly true for people who have learning disabilities and for certain gifted underachievers. But output problems also mask the capacities of children who, despite very retarded performance, do in fact elaborate better than they can convey the product of their thinking. Here egocentric modes of communication, lack of verbal tools to communicate, and impulsivity are often the reasons why sound thinking ends up in failed responses.

Instrumental enrichment, by the nature of its tasks, by the constant feedback it provides, by its very slogan ("Just a minute . . . let me think"), regulates the behavior of the individual, equips him with ways to better shape his responses, irrespective of whether he addresses them to someone else or to himself. In this we recognize the mediational interaction occurring between the O and the R, the organism and his responses, described in the chapters on mediated learning. The mediator helps shape the responses so they will really reflect the results of the student's elaborations.

Deficient cognitive functions are dealt with intensively in each of the instruments, but some instruments, such as Organization of Dots (see Figure 25), focus particularly on the correction of certain deficiencies responsible for retarded performance. Thus, these are usually the first ones to be implemented in the IE program. In this way, some of the most important operations of thinking are established early and facilitate the mastery of later tasks.

The second subgoal in the IE program, teaching verbal tools and operations, represents the "content" of the program, which is limited to the teaching of a vocabulary, concepts, relations, and the operations necessary to master the tasks in the program. These relatively difficult tasks require hundreds of new words related to shapes, objects, categorizations, relations, and types of operations that have to be mastered in order for the student to advance in his thinking ability.

For example, when equipping the child with the concept of "number" in order to solve the problems in Numerical Progressions (see Figure 33), the mediator will not make Numerical Progressions into a mathematics lesson. Rather, he will orient the child to the relations between the various numbers, help him find the rule that governs these relations, and then apply these rules to new situations.

The third subgoal, mediating intrinsic motivation through habit formation, is unique to instrumental enrichment and has been very powerful in shaping its nature, its length, its structure, and the way it is presented. Its purpose is to create an intrinsic need in the learner to use the modes of cognitive functioning he has been taught in diverse

Numerical Progressions

3. Complete the following progressions:

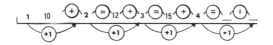

Figure 33. Numerical Progressions attacks an episodic grasp of reality by compelling the student to seek laws and stable superordinate relationships even in instances that seem to have no connection. The ability to anticipate and predict future events, explain the past, and construct new situations through generating rules based on past observations leads the student to a feeling of mastery.

situations. Few students with retarded performance are ever asked to use higher mental processes, to use analogies, to use precision in their responses. Teaching rules and principles without making sure that they become crystallized and automatized as an integral part of the active repertoire is not satisfactory. Using a "hit-and-run" approach offers very little chance that higher-order modes of thinking will ever be applied. Many children shed the rules and principles they have learned as they shed their lab coats at the exit of the chemistry classroom. This makes it imperative to consolidate the acquired learning, to turn it into an intrinsic need that will ensure its use under many circumstances.

The only way to consolidate what is learned and to shape activities into an intrinsic need system is by turning these activities into habits. In order to become habituated to focus automatically, to invest perceptually, to explore data systematically, to put together diverse sources of stimuli, to compare them, to categorize and group things, to divide them, the activities need to be crystallized.

Unfortunately, habit formation is usually offered through providing large doses of repetitive practice. This is seldom appealing to a learner and may actually impede his readiness to be involved in its acquisition. But how can we avoid the boredom of repetitive learning and still achieve habit formation?

We have structured our program to provide the learner with a multitude of similar but never identical tasks, a strategy sometimes referred to as capitalizing on relative novelty. The individual is asked to do something familiar, but in a slightly different way, requiring a rediscovery of the acquired rule and a readjustment of what he did initially. For instance, in the Organization of Dots (Figure 25), tasks are varied and repeated with slight variations each time. This is the reason that instrumental enrichment requires a substantial number of instructional hours over a period of two to three years. It is the consolidation produced through this repetition that modifies the cognitive structure of the individual and permits him to go beyond the acquired principles and skills, becoming steadily more efficient in his learning to learn.

The fourth subgoal, mediating insight, is the major task for the teacher. Here the principle of transcendence in mediated learning experience occurs. The learner and his peers search for the meaning in the processes they employed that enabled them to succeed, and for the relevance of these processes to situations other than those at hand. Insight is often referred to in the IE program as *bridging* or *transfer*. It is best done through tasks that are provocative and thereby elicit mediational interactions. Children guided by the teacher will start to search for divergent ways of application. It is often startling to see the wealth of divergent thinking strategies that can be produced by children, especially in interactive group situations. The 9-year-old boy, asked why he needs three strategies in order to solve the problem in the Organization of Dots (see Figure 25), answers (with the seriousness of an undertaker): "Well, if I have to go home from school and the only way I know is through the park, I am in trouble, because waiting there is the owner of a kiosk who I owe money to. If the only other way I know is through the back door of the school, I am in trouble because there are three guys waiting there to beat me up. So I need a third way, and l have to change *that* once in a while."

Strategy formation is often the product of insight. Thus, Aaron, who has a very hard time keeping his eyes fixed on the Representational Stencil Design poster (see Figure 31) while he mentally constructs the designs, owing to his hyperactivity, has learned the poster by heart and does the tasks extremely well. Insight is considered by many researchers as a key way to apply one's knowledge and skills to new situations. Teaching without insight seriously limits the generalizability of what is learned.

The fifth subgoal, producing task-intrinsic motivation, necessitates the use of tasks with a high level of complexity, tasks that demand representational thinking. Some of the students call it "mind-boggling." But this is by far preferable to "chewing" the tasks into small pieces and presenting them to the individual ready for easy consumption. Instead, the child is presented with challenging tasks, involving novelty and complexity, where neither previous experience nor a repertoire of specific skills is of great help. The most important finding resulting from the hundreds of studies done on IE all over the world is that this form of challenge has a strong appeal to children and they will seldom give up on a lesson of instrumental enrichment even when greatly tempted to do so. In fact, many students who drop out of school will request the right to complete the instrumental enrichment lessons owing to the fact that IE offers many of them an opportunity to excel after being an underdog in traditional schooling situations. In fact, some of the children with the most retarded performance in the classroom work very hard in instrumental enrichment lessons because, if they do well (and many of them do do well), they have an opportunity to compare favorably with those who are considered to be the best.

Moreover, teachers who have experienced the challenge of performing the instrumental enrichment tasks during their training create a greater rapport with, and empathy for, their students, as opposed to the usual situation where the teacher is "above" the student in all respects. This feeling of teacher–pupil partnership adds to the appeal of the tasks and makes the learner ready to do them without being reinforced with an external reward such as a grade or score. In fact, task-intrinsic motivation may sound familiar to those who recall the material earlier in this book on mediation of meaning. IE offers an opportunity for the student to enlarge his need systems beyond the immediate and elementary, leading eventually to doing things just for the sake of doing them—and doing them well.

Finally, the instrumental enrichment program fosters a feeling in the student of being a generator of information rather than someone who contents himself with reproducing, reevoking, or simply retaining things others have done for him. This feeling can produce important changes in his personality. Many retarded performers do not perform because they do not consider themselves called upon to produce anything that has not been formerly produced for them by others. Asked in what year she was born, Nada shrugged her shoulders, telling us to ask her mother: "I have never seen my birth certificate." When asked the date of the current year and how old she was, she proved to have the correct data. When asked, "When were you born," she exclaimed, "Of course, eighty-three minus sixteen," and gave the correct answer, 1967. The fact is that she had all the data and knew the operation of subtraction necessary to generate the required information. She even knew what she needed to do in order to answer. But she did not do it until pressed hard by our questioning because she did not consider herself a generator of information. As noted already instrumental enrichment does not seek the reevocation or reproduction of information. Its main objective is to generate new cognitive structures through adapting rules and principles previously acquired to new situations. The result, if properly interpreted by an individual, especially with the help of the mediating teacher, leads to the emergence of a different self-image.

Before moving on, let us introduce the remaining samples from the 14 IE instruments (see Figures 34–38).

What is the population for which instrumental enrichment is intended? Historically, instrumental enrichment was created to meet

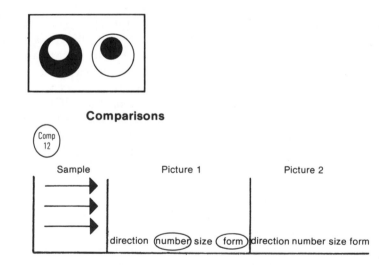

Figure 34. Comparisons induces an awareness of the importance and meaning of comparative behavior, establishes the prerequisite for comparison, and provides tasks for specific practice in determining similarities and differences. Students learn to compare two objects or events along the same continuum, using a common dimension. *Sample direction:* "Look at the sample. In each of the two frames, make a drawing that is the same as the sample *only* in those aspects indicated by the encircled words."

the needs of adolescents often referred to as culturally different and/or culturally deprived individuals. Originally, the program was employed with children who came to Israel from developing countries and who had neither the knowledge nor the ways of thinking necessary for adaptation to a technologically oriented society. They experienced particular difficulty in becoming integrated into the school system. Instrumental enrichment was proposed as a way to

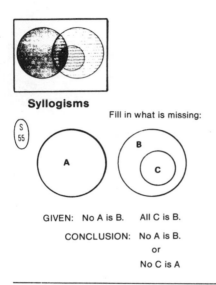

Syllogisms

Fill in what is missing:

GIVEN: No A is B.   All C is B.

CONCLUSION: No A is B.
or
No C is A

Look at the above diagram in order to solve the following problems.

1.

There is no machine (B) that works by itself (   )
Every computer is a machine (   )
Conclusion: There is no computer (   ) that works by itself (   )

2.

All who try (   ) succeed (   ).
No lazy people (   ) try (   ).
Conclusion: No lazy people (   ) succeed (   ).

Figure 35. Syllogisms focuses on the inferences that can be made from known relationships between sets and their members and the conclusion that can be drawn from them. Tasks require a more advanced level of abstract thinking but are based on learning acquired in earlier instruments. Syllogisms seeks to produce an intrinsically oriented need for deductive and inductive reasoning, inferential thinking, and logical proof.

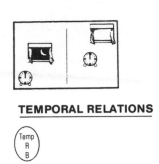

TEMPORAL RELATIONS

Temp
R
B

6. Two turtles were walking in the field. Both started off from a certain rock and walked to a well. Turtle A walked 35 feet (11 meters) in half an hour. Turtle B walked 35 feet (11 meters) in one hour.
Which one of them reached the water first? _____

Explain: _____

Figure 36. Temporal Relations teaches concepts and systems of reference by which students can understand time as both an object and a dimension. From the initial concept of time as a measurable stable interval, the focus is expanded to include the relativity of future, past, and present, and the unidirectional, irreversible flow from one tense to another. Divergent responses and exploration of alternatives are encouraged.

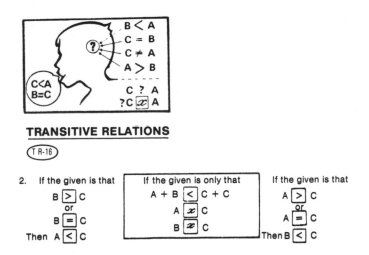

TRANSITIVE RELATIONS

T R-16

2. If the given is that
B $\boxed{>}$ C
or
B $\boxed{=}$ C
Then A $\boxed{<}$ C

If the given is only that
A + B $\boxed{<}$ C + C
A $\boxed{x}$ C
B $\boxed{x}$ C

If the given is that
A $\boxed{>}$ C
or
A $\boxed{=}$ C
Then B $\boxed{<}$ C

Figure 37. Transitive Relations, like Syllogisms, require sophisticated information processing and use of formal logic. The instrument explores the differences existing between members of ordered sets that can be described in terms of larger than, equal to, and smaller than. Equally important, the rules governing transitive thinking are presented.

ILLUSTRATIONS

Figure 38. Illustrations deals with the interaction among cognitive, affective, and motivational components of behavior. The instrument depicts absurd or humorous situations as well as those in which there is a strong link between objective reality and subjective perception. Situations lead to a perception of equilibrium and a subsequent search for an explanation for the transformations that occur from one frame to another.

prepare these adolescents to benefit from a regular classroom environment. After a long period of applying the IE program with adolescents and following up on its outcomes, we expanded the program to include populations of different ages, displaying a variety of exceptionalities. Hence, what proved to be helpful to culturally different and culturally deprived adolescents has proved to be no less meaningful to children classified as, for example, trainable mentally retarded, educable mentally retarded, learning-disabled, minimally brain-injured, or having Down syndrome.

THE INSTRUCTIONAL COMPONENT OF IE

A second major feature of the IE program is the nature of the instructional intervention, which is based on three conceptual frameworks: mediated learning experience (MLE), the list of deficient functions, and the cognitive map. MLE shapes the nature of the teacher–

student interaction, triggered by the tasks included in a particular IE instrument. The understanding of deficient functions allows the teacher to focus on the cognitive prerequisite most in need of change in an IE instrument. The cognitive map permits the teacher to analyze the characteristics of the task responsible for the failure of the child and to choose those tasks that will benefit him most. (The list of deficient functions and the cognitive map appear in Appendixes B and C.)

The following story illustrates how the instructional component of IE was administered effectively to an adolescent with Down syndrome. Marsha came to us at the age of 17, two years after having left school. She was literally vegetating at home, her only "activity" being the endless viewing of TV programs. She did not dare to cross the street by herself. Nor did she ever do any purchasing for herself, not even of the most basic articles. She could not use money because she did not know the coins and could not count. She could not recognize the numbers on a clock.

When first brought to us, she demonstrated a lack of readiness to learn, asserting that she could not and did not need to learn. It became obvious that underlying this uncooperativeness was a deeply ingrained feeling of helplessness. Her passivity was an impenetrable wall. It was obvious that she had to experience success in order to make her ready to become involved in learning tasks. But what would make these "Jericho walls" crumble? What kinds of "trumpets" would be necessary to bring them down?

Her instructors began with the Organization of Dots (Figure 25) from the IE program, using mediation directly and intensively. When Marsha was confronted with a square, her teacher, literally, had to take Marsha's hand and move it in order to teach her to trace the lines between the dots. Following intensive and repetitive exposure to simple reproductive tasks, her teacher was able to make Marsha overcome the huge motivational barrier that blocked her functioning. But motivation was not her only problem. In the more complex tasks of the Organization of Dots instrument, deficient cognitive functions hampering her reasoning ability had to be dealt with by anticipating difficulties and preparing her for the task. Thus, she was taught that the position of the square can change but that the square remains constant, rendering her perception more flexible, and enabling her eventually to find the square in a cloud of dots. Throughout the program, the meaning of her achievements was constantly interpreted to Marsha. Reinforcement of each success became a source of readiness to confront new and challenging tasks. Whenever she succeeded, Marsha repeated one of her favorite expressions, "No, I am not *meshugge*, I can do it."

But her difficulties were far from being overcome. In order for Marsha to master such tasks as Orientation in Space (Figures 28 and 29) or tasks dealing with Analytic Perception (Figure 26), systematic, exploratory search behavior had to be induced. Once Marsha experienced enough of the taste of success, she became "addicted" to the activities of instrumental enrichment. At the same time, her personality became more adaptive, more open, more ready for adventures. She started to travel by herself and even dared to go out and buy a snack for herself, though we had to supply her with the exact sum needed for a purchase because she still could not count or recognize the value of the various coins.

After a long period of intense instrumental enrichment activity, her teachers began to attack Marsha's most difficult area of learning: the acquisition of reading. She had great difficulty associating sounds of letters with their visual representation, owing not only to deficient learning processes but also to her defensiveness, which had become a pervasive way of avoiding challenging learning situations. But after two years of very intense work, Marsha became an avid and proficient reader. As a matter of fact, it became a very familiar scene to watch Marsha reading while she ate, obviously enjoying reading thoroughly.

Even after Marsha's decoding skills improved substantially, comprehension and verbal expression difficulties continued. After a lengthy investment in speech and language therapy and with the support of language-oriented IE instruments, Marsha was able to speak quite well. Furthermore, she was able to apply what she learned in IE Comparisons lessons (see Figure 34) in categorizing people, objects, and historical events. Marsha's self-confidence grew steadily, accompanied by newfound abilities to relate effectively to peers. In fact, she often assumed the role of mediator among her peers.

In mediating, the teacher does not merely dispense IE tasks, but, using the principle of transcendence, he or she will ensure that the rules underlying the task are applied by the learner to future tasks.

Figure 39. Building and promoting cognition and motivation through mediation.

The teacher will use each successive IE session as an opportunity to build and promote higher cognitive abilities and increased motivation (see Figure 39).

Following is a segment of a lesson in Instructions in a sixth-grade class. In it the emphasis is on mediation for individuation and psychological differentiation, mediation for meaning, and mediation for transcendence. Note that the discussion centers on the process by which the students arrived at their responses. The teacher is not content with merely comparing the various answers, but investigates with the students the similarities and differences among the responses, examines the reasons for divergences, and shows them how to make ambiguous answers more precise (see Figure 40).

TEACHER: Let's now look at task number five. Who will read the instructions aloud? Will you, Gail?

GAIL: Draw two squares so that one is in the upper right and the other is on the upper left of the frame. Below the square on the left, draw a circle.

TEACHER: Thank you, Gail. Who will come to the board and show us how he or she has followed the instructions? Very nicely done. Does somebody have another

5. Draw two squares so that one is in the upper right and the other is in the upper left of the frame.

Below the square on the left, draw a circle.

Figure 40. Task Number 5 from the IE program: Instructions.

way? Yes, Janet? That is also correct. Is there another way? Does somebody have another way? That is also correct. OK. We have three drawings on the board and all three are correct according to the instructions. Let's now compare the three drawings.

NELL: Well, in the first two drawings, the position of the two squares is similar and so is their size. So are the circles.

TEACHER: Can you be a little more explicit?

NELL: I mean the size of the squares is all alike and so are the circles in their size and their position.

TEACHER: On the left side?

JIM: In all three drawings, there are squares and circles on the left side.

RONALD: The difference between them is in the size of the squares and in the size and position of the circles.

TEACHER: Very good. My question is why did you all draw the squares in the same place, and yet you drew the circles in different sizes and in different locations in relation to the square on the upper left?

JOE: The squares are drawn in the same place because the instructions tell us that one must be on the upper right and the other on the upper left. It doesn't say anything about their size.

TEACHER: This means that the formulation of "upper right" and "upper left" precisely defines the location of the square. What about the circle?

LILA: The size and location of the circle is not defined in an accurate manner.

TEACHER: The instructions say that we should draw a circle below the square on the left.

LILA: Well, one can understand the instructions "below the square on the left" in a number of alternative ways.

ROSA: The instruction is not precise. It is ambiguous.

TEACHER: A beautiful answer! The reason all three drawings on the board are correct although they differ from one another is because the instruction can be carried out in a number of different ways. Could we possibly make this instruction clearer and more precise?

ANN: Draw a circle in the left corner below the left square.

TEACHER: Yes, Ann said, "Now draw a circle in the left corner under the left square."

TOM: Or we can also say, "below the left square in the middle of the frame."

SANDY: There is also the possibility of saying, "Draw a circle a few centimeters below the left square."

TEACHER: "Draw a circle below the left square, close to it," or "approximately two centimeters below it." What did you do in order to make your instructions more precise?

SANDY: We added details.

TEACHER: Can I have a volunteer formulate an instruction that we can examine for its precision? No ideas? OK. Let's suppose that I would like to have my purse that is in the teachers' room. Who can formulate an instruction to get it? Gail?

GAIL: Please bring me my bag from the teachers' room.

SANDRA: No. You have to tell its color and where to find it. For example, "Please bring me the brown bag that is on the chair."

MICHAEL: But which chair has to be noted. "On the first chair on the left side as you enter the room."

TEACHER: What did we do in order to correct and improve the instructions?

BETTY: We added details.

TEACHER: Very good. From the examples on the board, we have seen that it is possible to carry out an instruction in a number of different ways and still be correct. If we want the instruction to be carried out exactly the same way, we must add details. What principle can we derive from this?

CHARLES: The more detailed an instruction, the more clear and precise it is.

TEACHER: Yes, very good. Where in day-to-day life situations is it important for us to formulate precise and clear instructions?

GEORGE: For instance, when we describe how to go to a given place. Or where a place is, like in geography.

DAVID: In a military action, the instructions given to artillery have to be exact.

MONICA: It is important that an instruction be clear and precise when I am taking medicine. I should know how much to take and how often to take it.

TEACHER: And then?

LONICA: It is important that I read the instruction and follow it precisely.

TEACHER: Very nice.

ANN: But aren't there times when it won't bother us if the instructions are vague?

TEACHER: This is a very appropriate and interesting question, Ann. Class?

LOUIS: Before a field trip, the teacher tells us to come with comfortable shoes, but it doesn't matter to her which ones.

RITA: In instructions to bring along bag lunches for lunch and dinner, it doesn't really matter how much and what.

TEACHER: You're correct. Now, let's practice a bit. Start with an instruction that is broad and therefore vague; then make it well defined and therefore more precise.

To apply the IE program effectively, a teacher will have to attend a training program where he will obtain a thorough understanding of the SCM theory, identify with its belief systems, and appreciate the importance of the goals set forth by the SCM program. Most of all, he will have to master the IE tasks in order to be able to mediate them to his students. Such mastery cannot be achieved without becoming trained through a mediational experience with IE offered by a trainer specially qualified for this purpose.

The nature of the IE tasks is marked by a level of complexity that has seldom been offered to retarded performers. Rather than providing the typical rote types of tasks, the program will demand organization, require abstract thinking, tease out inferential thinking, insisting always on a meaningful contribution from the learner. In many respects, the tasks presented in the IE program appeal to a flexible type of thinking rather than to crystallized thinking. This does not mean, however, that crystallization and automatization of the thinking process will not come in as a very important result of the learning activity. But the tasks themselves demand fluid processing.

The IE program is best applied in the framework of the school curriculum, providing that a school's teachers have become convinced that unless their students possess the prerequisites of learning, the effects of their teaching basic school subject matter will be minimal at best. Equipped with the prerequisites of learning, students in IE will be in a much better position to benefit from the other parts of the curriculum. In fact, soon after they start the program, many teachers discover that IE promotes cognitive changes in the child that enhance and accelerate academic instruction substantially. Note, however, that IE is not meant to directly make the individual a better reader, even though better reading often accompanies IE proficiency, as has been shown in some of the experiments done with the IE program in the field.[1,2] No one should be told that IE will, *ipso facto*, teach a child to read. The child must learn the actual elements and processes of reading in order to know how to read! He has to learn math elements and operations in order to know how to do math! But using IE may facilitate the learning of reading and math because of the cognitive structures and processes learned through IE that may trigger, complement, and act as a catalyst for academic achievement.

Sam is a good example of this outcome. He was considered mentally defective with difficult behavioral problems. He completed a ninth-grade class for students classified as educable mentally retarded without being able to identify any of the letters of the alphabet or a single numeral. All of his teachers had given up on him.

Beginning the IE program was a real struggle. Sam would not accept any kind of mediation that would enable him to learn to do a task. When first presented with four dots to be turned into a square, he barely looked at the model square but started to draw lines in a random way. Attempts by the mediator to orient him to look at the drawn model were met with temper tantrums.

The first step was to make him perceive the elements of the task. Mediation on this level required capturing Sam's eyes, prompting him to follow his own finger as he was tracing the square with the mediator's hand-on-hand help. Once this behavior was learned through repetition, he was encouraged to do it by himself. It was only then that the pencil was given to him, but the mediator needed to continue guiding Sam's hand to connect the dots.

Sam's fleeting perception and lack of interest severely limited his overall performance. These were improved through a series of mediating questions: "How many dots are here? Which one of the squares is the same as this one? Which square is like this one but just a little bit different? How are the squares, rectangles, and triangles different?" He counted in an unsystematic way. Shown four dots and asked how many dots there were, he started to count each dot, lost count, and began the count again. (This behavior is typical of deficient functions on the input level—e.g., blurred perception, unsystematic explorations, lack of precision.)

On the elaborational level, Sam's lack of comparative and summative behavior became the target for mediation. The mediator's intervention helped establish modes for selecting relevant stimuli from among the surrounding ones. By focusing on a circumscribed part of the page and giving it meaning as the target of his activity, the mediator helped Sam's performance to become more purposeful.

Eventually, Sam not only became proficient in IE tasks, he also learned to read, a skill facilitated by becoming able to coordinate his eye–hand movements, attending and focusing on stimuli, and similar improvements. The feeling of competence mediated to him, combined with a growing capacity to understand and accept criticism, opened the way for learning that has modified Sam's level of cognitive functioning and his entire personality in a substantial way.

After 20 years, the application of IE and the large body of research that has accompanied its use have generated a number of techniques differing in certain dimensions from its classical use. For instance, MLE has been applied in the classroom by specially trained teachers without the use of IE instruments.[3] MLE is also being applied on a large scale with parents and professionals in Israel[4] and with parents of children at risk.[5] In the United States, a cognitive curriculum for use in early childhood programs, partly based on the theoretical and applied systems of structural cognitive modifiability, has been developed.[6] Additionally, attempts are being made to use the materials, principles, and methodology of MLE in the rehabilitation of physically handicapped people, especially for people with brain damage following trauma.[7]

The versatility of the IE program, usable in classrooms, in tutorial and remediational situations, and with persons of different ages and varying levels of functioning, stems from the fact that IE does not deal with a specific content or require a particular repertoire of skills as a condition for its use. The very limited literacy demands made on students (certain instruments can be done without knowing how to read, e.g., Organization of Dots, Orientation in Space, Analytic Perception), as well as its controlled vocabulary, turns IE into a program that is easily translated into other languages and can be applied in many different cultures.

Furthermore, the IE program appeals to gifted children no less than to the retarded performer. Also, properly prepared teachers using the IE program show enthusiasm similar to that of their students. They feel challenged by the task, happy to see success and to be "modified" in some of their own cognitive deficiencies (which they become aware of during their training and even more so during its application). Indeed, this is an important by-product of the IE program. The teacher/mediator who experiences the changes produced by the program in a direct way will find that his belief in the modifiability of children increases greatly. This in turn will make him more ready and able to elicit behaviors that were not present in his students' initial repertoire. Many teachers who are feeling professionally "burned out" remark that after learning how to use IE, they find that their interest in teaching has been renewed.*

The program is currently being used with a variety of special education populations, with gifted underachievers, in special education and regular education classrooms, and in clinics and rehabilitation programs in about 25 countries. It has been translated into eight languages (Hebrew, English, French, German, Italian, Spanish, Dutch, and Arabic) and has been the subject of numerous research and evaluation programs. For example, a research project on IE that was done in Israel showed a very important outcome.[1] Two groups were compared: One group received 300 hours of IE over a period of two years as a partial replacement of their regular program; the other group received 300 hours of reading, writing, and arithmetic added to their regular program over the same period of time. The groups were drawn from culturally deprived retarded performers, aged 12 to 15. Their IQs ranged between 60 and 90, and their scholastic deficits ranged from three to five years, rendering them ineligible for education in a regular classroom. A large number of them were functionally illiterate. They were placed in a preparatory class program with the goal to mainstream them after a period of two years. IE was used at the rate of 5 hours per week, and all 14 of the instruments were taught.

The two groups, after the first school year, showed significant cognitive differences favoring those who were offered the IE program. The differences became even greater at the end of the second year (the end of intervention) (see Appendix D). It is interesting to note that despite the fact that the experimental group received 300 hours less in basic school skills, they did not fall behind the contrast group, which had received 300 hours more of that type of training. In fact, in some cases, the IE group performed better than the contrast group in the achievement tests used for evaluation. However, what was most striking was what happened when the two groups were compared two or more years after completing the program. The differences between the two groups, favoring the IE group, were not only sustained but increased meaningfully and in certain cases even

*Training sessions in IE and LPAD are available to teachers in several countries, including Israel, the United States, and Canada. Institute personnel will be glad to supply information about these training sessions. (The address of the institute is in Appendix G.)

JUST A   MINUTE ...
LET ME THINK !

Figure 41. Motto of the IE program.

doubled (see Appendix D). This lends support to our contention that
the changes produced in the individual exposed systematically to the
IE program are revealed not only in an increase in the quantity and
quality of information but also in an increase in the *capacity* of the
individual to benefit from future learning opportunities. Indeed, this
is what IE is meant to do. And this is also what—in our view—the
goal of education should be—that is, rendering the individual more
modifiable, increasing his ability to cope with the continuously and
rapidly changing world in which he and we can live if we heed the
motto of the instrumental enrichment program: "Just a minute . . .
let me think!" (see Figure 41).

CHAPTER 13

Shaping Modifying Environments

This third applied system derived from the SCM theory helps to ensure that the modifiability discovered through the mediated use of the LPAD, and increased through mediated use of the IE program, will be materialized as fully as possible. If a modifying environment is not made available, the structural cognitive modifiability created through LPAD and IE efforts will dissipate, perhaps collapsing altogether.

With this understanding, what are the attributes of a modifying environment? First, a modifying environment is marked by a high degree of *openness*, where individuals with retarded performance have equal access to the full array of society's opportunities. Equality, in this instance, is based on the universality of human needs, such as for privacy and respect, not the dividing up of goods. At the same time, a modifying environment sets relatively "equal" responsibilities for every person and then provides what is necessary to enable each individual to fulfill these responsibilities. It is similar to the normalization principle,[1] which emphasizes making conditions available to people with retarded performance that are as close as possible to those available to all citizens in general.

Second, a modifying environment creates conditions of *positive stress* to which the individual needs to adapt. It is only to the extent that reasonable stress-generating requirements are laid on the individual, and the rewards following adaptation are meaningful for his existence, that modifiability becomes realized.[2] The protective environment usually offered to people with retarded performance in the special class, in the sheltered workshop, and in the summer camp for "handicapped only" can lead to the stagnation of their adaptive forces. The modifying environment uses protective services only as frequently and as long as is absolutely necessary.

Third, a modifying environment offers a *planned and controlled encounter with tasks that are new*, producing a positive tension between what is known and what has still to be learned, what has been mastered and what has still to be mastered. The purpose of mediating to the individual with retarded performance is to increase his adaptive capacity for new situations. Setting the individual with retarded performance in an overly predictive environment will be counterproductive. Adaptation to conditions of life entails the need to change oneself substantially and rapidly so as to succeed in unexpected situations. The "easy" comfort that passive acceptance offers in the present will likely become a source of great discomfort in the future. Protecting the individual with retarded performance from competitive employment in order to spare him stress is certainly humane, but it is not a constructive way to help him modify himself toward meeting higher levels of functioning. Observing the way some employees with retarded performance are unchallenged by employers and peers, we can understand their low level of efficiency and lack of motivation and why they are—at best—tolerated, rather than being sought after for what they contribute. Sometimes employers and peers avoid creating even the pressures necessary to make the individual feel that he is needed, that it matters if he works well, that it is important if he is on time to work. Everyone involved in modifying a vocational situation needs to understand that job requirements have to be shaped along with creating changes in the individual's readiness to respond to them. Indeed, environmental conditions must be created that make modifiability essential!

The fourth attribute of a modifying environment is *individualized/specialized/customized* instruction and mediation. A potential world champion baseball team receives the modifying adoration of its fans; at the same time, however, team members continue to have their individualized skills (hitting, base running, catching) sharpened. A gardener modifies (cultivates, waters) his whole plot of land; at the same time, he individualizes the type of fertilizer he puts on his tomatoes versus what he applies to his lettuce. A new restaurant owner, interested in modifying the total decor of the dining environment, also individualizes each dish on the menu.

As with baseball, gardening, and restaurant operations the successful educational experience must contain both a modifying atmosphere *and* individualized skill development opportunities to enhance the modification. Each complements the other; each is essential to the other.

That modificational pressure has to be administered with care, sympathy, and love goes without saying. That it is not done easily should also be clear. Yet without active modification there is no way to help the person with retarded performance become able to adapt maximally.

To illustrate the shaping of modifying environments, we will focus on three major periods/events of life: (1) the early years (shaping a modifying family/home environment), (2) the school years (shaping modifying integrated student interactions), and (3) the adult years (shaping modifying links between work, leisure, and homemaking in the community).

THE EARLY YEARS: SHAPING A MODIFYING HOME/FAMILY ENVIRONMENT

David was born with an injured brain caused by lack of oxygen during a long and complicated delivery. In his first month of life he appeared to be developing quite normally, to the delight of his mother and father, but gradually he became uninterested in his environment, spending increasing periods of time sleeping or just lying in his crib gazing at the ceiling. Two months after his birth, David's parents went from clinic to clinic, searching for a cure for their son's listlessness. The well-meaning advice they received de-emphasized the severity of the problem ("Don't worry, he'll outgrow his problems; wait and see what he's like in another six months") or suggested they depend on the influence of objects in his environment to improve his development ("Put lots of toys in his crib to stimulate his interests").

Now, five months after David's birth, his parents no longer believe that he will outgrow his problems or that putting toys in his crib will do much to promote his interest. In fact, they feel helpless to do anything further for him, so they now accept him as he is, leaving him by himself, in his crib, for longer and longer periods of time.

One of the keys to improving David's situation is to help his parents take an active modification approach to interacting with him, using mediated learning experiences as effectively as possible. Not that David's brain damage will disappear through active modification, but his thinking ability and learning capacity will improve through its influence. And, equally important, his parents will feel good about doing something that has meaning and relevance for them, helps them avoid the feeling of helplessness, and is rooted firmly in sound principles of child psychology, cultural anthropology, and education.

There are many important factors, both in David and in his environment, that affect the course of his cognitive development. Moreover, each of the factors (e.g., genetic, physiological, biological, cultural, economic) interacts with the others. The total effect will be either amplified or dampened by the quality and amount of human interaction to which he is exposed. In this regard, one researcher[3] observed that mothers of competent infants spent more time engaging their infants, stimulating them intellectually, and facilitating their activities by interacting with them than did mothers of infants with disabilities. Another researcher[4] showed that a mother's early perception of her newborn infant has a long-term effect. (In the study, all of the infants were healthy but were born prematurely.) A mother's perception of her baby—for example, her satisfaction with its appearance—was correlated strongly with how well the child was doing developmentally at the age of 1 year, and even 10 years later.

One of the authors' colleagues, Pnina Klein, asserts that the process of mediated learning experience (MLE) is called for to explain developmental complexity and individual differences.[5] Explaining that MLE begins with interactions on a preverbal level, she describes how later through verbal mediation the baby learns to benefit from experiences that he has not actually undergone. For example, mediation of awareness of the past, made possible through enlarging the child's time–space understanding, enables the child to expand his comprehension, eventually being able to understand his grandfather's death (and eventually anticipate the end of his own life). Generally, the more mediation the young child receives, the more he becomes capable of learning from future experience and being modified by it. In fact, the child who receives MLE develops a *need* to seek mediation, to *expect* events to have meaning, to *search* for relations, to *go beyond* the information provided by his senses at any given moment. There is, however, an optimal level of MLE. Too much mediation can be deleterious to development since it may leave no time for the child to apply newly acquired cognitive abilities (structures) in new learning situations. Thus, the ultimate goal of mediated learning is not solely to make the child a skillful recipient of mediation but also to make him able to learn directly from the environment and, ultimately, to direct his own learning experiences.

In a study of early mother–child or father–child MLE interaction, Klein explored the meaning of the first five criteria of MLE: (1) intentionality and reciprocity, (2) transcendence, (3) mediation of meaning, (4) mediated feelings of competence, and (5) mediated regulation of behavior, as they take form in interactions between parents and their very young children. (For descriptions of each of these, see Appendix E. See also Appendix A and Chapters 3–6.)

All of these types of MLE can be transmitted early in the child's life, including the mediation of meaning, which is often believed to depend on verbal expressions. For example, meaning of a certain sight or musical tone is mediated nonverbally when a mother stops what she is doing, closes her eyes, and, with a facial expression of contentment, rocks with her child in her lap to the sound of the music.

Up to this point, we have discussed MLE as it relates to young children with mild to moderate disabilities or whose environments are not optimal for some reason. But what does MLE have to offer parents whose young children have severe/multiple disabilities?

In a situation where a child has severe and/or multiple disabilities, specialized/customized/individualized types of active modification will need to be implemented in order to enable or support mediated learning. For instance, a child who has muscle control problems (such as occurs with cerebral palsy) will present mediational interaction challenges for his parents. But if a customized chair is built, one that supports the child in an upright position and provides Velcro foot straps to facilitate torso control and arm movement, parents' attempts to mediate will be greatly facilitated. Similarly, suppose that a child has a severe hearing loss. The child's parents, wishing to mediate, can learn to interact with their child by using nonvocal communication (sign language), or they may employ a communication board on which appear printed pictures of important objects in the child's environment to which the child can point in order to convey his desires.

In both of these examples, parents implement specialized active modification in conjunction with MLE because serious sensory, motor, cognitive language, or health disabilities often inhibit the standard type of mediation.

A short, illustrative list of other specialized active modifications, some of which will be provided by surgeons, speech therapists, occupational therapists, physical therapists, dentists, ophthalmologists, special educators, and psychologists, follows.

Modifications for Severe Vision and Hearing Problems

1. Surgery to correct retinal detachment, which will, in turn, facilitate visual mediation by parents.
2. Orientation and mobility training to teach the child with severe visual disability how to move about in the home safely and efficiently, facilitating mediational interactions.
3. Fitting a binaural hearing aid to an infant who has a severe hearing handicap to enable his parents to mediate vocally.

Modifications for Severe Physical and Health Problems

1. Helping the child with a severe physical disability to assume a normalized posture through positioning, splinting, bolstering, and bracing to facilitate mediation.
2. Prescribing medications to control epileptic seizures and teaching parents how to monitor their dosage so as to make the child accessible to a mediating interaction.
3. Providing surgery to repair a cleft lip or cleft palate and then assisting parents to communicate more effectively with their child.
4. Teaching parents to use adaptive equipment (e.g., standing tables, special wheelchairs, prone boards) to promote mobility and range of motion, which will, in turn, facilitate mediation attempts.

Modifications for Severe Cognitive and Social/Emotional Handicaps

1. Using selected behavior modification techniques—e.g., shaping, task analysis, physical guidance, modeling—to promote specific task acquisitions that will, in turn, enable MLE across many tasks.
2. Judicious use of drug therapy to reduce hyperactivity, marked aggression, and self-destructive behaviors, making mediation more effective.

Several other professionals have also noted the necessity of specialized forms of active modification to enable fruitful parent mediating interactions, observing that infants who resist cuddling tend to induce their parents to leave them alone,[6] and that fussy babies tend to make their parents frustrated and distraught.[7]

Sometimes even basic mothering interactions can be at risk in the newborn period, as shown in the following account[8]:

> The delivery had been complicated, and the child had an Apgar score of only 5 at one minute and 8 at five minutes. A few hours after birth, the child was examined by a pediatrician and was thought to be normal.
> The nurse gave the swaddled baby to the mother and left the room. The mother immediately unwrapped the baby. Looking pleased with what she saw, she laid the infant against her arm in order to begin breastfeeding. When placed in the supine [on his back] position, the infant went into slight extension of the trunk (probably a sign of cerebral irritability). The mother touched the baby's cheek, using the rooting reflex properly. But when the infant's head turned toward the nipple, this activated a definitely abnormal asymmetrical tonic neck reflex. The baby's arm on the chin side went into extension, as if he were "straight-arming" the mother. By now the mother was exasperated and the child, still hungry, was crying, which intensified the primitive reflexes. (p. 78)

In instances such as the situation just described, the most important goal of early mediation should be to reorchestrate an inharmonious parent–child relationship. To approach this goal, parents can gain specific insights into their child's handicap and, subsequently, stimulate their child's development more fully. This was a crucial issue in three studies with blind babies and their mothers[9–11] showing that parents who had been competent with their sighted babies often failed to learn their blind baby's mode of communication. Because a blind baby cannot see someone smiling, parents were advised to talk in a brightened ("happy") voice with their child. When this advice was followed, blind babies began to smile in response to their parents' vocalizations at approximately the same age that sighted babies smiled in response to their parents.

In the past, early childhood educators have often focused on the child with a handicap as the target of their intervention efforts. Currently, however, early educators have taken a very different position, one that says essentially, "Unless the child's parents and other family members thrive, the child with a handicap will not thrive." A key to mutual thriving is to assist parents in assuming an individualized, active modificational role, one that is given life and meaning through mediation.

THE SCHOOL YEARS: SHAPING MODIFYING INTEGRATED
INTERACTIONS

In recent years there has been a strong movement in the United States toward integrating school-age children with retarded performance in regular schools, trusting that *mutual* benefits would occur if integrated programming was done wisely.

Until the mid-1970s children with disabilities usually received schooling in segregated settings such as special schools or state-run residential institutions. Then, in 1975, a public law (PL 94-142, the Education for All Children Act) was passed, coming into being largely through the efforts of parents in organizations such as the Association for Retarded Citizens (ARC). This law declared that *all* children have a right to a free, appropriate public education in the *least restrictive environment*. The word *all* and the phrase *least restrictive environment* have created unprecedented opportunity for those seeking to integrate children with retarded performance in regular education settings. In capitalizing on these opportunities, we should take note of several distinct advantages of integrated services as conceptualized by a well-known special educator, Luanna Meyer.[12]

First, historically, local public schools have been reluctant to enroll children with retarded performance, particularly those with serious physical, emotional, and sensory disabilities. It was easier, and some believed better, to set up something separate. But even if a segregated school offers specialized services that seem to meet the needs of students who attend a self-contained program, this compromise of the individual's right to associate with nonhandicapped peers is neither justified nor necessary, given that specialized services can almost always be provided effectively within a regular public school. There should be "room" for children with disabilities in the regular school, just as there is room, with no questions asked, for normal children in those regular schools.

Second, the value of strong, positive peer interactions as the "heart" of good integration programming should not be underestimated. Friend-to-friend interactions provide a context for the practice of skills that may have been learned from a teacher or parent. Furthermore, since the ultimate goal of nearly everything we teach is to establish functional ability in the student, why not put our instructional efforts into teaching the skill where we really want it to occur? If this is to happen, more instruction must take place in the context of the neighborhood 4-H club, scout troop, local park, nearby fast-food restaurant, and other such places.[13]

Third, a strong emphasis has often been placed on preparing the person with retarded performance for independence. But is this emphasis realistic? Very few normal people are completely independent; most are part of a variety of complex and mutually beneficial, interdependent support networks at home, school, work, and other places. For example, family members "negotiate" the complementary roles they assume at home; that is, there are some things that each spouse cannot do, and/or dislikes doing, so "jobs" are negotiated accordingly. In fact, many things are not done in many households by either spouse—for example, fixing the plumbing, car, refrigerator, or furnace. Why then do some educators continue to group persons with disabilities in self-contained programs, expecting the individual with a disability, or even groups of persons with disabilities, to become more independent while still in an isolated environment? If our goal is to reflect normalized patterns of *interdependence,* educators can no longer avoid the crucial obligation to prepare normal people to include individuals with disabilities in "their" environments. If children of every ability level have grown up together and have seen one another in every imaginable context, children with disabilities can graduate into an adult world that consists of normal people who have learned the skills and attitudes needed to include persons with disabilities, for *mutual* benefits.

Fourth, the prevailing social interaction pattern of persons with disabilities is often "top-down"; that is, an authority figure (a teacher, a parent), no matter how kindly, creates and enforces conditions to which the child must respond. While some of these top-down interactions are nurturant, many of them are situations where the child with retarded performance meets the demands of another person. In interactions with nondisabled peers, however, the child with disabilities can be involved in a friend-type relationship. One could argue, of course, that peer friend opportunities are also available among children with disabilities, but the reality of the situation is that the more disabled a child is, the more difficult it is for him to initiate and maintain interaction opportunities. Hence, under conditions that the mediating adult orchestrates, normal peers can extend the social and cognitive skills of children with disabilities dramatically and, in the bargain, learn some valuable things about themselves and the worth of *every* person.

How does one begin and maintain a successful integrated program? Factors identified as important to beginning successful school and nonschool integration efforts include securing parent and administrative support, integrating people with disabilities into settings frequented by normal peers whose ages are similar, and resisting pressures to place a disproportionate number of persons with disabilities in a program. Other factors include creating an integration task force to develop a long-term integration plan, appointing a facilitator to take responsibility for organizing and coordinating integrated programming on a day-to-day basis,[14,15] and cultivating cooperative interactions between disabled and nondisabled participants and between regular and special education teachers.[16-18]

The most important factor in creating a successful integrated program is to prepare activities for cooperative, peer friendship, interactions. To accomplish this, the adult should create small, cooperatively structured groups, perhaps a group containing one student with disabilities and two or three nondisabled students, or by pairing each individual with disabilities with a nonhandicapped person.

In peer tutoring programs, nondisabled students typically receive instruction on how to serve in a role that essentially parallels that of the teacher; that is, they interact with their peers in a top-down, "vertical" manner. In contrast, a peer friendship program encourages peers to develop relationships in the context of socializing activities. Peer friends interact in a "horizontal" manner, with an emphasis on cooperative participation.[19]

Differences between the two techniques raise interesting questions for educators and recreation professionals. At first, it may appear to be an "easy decision": The program is tailored according to the outcome desired—academic skill acquisition or social interaction—whereupon a peer tutoring approach is used if the primary objective is the acquisition of academic skills; if social interaction is the main objective, a peer friendship program is used. But making a choice between the two may not be necessary. We opt for concentrating initially on the facilitation of friendships. Then, later, there is nothing wrong with one friend tutoring another in how to play a new game or increase flash card recognition ability. However, the fundamental basis of the relationship should continue to emphasize friend-type interactions.

The next step in creating positive integrated interactions is for the adult instructor to select learners with retarded performance, asking:

Do peer age differences matter? What accommodations need to be made for severe physical, sensory, intellectual, or behavioral disabilities? How important are the requirements of the task itself? Our findings[20] support encouraging cooperative interactions between similarly aged peers, regardless of level of ability. However, activity adjustments will need to be made and normal peers must be given training regarding how and when they should assist. This judgment will be facilitated once they know their special friend better and have been assured that it is no more their "duty" to do everything for this peer than it would be for any other. In fact, normal peers will need to be assured that their friends with disabilities need to learn about the real world of natural cues, corrections, and consequences. For instance, in the real world, when playing a game with another person, friends usually take turns. Additionally, real-world friends don't let their buddies pull their hair but may respond with a sharp "no" or by walking away. Normal peers need to know that it is acceptable for them to assert their rights when interacting with their friends with disabilities, just as they do with their nonhandicapped friends.

Next, the adult in charge will need to create opportunities for nondisabled peers to participate in voluntary integrated programming activities. Activities that are particularly conducive to special friend social interactions are those that have modest academic expectations and embody high socialization opportunities. Examples of these types of activities follow:

1. Provide opportunities for peer interactions during non-academic time, such as recess, lunch, study hall, homeroom, or open periods.
2. Integrate students with disabilities into portions of the curriculum in which they can participate easily with nondisabled peers. These might include music, art, social studies, and physical education classes.
3. Provide an opportunity for students with disabilities to engage in job-training opportunities around the school with nondisabled peers. Typical jobs might be working together in the library or school office, filling the soda machine, or buffing floors.
4. Assist students with disabilities to join regular school clubs and organizations such as pep club or a socially oriented organization.

5. Assist students to participate in afterschool/community activities such as Campfire Girls, Boy Scouts, 4-H, open swim at the local YMCA, or activities at the neighborhood recreation center.

The next thing that the adult will need to do is to prepare the environment for cooperative interactions. Is the classroom space accessible to wheelchairs? Do environmental demands exist that will be problematic for learners with severe handicaps? Are there physical, language, social, cognitive, or academic barriers that will need to be circumvented or adapted to for partial participation? If any of these questions receive an affirmative answer, the adult will need to make adaptations and accommodations accordingly.

The environment should be carefully arranged so as to allow persons with disabilities to do as much as they can on their own. As was said earlier, a balance must be struck between independence and interdependence. Photography is a good example of an activity that lends itself very well to both independent (solo) and interdependent (cooperative group) activity. For instance, an adult volunteer could train adolescents (attending an integrated 4-H club) to take photographs independently (e.g., load film into the camera, operate it, turn film in for processing). This would be appropriate since photography is an activity that can be engaged in naturally on an individual basis. Additionally, however, the adult leader could plan a cooperative get-together for the purpose of creating a club photo album, where each member contributes at least one favorite photograph, and where, in small integrated groups, pages are laid out to represent club themes. Afterward, club members continue to work together in miniteams, preparing—and photographing—food items that they assemble for a pizza party, before and during which the adult in charge can do a number of things to promote cooperative interactions:

1. Create pairs or small groups of pizza makers comprising both disabled and nondisabled individuals. Groups of three or more should contain a greater number of nondisabled than disabled participants.
2. Arrange ingredients of the pizza so that everything needed by the dyad or group is in one small area rather than scattered around the room. This will help keep members close to one another.
3. Develop directions for the task in such a way that an interde-

pendent (cooperative) effort, rather than independent (solo) effort, is emphasized. For example, emphasis should be given to the fact that the intent is to create a pizza to which *each* group member contributes. Additionally, directions can emphasize dual participation (e.g., "John, why don't you hold the sausage while Doug slices it" or "If Sara turns the pizza, Beth can sprinkle the cheese on it").

4. Emphasize the importance of enjoying the activity rather than focusing on the speed and/or accuracy with which it is accomplished.

In order for the pizza making to be a successful cooperative activity, the adult in charge will need to prepare nondisabled participants to be effective as cooperative friends. One of the first things is to emphasize that, as much as possible, they should interact with their disabled special friend as they would with their nondisabled friends. For example, they are not expected to do all of the work while their friend with a disability watches; however, peers without disabilities should be informed that their peers with disabilities may need assistance in order to join actively in pizza making. Some tips for the nondisabled peer to use in helping include the following:

1. *Stay close* to your friend when you are preparing a pizza together.
2. *Smile* and *talk pleasantly* to your friend and try to maintain *eye contact* when talking to him.
3. *Encourage* your friend to take part in the activity. Invite him to put pepperoni on the pizza with you or to open the tomato sauce while you knead the dough. Make the activity enjoyable and let your friend know that you are having a good time.
4. *Take turns.* Your friend with a disability may not be used to taking turns, so be patient; don't jump in too quickly or help too much. But when he appears to be confused, loses interest, or shows signs of frustration, that's a clear signal that help is needed.
5. *Assist* when needed. Since your friend won't always know how to do something, the following steps can help him to participate:
   a. *Give words of encouragement* so that your friend will want to try the task with you.
   b. *Explain* how to perform the task.

c. *Show* your friend how to perform the task, continuing to explain how to do it.

d. *Guide* your friend through the task by gently moving his arm toward it, or by actually moving your friend's hand to perform the task with you, continuing to explain how to do the task.

6. *Say something pleasant as an activity ends* so that your friend will want to come back again to be with you.

Our group of researchers has found the use of the Special Friends[21] curriculum to be helpful in preparing nondisabled children to be peer friends.[22] (See Appendix F for a description of components of the Special Friends curriculum.)

Next, the leader should decide what role to adopt in facilitating social interactions. In this regard, Meyer and her associates[23] investigated the effects of different levels of teacher supervision on the social play of children with autism and their nonhandicapped special friends. They found few differences in children's interactions as a function of intrusive versus nonintrusive teacher roles, and suggested that teachers may be able to reduce or discontinue their level of intervention involvement once children are acquainted with each other. In a similarly oriented study,[24] the effects of two types of teachers' verbalizations in social interactions with children with and without serious handicaps were compared. In one condition, teachers provided prompts or words of praise for cooperative behavior, while, in the other, teachers provided only casual comments—that is, comments about the weather, weekend plans, and other subjects—during the program. Initially, rates of social interaction behaviors were higher in the condition in which teachers prompted or rewarded social play. However, differences disappeared by the middle of the study, and, by the end, the favored condition was one in which teachers made only general, friendly comments during activities. The researchers recommend that teachers modify their interventions on the basis of the needs of the children involved and the type of activity in which they are participating. One way teachers can accomplish this is to observe pairs or groups of students with and without disabilities as they begin interacting. By noting the types of cooperative behaviors that occur, and that do not occur, the teacher can tailor intervention efforts to suit the needs of each pair or group.

Additionally, teachers can provide individualized instruction that will promote participation of students with retarded performance, such as showing them how to use a piece of equipment or engage in an activity, providing verbal or modeled directions or physical prompts,[25] or suggesting different ways to accomplish an activity. Students with retarded performance can often receive specific instruction "on the side," that is, between interaction sessions, in creating a modifying integrated environment (see Table 4 for examples illustrating what we mean). To promote the skills shown in Table 4, a mediating teacher will find the use of a task analysis to be very helpful, particularly if a skill has a number of steps that follow a predictable sequence.

TABLE 4. Individualizing Instruction of Person with Retarded Performance to Maximize the Opportunities of an Integrated Program

Individualized instruction needed	Integrated programming desired
1. Individual skill training in table manners (e.g., use of eating utensils, way to use napkin, posture)	1. Attending an integrated birthday party
2. Individualized skill training in independent use of bus to travel back and forth to 4-H program (e.g., practice in speedy identification of correct bus number, practice in proper way to stand in line)	2. Meeting with members of an integrated community 4-H club
3. Individual skill training in maintaining good oral hygiene (e.g., proper brushing and flossing, identification of when to use a mouthwash)	3. Playing a table game with a friend at his home
4. Individualized articulation training to improve communication ability	4. Promoting mainstreaming opportunities in regular classes
5. Individualized training in indicating food preferences using cards instead of verbalizations (individual does not have intelligible language)	5. Facilitating the ability to go with a friend to a place like McDonald's and order food
6. Individualized training in how to shower independently (e.g., remove clothes and place on bench in front of locker, enter showering area without slipping, turn on water and adjust temperature)	6. Promoting ability to be part of a regular gym class

Sometimes teachers will need to redirect students with retarded performance in how to participate in an activity appropriately, such as providing instructions that redirect a student's attention to his partner or group, or commenting on the enjoyment and excitement others show.

The rewards for participation in peer friendship interactions should come largely from the social exchange between participants and not from the words of praise provided by the teacher. Hence, if emphasizing peer friendship, teachers should avoid thanking the regular education students for doing such a good "job" and reminding them of what to do the next time they "work" with their friend.

When learners with and without disabilities are involved in programs emphasizing integrated cooperative interactions and peer friendship, we can expect to see significant increases in the frequency of positive social interactions between learners with and without handicaps. Such increases have occurred in a variety of studies involving integrated outdoor camping,[26] integrated art activities,[27,28] integrated recreational bowling,[29,30] integrated school activities,[31,32] integrated playground programs,[33] integrated physical education activities,[34] and an integrated sports camp.[35] We also find significant increases in the acceptance by nondisabled peers of learners with disabilities during integrated activities.[36–41]

Regarding staff members' attitudes, in a recent study,[42] pre- and postattitudinal ratings were collected from staff members participating for the first time in an integrated camping program (for 20 years, the camping program had been operated on a segregated basis). Postcamp ratings of several attitudinal dimensions, such as desire for more integration, showed significant change in a positive direction.

And looking to outcomes related to the promotion of skill development and appropriateness of behavior by learners with severe disabilities in integrated settings, a number of studies have shown that significant improvement occurs.[43,44]

As education's capacity for accommodation grows, "special friends" should gradually become, simply, "friends." At the same time, however, individualized special education services must not be abandoned. Rather, special educators will need to develop and refine strategies for delivering individualized services to children in regular education settings, separating them from groups of nonhandicapped peers only when absolutely necessary.

THE ADULT YEARS: SHAPING A MODIFYING COMMUNITY ENVIRONMENT

Graduation into successful adult community living involves ability to thrive in at least three environments: work, living arrangement, and leisure. Each of these supports the others, the way the three legs of a tripod support the whole structure.

In contrast to how normal adults negotiate their way through these life spaces fairly independently, the person with retarded performance will need both mediational assistance and individualized skill training, similar to what was described in the section on schooling just completed. For, while the regular community has modifying qualities in and of itself, it can be a bewildering and, occasionally, even hostile environment for the person with retarded performance if he is not properly skilled and supported. That this is true should be apparent in the relatively high "fallout" rate among segments of the normal population, such as we see in the increasing incidence of drug use, runaways, and unplanned pregnancy among teenagers, and the high number of expressions of loneliness and helplessness in society's elderly people.

The interrelations of work, socialization and recreation, and self-care in the successful community living of people with retarded performance are illustrated in the following:

R. is doing well in his job at the neighborhood laundry, where he skillfully sorts and folds clothing. But at his apartment he is unable to set his alarm clock reliably. Consequently, he has a record of tardiness and is about to lose his job.

C. has sloppy work habits. She packs plastic items in a box at a factory, looking at a photo that signals what items are to be packed in which box. A spot check of her work shows that some boxes have too many or too few items. Her fellow workers are becoming increasingly unhappy with her because she is causing them extra work on the assembly line. They have just signed a petition requesting that she be fired.

H. is doing well on his job and is living independently at a rooming house. However, he has no friends and has few skills in leisure activities or in cultivating friendships. His loneliness is becoming a problem, manifested in an increasing number of days of missed work and a marked deterioration in his housekeeping habits. His landlord is threatening to evict him.

In each of these cases, a solution to the problem is related to a combination of factors. Hence, those who are interested in creating a modifying adult environment should attend to all of these factors.

Since success is ultimately measured by how students function in a community, secondary education must be community referenced; that is, it should stress age-appropriateness, functionality, integration, and normalization, and should take place out in the community itself as much as is feasible.

A number of researchers have developed community-referenced techniques that are dynamic and creative, yet appropriate for youths with retarded performance.[45] For instance, *environmental inventorying* is a helpful technique, similar to what anthropologists do: that is, they create a set of meticulously detailed and thorough set of observations about the environment in which they are interested. The vocational counselor who is interested in giving a young adult a work tryout in a cafeteria should visit the place and "shadow" a seasoned employee whose skills the counselor wants his client with retarded performance to have. He should not only make detailed notes about the discrete job operations; he should observe how workers punch time cards, take coffee breaks, and function in the "chain of command." Operations that may need adaptation because they are beyond the capability of his client should be described in detail. For example, a client's weak left arm, which is the preferred one to use at the particular dishwasher, will necessitate the attaching of a handle permitting right-hand use. (The counselor writes in his book: "No problem. A large iron gate handle will work fine.") The counselor should check to see how and where workers eat lunch (he may, depending on the "social conventions" of the employee lunchroom, provide training in when to talk and when *not* to). Careful notes should be made about how his client will get to work since training in the efficient use of the bus will be as important to his client's employment success as the actual job skills themselves.

Similar environmental inventories should be done for the client's living and recreational environments.

Task analyzing can also be a useful training technique. For those who have purchased a bicycle for a child from the department store catalog, a task analysis often takes the form of a blown-up drawing of the unassembled bicycle, accompanied by a sequenced, step-by-step description of where each part goes.

For the vocational counselor of a young adult with retarded performance being trained to work at the cafeteria, a task analysis is a sheet of paper containing the sequence of steps the employee must follow to complete a job operation successfully. (It is actually a subcomponent of the environmental inventory just described.) For instance, a task analysis might be designed to teach the specific steps required to use the time clock or to operate the dishwashing machine. Once the task analysis is developed, with spaces provided for individualizing teaching as needed, the counselor should run his client through the steps without instruction, noting which steps he can and cannot do independently and well.

Construction of the environmental inventory, and task analysis development and implementation should occur out in the actual community job site. The reason for not doing it in a simulated manner, or in a similar but not actual setting, is that people with retarded performance do not generally transfer what they learn to tasks that are even slightly different from the ones learned originally, unless they are especially framed for such transfer by mediated learning experience. Hence, it is unrealistic to expect that training in the use of a dishwasher at home will transfer fully to the use of an industrial dishwasher at the cafeteria. Furthermore, if transfer of skills is required, mediational interaction will include teaching transcending components that foster the learning to be transferred, an investment in structural cognitive modifiability.

In mediating during vocational training, the counselor will introduce each step of a task analysis without providing training. Steps that are not done independently should then be taught through verbal directions, modeling, and, if needed, physical guidance. When errors occur, they should be corrected immediately; likewise, where success is achieved, verbal praise should follow promptly. Gradually, as skill increases, the counselor will withdraw mediation until the client shows independent mastery over all of the steps of each task analysis and over the whole cafeteria environment.

The IE program and job-related academic instruction should continue if at all possible even though the person with retarded performance is on a job site in the community. Often, the authors have found that IE is a continuing source of stimulation to the working adult with retarded performance, complementing the functional academic instruction related to the job, and often the job operations as well. Structural changes in cognitive ability are bound to have a salutary affect, not only on employability but on living in the community successfully and using spare time more productively.

In closing this section, we want to alert the reader to Appendix G, which contains a list of resources that will be of help in making decisions of this type. Appendix G contains lists of resources in other areas related to shaping a modifying environment as well.

In summary, shaping a modifying environment should begin in the early years in a family, continue through modifying integrated activities during the schooling years, and assume possibly its most important form—in the community, job, living arrangement, and recreation site—during the adult years. In all of these settings, the mediating adult plays a critical ongoing role, utilizing dynamic modes of assessment and instruction such as LPAD, IE, task analysis, and special friends programming as vehicles for producing structural cognitive modifiability.

A Futures Perspective
The Need to Modify Society as a Whole

Over the years, given the results obtained from the LPAD, we have been able to convince progressive and, in certain cases, even conservative administrators, teachers, and employers to accept thousands of people with retarded performance into their programs, supporting them with the IE program and other interventions. But, paradoxically, the large number of successes we have had is also a source of frustration and dissatisfaction for us. How much *more* could be done for large numbers of individuals with retarded performance if more segments of society would change from a passive-acceptant approach to an active-modificational approach.

Zivi, a person with Down syndrome whose capacity and readiness to learn and to reason logically amazed all those who knew him, became very depressed after all attempts to find employment had failed. He said, "Wherever I turn, I don't see anything but zeroes, big zeroes, lots of zeroes, nothing but zeroes." Changing the individual and his peer group without changing the social system on which they depend will not only hamper the materialization of modification goals; it may even worsen the condition of those who have become aware of what the world could offer them but does not.

A story goes that a man working very hard for human rights came home after a hard day of work. As he fell asleep, he dreamed that an angel announced that he was being condemned to the eighth department of the inferno. Asked what the eighth department is like, the angel granted him the right to see it. When he arrived there he heard someone complaining that the world there was too cold to live in. Seeing a mountain of snow—the source of the cold—the man decided that he would melt the snow with the heat of his own body.

He took off his shirt and approached the mountain. Hour by hour the warmth of his body turned the melting mountain of snow into a stream of water. When all of the snow was gone he put on his shirt, full of happiness about what he had achieved. Then, to his horror, he saw that the melted stream had become a large lake of ice! The cold became even more bitter than before. The moral of this story is that societal changes earned in one area may be worthless, and in certain cases damaging, unless society as a whole is changed.

An illustration of this problem can be seen in what happened to efforts made to desegregate the education of black children in the 1960s by placing them in white schools. Black children were indeed enrolled in white schools, but once there, they were frequently placed in special classes for educable mentally retarded children. Having earned the right to an "integrated" school, they were segregated in it, with a disability label that was possibly more damaging to their educational opportunities than their minority status.

Likewise, sometimes those who have attempted to improve the destiny of children with retarded performance by integrating them into the educational mainstream have not always taken care to provide the type of instruction necessary to ensure acceptance into the larger group of peers. This preparation has to include stimulation of cognitive, social, and motivational factors, all of which are associated with an individual's profiting from integrated education.

For many individuals with retarded performance, there is still the big zero, the many zeroes, and sometimes "nothing but zeroes," as Zivi put it so dramatically. The sources of failure lie in the halfhearted and fragmented nature of modification efforts. The "snow melter" melted the mountain of snow but didn't think of ways to warm up the entire atmosphere. With his naïveté, he worsened the very condition he tried to improve.

Passive-acceptant belief systems are derived partly from political attitudes and partly from the assessment requirements laid upon a discipline in order to become accepted into the "scientific" community. The belief that intelligence is a "real thing" (is reified) often leads to the assumption that it can be measured with a high degree of accuracy and forecasting validity (envied by the physical sciences, which have given up on such requirements for portions of their science).

Melting the mountain of snow for people with retarded performance will have to be accompanied by efforts to shape modifying environments so that they will not only allow for substantial changes in the individual to occur but will actually encourage these changes by setting conditions required for their thriving in society. This will require promoting belief systems, such as active modifiability, which emphasize the need to help *all* individuals improve the quality of their lives by modifying their cognitive functioning,[1,2] and which lead to the improvement of society as well!

Mediated Learning Experience
Criteria and Categories of Interaction

This appendix is a brief blueprint of the encoding of MLE interactions according to their mediative meaning. It represents for didactical purposes a shortened version of suggested categories. As such, it is not to be considered as either exhaustive or definitive.

I. CRITERIA OF MEDIATED LEARNING INTERACTIONS

1. Intentionality and reciprocity
2. Transcendence
3. Mediation of meaning
4. Mediation of feelings of competence
5. Mediated regulation and control of behavior
6. Mediated sharing behavior
7. Mediation of individuation and psychological differentiation
8. Mediation of goal seeking, goal setting, goal planning, and achieving behavior
9. Mediation of challenge: The search for novelty and complexity
10. Mediation of an awareness of the human being as a changing entity
11. Mediation of an optimistic alternative

II. CATEGORIZATION OF MEDIATED INTERACTIONS

1. Mediated focusing
2. Mediated selection of stimuli
3. Mediated scheduling
4. Provoking (requesting) mediation
5. Mediation of positive anticipation
6. Mediated act substitute

Based on Feuerstein, R., Rand, Y., Hoffman, M., & Miller, R. (1980). *Instrumental Enrichment* (Chap. 2). Baltimore: University Park Press.

7. Mediated imitation
8. Mediated repetition
9. Mediated reinforcement and reward
10. Mediated verbal stimulation
11. Mediated inhibition and control
12. Mediated provision of stimuli
13. Mediated recall short-term
14. Mediated recall long-term
15. Mediated transmission of past
16. Mediated representation of future
17. Mediated identification and description—verbal
18. Mediated identification and description—nonverbal
19. Positive verbal response to mediation
20. Positive nonverbal response to mediation
21. Mediated assuming responsibility
22. Mediated shared responsibility
23. Mediation of cause-and-effect relationship
24. Mediated response—verbal
25. Mediated response—motor
26. Mediated discrimination and sequencing
27. Mediation of spatial orientation
28. Mediation of temporal orientation
29. Mediation of comparative behavior
30. Mediated fostering a sense of completion
31. Mediation of directing attention
32. Mediated association and application
33. Mediated critical interpretation
34. Mediated deductive reasoning
35. Mediated inductive reasoning
36. Mediation of developing inferential thinking
37. Mediation of problem-solving strategies
38. Mediated transmission of values
39. Mediation of need of precision on input levels
40. Mediation of need of precision on output levels
41. Mediation of need for logical evidence on input levels
42. Mediation of need for logical evidence on output levels
43. Mediation of systematic exploration
44. Mediated confrontation of reality
45. Mediated organization of stimuli
46. Mediation of cognitive operation—verbal
47. Mediation of cognitive operation—motor
48. Mediation of perception of feelings—verbal
49. Mediation of perception of feelings—nonverbal
50. Mediation of reciprocity

Deficient Cognitive Functions

Inadequate mediated learning experience leads to cognitive functions that are undeveloped, poorly developed, arrested, impaired, or seldom and inefficiently used. The locus of such deficiencies may be peripheral (in the gathering and communication of information) or central (in the elaboration of information), and often reflects attitudinal and motivational deficiencies, lack of learning sets, and lack of internal needs rather than structural incapacity. Evidence of the reversibility of the phenomenon has been provided by clinical and experimental work, especially through dynamic assessment. Clinical use of the learning potential assessment device (LPAD) has also enabled us to establish a partial inventory of deficient cognitive functions, which we have categorized into *input, elaboration,* and *output* phases of the mental act. The severity of the impairment at one phase may affect the ability to function at another, but not necessarily. For example, deficiencies at the input phase may also affect the ability to function at phases of elaboration and/or output. There may be highly original, creative, and correct elaboration that nevertheless yields wrong responses because it is based on inappropriate data at the input phase, or because it cannot be adequately expressed at the output phase.

Impaired cognitive functions that are found at the *input* phase include impairments in the quantity and quality of data gathered by a person confronted with a given problem, object, or experience. They include the following:

1. Blurred and sweeping perception.
2. Unplanned, impulsive, and unsystematic exploratory behavior.
3. Lack of or impaired receptive verbal tools that affect discrimination (e.g., objects, events, and relationships are not appropriately labeled).
4. Lack of or impaired spatial orientation and lack of stable systems of reference by which to establish topological and Euclidian organization of space.
5. Lack of or impaired temporal concepts.
6. Lack of or impaired conservation of constancies (e.g., size, shape,

quantity, color, orientation) across variations in one or more dimensions.

7. Lack of or deficient need for precision and accuracy in data gathering.
8. Lack of capacity for considering two or more sources of information at once. This is reflected in dealing with data in a piecemeal fashion rather than as a unit of facts that are organized.

Impaired cognitive functions found at the *elaboration* phase include those factors that impede the efficient use of available data and existing cues. They are as follows:

1. Inadequacy in the perception of the existence of a problem and its definition.
2. Inability to select relevant, as opposed to irrelevant, cues in defining a problem.
3. Lack of spontaneous comparative behavior or the limitation of its application to a restricted need system.
4. Narrowness of the mental field.
5. Episodic grasp of reality.
6. Lack of need for the eduction or establishment of relationships.
7. Lack of need for, and/or exercise of, summative behavior.
8. Lack of or impaired need for pursuing logical evidence.
9. Lack of or impaired inferential hypothetical ("if") thinking.
10. Lack of or imparied strategies for hypothesis testing.
11. Lack of or impaired planning behavior.
12. Lack of or impaired interiorization.
13. Nonelaboration of certain cognitive categories because the verbal concepts are not a part of the individual verbal inventory on a receptive level, or because they are not mobilized at the expressive level.

Impaired functions found at the *output* phase include those factors that lead to inadequate communication of insights, answers, and solutions. It should be noted that even adequately perceived data and appropriate elaboration can be expressed as an incorrect or haphazard solution if difficulties exist at this phase. Deficiencies include the following:

1. Egocentric communication modalities.
2. Difficulty in projecting virtual relationships.
3. Blocking.
4. Trial-and-error responses.
5. Lack of or impaired verbal or other tools for communicating adequately elaborated responses.
6. Lack of or impaired need for precision and accuracy in the communication of one's responses.

7. Deficiency of visual transport.
8. Impulsive, random, unplanned behavior.

The deficient cognitive functions play a critical role in the process orientation of dynamic assessment and educational intervention. The LPAD examiner, as well as the educator, must be thoroughly familiar with them in all of their manifestations to pinpoint the source of subjects' difficulties.

APPENDIX C

Cognitive Map

Another important way to conceptualize the relationship between the characteristics of a task and its performance by a subject is the *cognitive map*. This conceptual model is not a map in the topographical sense but a tool by which to locate specific problem areas and to produce changes in corresponding dimensions. The cognitive map describes the mental act in terms of seven parameters that permit us to analyze and interpret a subject's performance. The manipulation of these parameters becomes highly important in the examiner–subject interaction and in the formation and validation of hypotheses regarding the loci of a subject's difficulties. The seven parameters are as follows.

1. *The universe of content around which the mental act is centered.* The competence with which subjects deal with a specific body of content is directly related to each subject's experiential, cultural, and educational background. Certain content may be quite unfamiliar to a subject and thus may require such an intensive investment for its mastery that it is no longer useful for providing information about the cognitive functions and operations it involves, the real target of the assessment. Manipulation of the content in both assessment and intervention will become a source of insight for change.

2. *The modality or language in which the mental act is expressed.* The modality, which may be verbal, pictorial, numerical, figural, symbolic, graphic, or any combination of these and other codes, will affect subjects' performance. The parameter of modality is important owing to the fact that the elaborative capacities revealed by subjects on any single modality may not reflect reliably their capacity if the task were presented in another modality. For example, a subject may be able to complete a mathematical operation successfully when the problem is presented in numbers and signs and fail when the same problem is presented in a verbal modality.

3. *The phase of the mental act.* The mental act can be broadly divided into three phases: *input, elaboration,* and *output.* Although there is an interrelationship among the three phases, a greater or lesser emphasis may be placed on one or another of them by the requirements of a particular mental

act. The isolation of the phase (and of the strengths and/or deficiencies of the cognitive functions it contains) helps to locate the sources of inadequate responses and to determine the nature and extent of mediation the examiner must provide.

4. *The cognitive operations required by the mental act.* A mental act is analyzed according to the rules or operations by which information is organized, transformed, manipulated, understood, and acted upon to generate new information. Operations may be relatively simple (e.g., identification or comparison) or complex (e.g., analogical thinking, transitive thinking, or logical multiplication).

5. *Level of complexity.* A mental act is analyzed according to the number of units of information upon which it centers, in conjunction with the degree of novelty or familiarity of the information to the subject.

6. *Level of abstraction.* The conceptual or cognitive distance between a given mental act and the object or event upon which it operates defines the level of abstraction. For example, the mental act involved in sorting by producing relationships among objects through perception and motor performance (i.e., concrete–abstract) represents a lower level of abstraction than does a mental act involving an analysis of the relationships among relationships (i.e., abstract–abstract).

7. *The level of efficiency with which a mental act is performed.* The level of efficiency of a mental act can be measured objectively by the rapidity and precision with which it is performed, and by the subjective criterion of the experienced amount of effort invested in the performance of the task. The level of efficiency is a function of the degree of crystallization of the mental act and the recency of its acquisition. Processes that are recently acquired and not yet automatized are more vulnerable and less resistant to a variety of interfering factors. Lack of efficiency may be due to difficulties in one or more of any of the other six parameters, as well as to a host of physical, environmental, affective, and motivational factors that may be transient and fleeting or more pervasive. This parameter is not to be confounded with the question of the subject's capacity, although in conventional psychometric procedures there is very frequently confusion between the two.

The cognitive map is used extensively during dynamic assessment and systematic cognitive intervention. It plays a critical role in the construction of materials, in their selection and manipulation during the assessment, in the mediated learning interventions, and in the interpretation of subjects' performances.

The relationship between the theory of structural cognitive modifiability and the learning potential assessment device is circular. To some extent the operational elements and theory of structural cognitive modifiability have been derived from our work with the learning potential assessment device, while the LPAD represents an application of the theory of structural cognitive modifiability.

Results of Using the IE Program Experimentally

Figures 42 and 43

Figures 42 and 43 (on the two pages that follow) provide a graphic summary of findings taken from a follow-up study by Professors Rand, Tannenbaum, and Feuerstein on the long-term effects of the IE program as it influenced adolescents classified as low-functioning and culturally deprived.

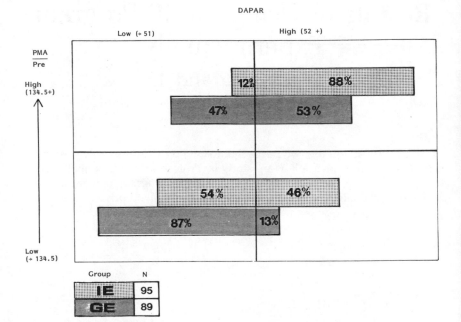

Figure 42. Instrumental enrichment: Follow-up study. Percentages in categories of PMA-pre and DAPAR-post (high vs. low) ($N = 184$). PMA = primary Mental Abilities test by Thurstone; DAPAR = an army intelligence test used in Israel; IE = instrumental enrichment, experimental group; GE = general enrichment, comparison group; and High and Low = means obtained by the total study populations on both tests. *Note*. All differences between IE and GE groups are statistically significant ($p < .01$).

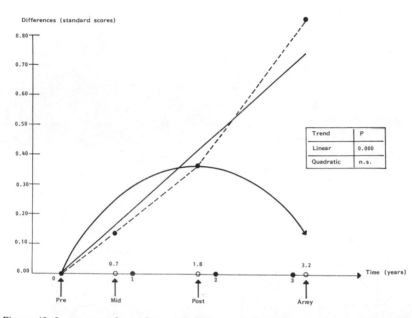

Figure 43. Instrumental enrichment: Follow-up study. Differences between IE and GE groups on PMA and DAPAR mean standard scores at pre, mid, post, and follow-up stages, versus linear and quadratic models ($N = 163$). This figure presents findings in terms of standardized difference (z) scores. The linear curve reflects theoretical differences if the differences increase continuously. The quadratic curve reflects what is usually found in intervention experiments after termination of the experimental program. The broken line represents the actual findings of the experiment. Results show that differences between IE and GE groups continue to increase over time, coming very close to the "ideal" linear curve.

Criteria for Observation of Mediated Learning Experience in Infancy and Early Childhood

As Suggested in a Study by

Pnina S. Klein
Bar-Ilan University, Ramat-Gan, Israel

INTENTIONALITY AND RECIPROCITY

Intentionality may take one, some, or all of the following forms:

- Verbal "reading" of the child's states (i.e., "You look as though you are going to sleep" or "You look wide awake"), then changing behavior in line with identified state.

- Making efforts to alter stimulation or way of toy or object presentation to meet the child's needs (e.g., changing distance from child, reduction of background disturbance, order of presentation, simplification, amplification).

- Reinforcing or "inviting" specific responses from the child.

- Catching and holding child's visual attention.

- Responding to child's vocalization or visual search.

- Repeating a sequence of movements with the intention of having the child focus on them or imitate them.

- Inviting expectations (leaving time or space between repeated actions waiting for response).

Reciprocity may be seen when a child invites a response from the adult and he/she responds. Invitation of response could be vocal or nonvocal (i.e.,

The criteria are based on the theoretical model of Reuven Feuerstein.

stress signs such as tensed body movements) or through positive invitation
(i.e., smiles and laughter desirable to caretaker).

- There is a mutual gaze between the child and the adult.
- Both child and adult focus on one stimulus.
- There is an actual observed behavior of the child in line with
mediation.

TRANSCENDENCE

Transcendence is seen when an adult uses, or creates, a situation in
which there is an immediate need for adult–child interaction that goes beyond the satisfaction of that need. For instance, mediating transcendence
during feeding could include mediating information about food, such as
taste, kind, temperature, where it comes from, what it does for the child, the
need to be thankful for food.

- Transcendence around bathing or diapering could include mediating
  the pleasure of being touched, handled, providing information about
  water, soap, parts of the body, temperature, space.
- Transcendence from the present situation and present needs into the
  past and future related to that situation.
- Mediation of space and time orientation: A child may carry out a task
  requiring temporal or spatial orientation but remain unaware as to the
  signs or methods of orientation in time and space unless these are
  mediated to him (i.e., setting stable landmarks for spatial orientation,
  such as window, door, building).
- Mediated critical interpretation: Reviewing collected information and
  posing questions (Is it possible? Is it correct?) on the basis of comparisons with previous experiences, testing hypotheses, and mediation
  of ways for seeking information (i.e., through an adult or other
  references).
- Mediated inductive and deductive reasoning.
- Mediation of comparative behavior: Demonstrating or encouraging the
  child to compare concretely or representationally, between objects or
  experiences.
- Mediation of short- and long-term memory: Pointing out strategies for
  improving remembering (i.e., clustering, quick repetition, classification, comparisons and contrasts, and the use of multisensory input).
- Mediation of strategies for memory search and recall (i.e., use of key
  words or parts of perceptions and associations).

MEDIATION OF MEANING

- Mediation of affect in relation to people, objects, and activities through facial expressions of excitement, variations in vocal intonation, repetition, utterance of a vocal sound of appreciation of wonder.
- Mediation of cultural values: Verbal or nonverbal in the above manners.
- Nonverbal signs of identification (i.e., pointing toward something, focusing one's eyes in attempting to focus child's eyes).
- Relating to past experience (i.e., "You have one like that at home," "Daddy brought you one," "It looks just like Susan's").
- Relating to future: Mediating the creation or definition of a goal for future activities.
- Mediation of cause and effect: Through repetition of cause–effect sequences with isolation and exaggeration of the links between the cause and the effect.
- Mediation of the meaning of learning: "It is fun to learn new things."

MEDIATED FEELINGS OF COMPETENCE

Verbal praise and encouragement ("Nice going!" "Great!" "Try to do it with me") or nonverbal encouragement (i.e., attentive looking, clapping hands, smiling or laughing to the child, in combination with

- Pointing out, verbally or nonverbally, the component or components within a particular sequence of behaviors, which led to success on a particular task and/or
- Scaling the child's success in performing against an adult's model or as compared with the child's previous experiences (i.e., "What you did is great, you are improving"—specifying in what way—or "Although it doesn't look exactly like David's picture, you did very well, you used many colors and you filled up almost the entire page").
- Mediation of competence around learning (i.e., "You learn fast").

MEDIATED REGULATION OF BEHAVIOR (IN PERCEIVING)

- Mediated orienting behavior: verbal and nonverbal (i.e., guiding child's focus with adult's eyes, guiding focus through pointing); mediated holding of attention (i.e., through repeated orientation attempts and variation in task).
- Mediation of the need for precision and accuracy in perception (as opposed to a fleeting perception or satisfaction with partially precise

perceptions): "Did you see what it was—a cow? Not exactly—let's look again."

- Mediating the need to organize perceptions (i.e., through verbal or other identification, sequencing in relation to other experiences, or simultaneous comparisons).

- Mediating the need to be systematic in exploration of a stimulus field (the need for planning, i.e., scanning a visual field systematically).

MEDIATED REGULATION OF BEHAVIOR (IN PROCESSING INFORMATION)

- Mediating definition of the problem prior to any attempt to solve it.

- Mediation of the need to explore possibilities for a solution prior to any attempt to solve the problem.

- Mediation of a plan of action when solution of a problem appears to require more than one or two steps.

MEDIATED REGULATION OF BEHAVIOR (IN EXPRESSIVE BEHAVIOR)

- Mediating inhibition and control: mediating the need to think before acting (i.e., adjusting the speed of actions needed to the characteristics of the task); weighing task demands against child's abilities, and expressing the need for an active and systmatic search for a solution.

- Mediating the need for precision in output as opposed to responses vaguely meeting task demands.

- Mediating the need for nonegocentric responses (e.g., rewarding socially acceptable behaviors).

- Mediating ways to avoid blockage of responses (e.g., through pointing out of the availability of other paths to achieve an objective).

- Provoking requests for mediation (i.e., creating situations in which the child is encouraged to ask for adult's assistance or to ask questions).

- Mediating the need to express oneself in a way that will be acceptable and understandable by others (e.g., "I want wa wa." "What do you want? Say it so the lady will understand. Ask her for *water*").

Examples of Content Based on the Special Friends Curriculum

How Do We Play Together?

Discuss how friends take turns, say nice things to each other, help each other out when a task is hard, stay close to each other when playing, smile at each other, and so forth. In other words, the cooperative interaction techniques that they have been taught to apply during the integrated activities can be discussed and elaborated upon during discussion sessions.

How Do We Communicate?

Discuss communication and guidelines for using it effectively (eye contact, talk slowly, allow time for a response, try another way if your friend does not understand you, and don't give up). Nonverbal communication, such as the use of often-used, simple manual signs (e.g., "hello," "good," "you," "me") can be introduced as well.

What Is a Prosthesis?

Discuss the use of tools (e.g., ladder, paintbrush) that nondisabled people need in order to do tasks (e.g., paint a house) they would not be able to do or do as well without the tools. Show examples of protheses—such as an artificial foot—and explain how they are like tools that everyone uses.

Voeltz, L. J., Hemphill, N J , Brown, S., Kishi, G., Klein, R., Fruehling, R., Collie, J., Levy, G., & Kube, C. (1983). *The Special Friends Program: A Trainer's Manual for Integrated School Settings* (rev. ed.). Honolulu: University of Hawaii Department of Special Education.

How Does a Person with a Disability Live?

Invite a person with a disability to come and talk about where he lives, how he moves from home to work, what he does on weekends, and so forth. Provide ample opportunity for questions.

What Is a Friend?

Discuss friendship in general. Ask participants to think about similarities and differences in their relationship with their special friend and their best friend.

Why Integration?

What are the benefits of integration for them? Discuss the positive and problematic aspects of having their special friend in their lunchroom and classes.

Resources

Appendix G is designed to be a guide for parents, teachers, educators, and other interested persons. It provides an introduction to relevant publications, organizations, agencies, and commercial outlets that are available for educational use with people who have retarded performance.

The reader should consider the following in perusing the resources:

1. The literature is just a sample of what is available; it is *not* an exhaustive list.
2. Any list of resources becomes outdated very rapidly.
3. Almost all of the books and articles listed are printed in English. A wealth of literature exists in other languages, such as French, German, and Hebrew.
4. Most of the organizations listed are located in the United States. Similar organizations exist in a variety of countries.
5. The part on selected vendors of equipment, supplies, etc., should *not* be regarded as an advertisement for, or endorsement of, any of the resources mentioned.

SCM THEORY, MLE, LPAD, IE

Books, Chapters, Articles

Feuerstein, R. (1970). A dynamic approach to the causation, prevention, and alleviation of retarded performance. In H. C. Haywood (Ed.), *Sociocultural aspects of mental retardation* (pp. 341–377). New York: Appleton-Century-Crofts.

This paper relates retarded performance to dynamic assessment, using LPAD.

Feuerstein, R., & Rand, Y. (1974). Mediated learning experience: An outline of the proximal etiology for differential development of cognitive functions. In L. Goldfein (Ed.), *International understanding: Cultural differences in the development of cognitive processes* (pp. 7–37).

This article lays the basis for the concept of mediated learning experience (MLE) and its implications for the development of individuals who are culturally deprived and/or have retarded performance.

Feuerstein, R., Rand, Y., & Hoffman, M. (1979). *The dynamic assessment of retarded performers: The learning potential assessment device, theory, instruments, and techniques.* Baltimore: University Park Press.

This textbook provides a thorough, detailed, and technical description of the SCM theory and its correlaries. Topics include passive acceptance versus active modification, administration procedures for the learning potential assessment device (LPAD), samples of the assessment tools, and other subjects.

Feuerstein, R., Rand, Y., Hoffman, M., Hoffman, M., & Miller, R. (1979). Cognitive modifiability in retarded adolescents: Effects of instrumental enrichment. *American Journal of Mental Deficiency, 83*(6), 539–550.

In this paper, empirical findings are presented on the efficiency of the IE program with low-functioning adolescents.

Feuerstein, R., Rand, Y., Hoffman, M., & Miller, R. (1980). *Instrumental enrichment: An intervention program for cognitive modifiability.* Baltimore: University Park Press.

This textbook's emphasis is on the instrumental enrichment (IE) program. Detailed descriptions of each of the 14 instruments are offered, along with details about mediated learning techniques to make IE effective.

Haywood, C., & Wachs, T. (1981). Intelligence, cognition, and individual differences. In M. Begab, C. Haywood, & H. Garber (Eds.), *Psychosocial influences in retarded performance* (pp. 95–126). Baltimore: University Park Press.

This chapter compares the SCM approach to other cognitive approaches, such as Piaget's, and examines the contribution of genetic and environmental factors to intellectual development.

Klein, P., & Feuerstein, R. (1985). Environmental variables and cognitive development. In S. Harel & N. Anastasiow (Eds.), *The at-risk infant: Psycho/social/medical aspects* (pp. 369–377). Baltimore: Brookes.

This paper presents evidence of the effectiveness of MLE for young children with mild disabilities who live in high-risk environments. Included also are details about the five basic criteria of MLE for young children.

Rand, Y., Tannenbaum, A. J., & Feuerstein, R. (1979). Effects of instrumental enrichment on the psycho-educational development of low-functioning adolescents. *Journal of Educational Psychology, 83,* 539–550.

This article describes how the IE program was used effectively with adolescents with retarded performance.

Savell, J., Twolig, P., & Rachford, D. (1986). Empirical status of Feuerstein's "instrumental enrichment" (FIE) technique as a method of teaching thinking skills. *Review of Educational Research, 56,* 381–409.

This article offers a very thorough (and highly technical) review of research findings resulting from the experimental use of the IE program on a worldwide basis.

Organizations

Inquiries about obtaining training in the use of IE and LPAD materials or ordering the IE instruments should be addressed to Professor Reuven Feuerstein, Director; Hadassah–WIZO–Canada Research Institute, 6 Karmon Street, Beit Hakerem, P.O. Box 3160, Jerusalem, 96308, Israel.

DOWN SYNDROME

Books, Chapters, Articles

Lane, D., & Stratford, B. (1985). *Current approaches to Down syndrome*. New York: Holt, Rinehart & Winston.

An excellent overview of knowledge and research concerning people with Down syndrome from birth to adulthood. Technical in spots, this book overall is very readable.

Pueschel, S. (1988). *The young person with Down syndrome: Transition from adolescence to adulthood*. Baltimore: Brookes.

This book emphasizes the transition from adolescence to adulthood and constitutes a practical guide for intervention in the areas of physical, social, mental, and emotional development. It is "parent friendly."

Pueschel, S., Tingey, C., Rynders, J., Crocker, A., & Crutcher, D. (Eds.). (1987). *New perspectives on Down syndrome*. Baltimore: Brookes.

Based on a national conference on Down syndrome that was sponsored by the Office of Special Education and Rehabilitative Services, Washington, D.C., this book provides a comprehensive look at research findings and "best practices" for people with Down syndrome in the United States.

Rynders, J. (1987). History of Down syndrome: Need for a new perspective. In S. Pueschel, C. Tingey, J. Rynders, A. Crocker, & D. Crutcher (Eds.), *New perspectives on Down syndrome* (pp. 1–17). Baltimore: Brookes.

This chapter approaches the history of Down syndrome from a values-oriented perspective.

Rynders, J., & Horrobin, J. (1984). *To give an EDGE: A guide for new parents of children with Down's syndrome* (2nd ed.). Minneapolis: Colwell Industries.

Now in its seventh printing, this useful handbook for parents is available from Colwell Industries, c/o M. Colwell, 123 North 3rd Street, Minneapolis, MN 55401.

Rynders, J., Johnson, R., Johnson, D., & Schmidt, B. (1980). Producing positive interaction among Down syndrome and nonhandicapped teenagers through cooperative goal structuring. *American Journal of Mental Deficiency, 85,* 268–273.

This research article provides evidence that structuring leisure activities for cooperative learning produces increases not only in positive child-to-child social interactions but in attitudinal dimensions too.

Stray-Gunderson, K. (1986). *Babies with Down syndrome: A new parent's guide.* Kensignton, MD: Woodbine House.

A comprehensive and sensitively written book that will be especially helpful to new parents of a baby with Down syndrome.

Organizations

National Down Syndrome Congress
1800 Dempster Street
Park Ridge, IL 60068

This outstanding parent-professional organization publishes a newsletter for parents (the *Down Syndrome News*), holds a national convention every year, and has been effective in promoting national legislation and advocating the rights of people with Down syndrome.

THE EARLY YEARS

Books, Chapters, Articles

Bricker, D. (1982). *Intervention with at-risk and handicapped infants.* Baltimore: University Park Press.

A book written in a technical fashion, it is an excellent compendium of research findings. It is one of the few technical references devoted entirely to infants.

Clarke, A. M., & Clarke, A. D. B. (1975). *Mental deficiency: The changing outlook.* New York: Free Press.

This book provides a thorough overview of ongoing research that helps to define mental retardation.

Connor, F., Williamson, G., & Siepp, J. (1978). *Program guide for infants and toddlers with neuromotor and other developmental disabilities.* New York, Teachers College of Columbia.

In this valuable book for teachers who have young children with cerebral palsy and other movement disabilities, the section on assessment and lesson planning is especially useful.

Deiner, P. (1983). *Resources for teaching young children with special needs.* New York: Harcourt Brace Jovanovich.

This is an easily understood book of helpful, practical ideas about stimulating young children who have a variety of disabilities with differing levels of severity.

Klein, P. (1980). *Human modifiability and the development of intelligence: An outlook for the future.* Ramat-Gan, Israel: Bar-Ilan University.

This book provides a comprehensive look at research surrounding the issue of human modifiability as it relates to cognition.

Rand, Y. (1980). Parent education and cognitive development in children: An issue in educational policy. In P. Klein (Ed.), *Human modifiability and the development of intelligence: An outlook for the future* (pp. 123–136). Ramat-Gan, Israel: Bar-Ilan University.

This article is one of the few that examines educational policy as it relates to the parents' role in stimulating their child's cognitive development.

Rynders, J., & Stealey, D. (1985). Early education: A strategy for producing a less (least) restrictive environment for young children with severe handicaps. In R. Bruininks & C. Lakin (Eds.), *Living and learning in the least restrictive alternative.* Baltimore: Brookes.

This chapter reviews the research on the effectiveness of early education for young children with a variety of severe disabilities.

Schiefelbusch, R. L., & Lloyd, L. L. (Eds.). (1974). *Language perspectives—Acquisition, retardation, and intervention.* Baltimore: University Park Press.

This book contains a series of articles pertaining to all kinds of issues in the area of language acquisition and its development in individuals who have retarded performance.

Wollins, M., & Gottesman, M. (Eds.). (1971). *Group care: An Israeli approach.* New York: Gordon & Breach.

Emphasizing the importance of the environment as an instrument for modifying and shaping the individual under various life conditions, this book contains a series of helpful chapters.

SCHOOL YEARS: INTEGRATION AND INDIVIDUALIZATION

Books, Chapters, Articles

Campbell, P. (1985). *Integrated therapy and educational programming for students with severe handicaps.* Akron, OH: Children's Hospital Medical Center of Akron.

This article describes how effective programming depends on the integration of therapeutic with instructional programming, promoting increasing student independence.

Fraser, B., & Hensinger, R. (1983). *Managing physical handicaps: A practical guide for parents, care providers and educators.* Baltimore: Brookes.

Useful information about physical disabilities is followed by practical techniques and tips for communication, handling, and movement of people with movement problems.

Reichle, J., & Keogh, W. (1985). Communication intervention: A selective review of what, when, and how to teach. In S. Warren & A. Rogers-Warren (Eds.), *Teaching functional language: Generalization and maintenance of language skills* (pp. 25–29). Baltimore: University Park Press.

This chapter is a comprehensive review of factors that need to be considered in choosing and using various communication intervention strategies. Emphasis is on functional use of communication.

Reynolds, M. C., & Birch, J. W. (1988). *Adaptive mainstreaming: A primer for teachers and principals.* White Plains, NY: Longmans.

This textbook provides suggestions on how special and vocational educators can work together to help prepare handicapped students for the world of work.

Schulz, J., & Turnbull, A. (1983). *Mainstreaming handicapped students: A guide for classroom teachers* (2nd ed.). Boston: Allyn and Bacon.

This volume provides basic information on disabling conditions, individualized planning, creating educational accommodations in academic and other curricular areas, and implementing individualized programs. The book is especially suited for regular education personnel who are just beginning to move into mainstreaming.

Snell, M. (1987). *Systematic instruction of persons with severe handicaps* (3rd ed.). Columbus, OH: Merrill.

This book is very well written and covers critical areas of instructing people with severe disabilities. Based on principles of behavior modification, topics covered include assessment, intervention strategies, handling medical emergencies, transporting people with severe movement difficulties, recreation, communication, functional academics, and employment.

POSTSCHOOL YEARS: WORKING, INDEPENDENT LIVING, LEISURE

Books, Chapters, Articles

Edwards, J. (1987). Living options for persons with Down syndrome. In S. Pueschel, C. Tingey, J. Rynders, A. Crocker, & D. Crutcher (Eds.), *New perspectives on Down syndrome* (pp. 337–354). Baltimore: Brookes.

This chapter discusses supported living and other programming techniques that promote community independence.

Hardman, M., Drew, C., & Egan, M. (1984). Adult and aging factors in exceptionality. In M. Hardman, C. Drew, & M. Egan (Eds.), *Human exceptionality: Society, school and family* (pp. 459–489). Boston: Allyn & Bacon.

This article provides a good discussion of "learned helplessness" and outlines strategies to avoid and/or overcome the problem.

Kokaska, C., & Brolin, D. (1985). *Career education for handicapped individuals* (2nd ed.). Columbus, OH: Merrill.

This book presents career education as a whole-life process for individuals with handicaps. Topics include teaching daily living skills, personal-social skills, and occupational skills, career and vocational assessment, and conducting career education programs.

Rusch, F., Chadsey-Rusch, J., & Lagomarcino, T. (1987). Preparing students for employment. In M. Snell (Ed.), *Systematic instruction of persons with severe handicaps* (3rd ed., pp. 471–490). Columbus, OH: Merrill.

A chapter that covers curriculum development, and employment models such as supported work, it moves to the important topic of the transition from school to work.

Schleien, S., & Ray, M. (1988). *Community recreation and persons with disabilities: Strategies for integration.* Baltimore: Brookes.

This book not only provides a compelling rationale for integrated community programming, it outlines a comprehensive plan for implementing such a program successfully, including how to inventory the community environment for obstacles, do a task analysis for a recreational activity, and build service networks.

Weisgerber, R. A. (1978). *Vocational education: Teaching the handicapped in regular classes.* Reston, VA: Council for Exceptional Children.

This book is designed to help vocational educators appreciate the regular class as a success-oriented climate for developing group and individualized instruction.

CUTTING ACROSS THE WHOLE LIFE SPAN AND ALL DISABILITY AREAS

Selected National Organizations

Alexander Graham Bell Association for the Deaf, Inc.
3417 Volta Place, N.W.
Washington, DC 20007

American Association on Mental Retardation
5101 Wisconsin Avenue
Washington, DC 20016

American Foundation for the Blind, Inc.
15 West Sixteenth Street
New York, NY 10011

American Psychological Association
1200 Seventeenth Street, N.W.
Washington, DC 20036

American Speech and Hearing Association
10801 Rockville Pike
Rockville, MD 20852

Association for Children and Adults with Learning Disabilities
4156 Library Road
Pittsburgh, PA 15234

The Association for Persons with Severe Handicaps
7010 Roosevelt Way, N.E.
Seattle, WA 98115

Association for Retarded Citizens
2501 Avenue J
Arlington, TX 76006

Council for Exceptional Children
1920 Association Drive
Reston, VA 22091

Cystic Fibrosis Foundation
3379 Peachtree Road, N.E.
Atlanta, GA 30326

Epilepsy Foundation of America
4351 Garden City Drive
Suite 406
Landover, MD 20785

Information Center for Individuals with Disabilities
20 Providence Street
Room 329
Boston, MA 02116

Muscular Dystrophy Association, Inc.
810 Seventh Avenue
New York, NY 10019

National Amputation Foundation
12-45 150th Street
Whitestone, NY 11357

National Association for the Visually Handicapped
305 East 24th Street
New York, NY 10010

National Association of Developmental Disabilities Councils
1234 Massachusetts Avenue, N.W.
Suite 103
Washington, DC 20005

National Association of the Deaf
814 Thayer Avenue
Silver Spring, MD 20910

National Easter Seal Society
2023 West Ogden Avenue
Chicago, IL 60612

National Epilepsy League
6 North Michigan Avenue
Chicago, IL 60602

National Federation of the Blind
1346 Connecticut Avenue, N.W., Suite 1346
Washington, DC 20036

National Foundation
March of Dimes
1275 Mamaroneck Avenue
White Plains, NY 10605

National Handicapped Sports and Recreation Association
4405 East-West Highway
Suite 603
Bethesda, MD 20814

National Head Injury Foundation
280 Singletary Lane
Framingham, MA 01701

National Information Center on Deafness
Gallaudet College
Kendall Green
Washington, DC 20002

National Multiple Sclerosis Society
205 East 42nd Street
New York, NY 10017

National Paraplegia Foundation
333 North Michigan Avenue
Chicago, IL 60601

National Recreation and Park
    Association
3101 Park Center Drive
Alexandria, VA 22302

National Society for Autistic Children
1234 Massachusetts Ave., N.W.
Suite 1017
Washington, DC 20005

National Society for the Prevention of
    Blindness, Inc.
79 Madison Avenue
New York, NY 10016

National Spinal Cord Injury
    Foundation
369 Elliot Street
Newton Upper Falls, MA 02164

National Therapeutic Recreation
    Society
3101 Park Center Drive
Alexandria, VA 22302

United Cerebral Palsy Association
66 East 34th Street
New York, NY 10016

Selected Vendors of Equipment and Supplies

Achievement Products
P.O. Box 547
Mineola, NY 11501

Sells many types of equipment, including items for positioning and adaptive feeding, and devices for early intervention programs.

Adaptive Equipment Company
11443 Chapin Road
Chesterland, OH 44026

Produces such products as adaptive chairs, prone boards, and bolsters.

American Guidance Service
Publishers' Building
Circle Pines, MN 55014

Produces instructional materials and assessment devices for people with handicaps of all ages.

Beckley-Cardy
1900 North Narragansett
Chicago, IL 60639

A good source for rhythm instruments and phonograph records.

Blue Grass Industries
Carlisle, KY 40311

Sells the Speedo Aqualift Swimsuit.

Childcraft Education Corp.
20 Kilmer Road
Edison, NJ 08817

Distributes adaptive eating utensils.

Community Playthings
Rifton, NY 12471

Produces specialized equipment for play and other needs of physically handicapped preschoolers, such as wooden toys and furniture.

Constructive Playthings
11100 Harry Hines Boulevard
Dallas, TX 75229

Manufactures curriculum materials, supplies, and equipment for early education purposes.

Cuisenaire Co. of America Inc.
12 Church Street
Box D
New Rochelle, NY 10805

Offers small wooden rods to use for early mathematics experiences.

Developmental Learning Materials
P.O. Box 4000
One DLM Park
Allen, TX 75002

Publishes teaching aids for skill development in communication and preacademic skills.

Edmark Associates
P.O. Box 3903
Bellevue, WA 98009

Publishes field-tested instructional materials for use with young children.

Everest and Jennings Inc.
1803 Pontius Avenue
Los Angeles, CA 90025

Sells the Zygo Communicator, an electronic visual communicator. The visual board can be controlled via touch, breathing, biting, etc.

Flaghouse Inc.
18 W. 18th Street
New York, NY 10011

Manufacturer of an exercise bike, game equipment (basketball, baseball, floor hockey), floor seat, shatterproof mirrors, weights, folding mats.

High/Scope Press
600 North River Street
Ypsilanti, MI 48197

Publishes materials emphasizing cognitive approaches to educating children.

Love Publishing Company
1777 South Bellaire Street
Denver, CO 80222

Publishes materials for professional development in assessment, intervention, and working with parents.

Motor Development Equipment Co.
P.O. Box 4054
Downey, CA 90241

Distributor of such items as prone boards and balance boards.

North American Recreation Convertibles, Inc.
33 Knowton Street
P.O. Box 758
Bridgeport, CT 06601

Offers net climbers, hollow building blocks, sand tables, crawl tunnel, hand-grip bowling balls, bowling ramps.

Pro-Ed
5341 Industrial Oaks Boulevard
Austin, TX 78735

Offers tests and other materials.

Pull-Buoy, Inc.
2511 Leach
Auburn Heights, MI 48057

Markets such products as aquatic kickboards.

Reader's Digest Services, Inc.
Educational Division
Pleasantville, NY 10570

Provides readiness materials.

Reading Joy
P.O. Box 404
Naperville, IL 60540

Produces games to develop prereading skills.

Research Press
Box 31773
Champaign, IL 61821

Offers materials for promoting language and self-help skills in young children.

SRA
Science Research Associates, Inc.
155 North Wacker Drive
Chicago, IL 60606

Publishes the DISTAR basal programs in language, reading, and arithmetic for young children with serious reading problems.

Weekly Reader Skills Book
1250 Fairwood Avenue
P.O. Box 16618
Columbus, OH 43216

Publishes basic language arts material for elementary education students.

References

CHAPTER 1

1. Feuerstein R., Rand Y., & Hoffman M. (1979). *The dynamic assessment of retarded performers: The learning potential assessment device—Theory, instruments and techniques.* Baltimore: University Park Press.
2. Feuerstein R., Rand Y., Hoffman M., & Miller R. (1980). *Instrumental enrichment: An intervention program for cognitive modifiability.* Baltimore: University Park Press.
3. Frankenstein C. (1968). *Psychodynamics of externalization: Life from without.* Baltimore: Williams and Wilkins.

CHAPTER 2

1. Scheerenberger, R. C. (1982). Treatment from ancient times to the present. In P. T. Cegelka & H. J. Prehm (Eds.), *Mental retardation—From categories to people.* Toronto: Charles E. Merill.
2. Itard, J. M. (1806). *The wild boy of Aveyron* (G. & M. Humphrey, Trans.). New York: Appleton-Century-Crofts.
3. Seguin, E. (1866). *Idiocy and its treatment by the physiological method.* New York: William Wood.
4. Farell E. (1908). Special classes in the New York City schools. *Journal of Psycho-Asthenics, 13,* 91–96.
5. Fernald, W. (1912). The burden of feeblemindedness. *Journal of Psycho-Asthenics, 17,* 87–111.
6. Goddard, H. (1912). *The Kallikak family: A study in the heredity of feeblemindedness.* New York: Macmillan.
7. Goddard, H. (1928). Feeblemindedness: A question of definition. *Journal of Psycho-Asthenics, 33,* 219–227.
8. Skeels, H. (1942). A study of the effects of differential stimulation of mentally retarded children: A follow-up report. *American Journal of Mental Deficiency, 46,* 340–350.
9. Gold, M. (1973). Factors affecting production by the retarded: Base rate. *Mental Retardation, 11,* 41–45.
10. Bellamy, T., & Buttars, K. L. (1975). Teaching trainable level students to count

money: Toward personal independence through academic instruction. *Education and Training of the Mentally Retarded, 10*, 18–26.

11. Bellamy, G. T., Wilson, D. J., Adler, E., & Clarke, J. Y. (1980). A strategy for programming vocational skills for severely handicapped youth. *Exceptional Education Quarterly, 1*(2), 85–97.

12. Wehman, P., & Hill, J. W. (1980). *Instructional programming for severely handicapped youth: A community integration approach.* Richmond, Virginia Commonwealth University.

13. Rusch, F., Chadney Rusch, J., & Lagomarcino, T. (1987). Preparing students for employment. In M. Snell (Ed.), *Systematic instruction of persons with severe handicaps* (3rd ed., pp. 471–490). Columbus, OH: Charles E. Merril.

14. Cottam, P., & Sutton, A. (1986). *Conductive education: A system for overcoming motor disorder.* London: Croom Helm.

15. Feuerstein, R. (1970). A dynamic approach to the causation, prevention and alleviation of retarded performance. In H. C. Haywood (Ed.), *Socio-cultural aspects of mental retardation* (pp. 341–377). New York: Appleton-Century-Crofts.

16. Hari, M. (1968). Address given at Conductive Education Conference on the Petö Method, Castle Prevy College, Wallingford, Oxford.

17. Picq, L., & Vayer, P. (1976). Education, pscho-motrice et arrieration mentale. Paris: DOIN.

18. Sutton, A. (1984). Conductive education in the Midlands, Summer 1982: Progress and problems in the importation of an educational method. *Educational Studies, 10*(2), 121–130.

CHAPTER 3

1. Feuerstein, R., & Krasilowsky, D. (1967). The treatment groups technique. *Israel Annals of Psychiatry and Related Disciplines, 5* (1), 61–90.

2. Arieli, M., & Feuerstein, R. (1987). The two-fold care organization: On the combining of group and foster care. *Child and Youth Care Quarterly, 16*(3).

3. Feuerstein, R., Krasilowsky, D., & Rand, Y. (1974). Innovative educational strategies for the integration of high-risk adolescents in Israel. *Phi Delta Kappan, 55*(8), 1–6.

4. Rey, A. (1968). *Epreuves mnemoniques d'apprentissage.* La Chaux-de-Fonds: Delachaux & Niestle.

5. Feuerstein, R., Richelle, M., & Rey, A. (1963). *Children of the Melah. Socio-cultural deprivation and its educational significance. The North-African Jewish child.* Jerusalem: Szold Foundation for Child and Youth Welfare (Hebrew).

6. Spitz, H. H. (1986). *The raising of intelligence.* Hillsdale, NJ: Erlbaum.

7. Reynold, C. R. (1987). Raising intelligence: Clever Hans, Candidec, and the miracle in Milwaukee. *Journal of School Psychology, 23*, 309–312.

CHAPTER 4

1. Gerber, M. (1985). A less stressful way of caring for infants. *Kiddie Kare, November/December*, 9–12.

2. Bruner, J. (1980). NIE Conference, Pittsburgh, Pennsylvania.

CHAPTER 5

1. Smilansky, S., Shephatia, L., & Frankel, E. (1976). *Mental development of infants from two ethnic groups.* Jerusalem: Henrietta Szold Foundation.
2. Bettelheim, B. (1950). *Love is not enough: The treatment of emotionally disturbed children.* Glencoe, IL: Free Press.
3. Emerson, L. E. (1986, August). *Feuerstein cognitive education theory and American Indian education.* Paper presented at the Mediated Learning Experience International Workshop, Jerusalem, Israel.
4. Lesser, G. H., Fifer, G., & Clark, D. H. (1965). Mental abilities of children from different social class and cultural groups. *Monographs of the Society for Research in Child Development, 30*(Whole No. 102).
5. Hunt, J. McV. (1961). *Intelligence and experience.* New York: Ronald Press.
6. Aebli, H. (1963). *Über die geistige Entwicklung des Kindes.* Stuttgart: Klitt.
7. Dennis, W. (1960). Causes of retardation among institutional children: Iran. *Journal of Genetic Psychology, 96,* 47–59.
8. Dennis, W. (1973). *Children of the crèche.* Englewood Cliffs, NJ: Prentice-Hall.
9. Flavell, J. (1963). *The developmental psychology of Jean Piaget.* Princeton: Van Nostrand.
10. Elkind, D. (1967). Cognition in infancy and early childhood. In Y. Brackbill (Ed.), *Infancy and early childhood* (pp. 361–394). New York: Free Press.

CHAPTER 6

1. Feuerstein, R., & Hoffman, M. B. (1982). Intergenerational conflict of rights: Cultural imposition and self-realization. Viewpoints in teaching and learning. *Journal of School Education, 58*(1), 44–63.

CHAPTER 7

1. Bert, C. (1983). *Le Monde de l'education,* 51–52.

CHAPTER 8

1. Fishler, K., Share, J., & Koch, R. (1964). Adaptation of Gesell Developmental Scales for evaluation of development in children with Down's syndrome (mongolism). *American Journal of Mental Deficiency, 68,* 642–646.
2. Hilgard, E. *et al.* (1979). *Introduction to psychology* (7th ed., p. 320). New York: Harcourt Brace Jovanovich.
3. Down, J. L. H. (1866). Observations on an ethnic classification of idiots. *London Hospital, Clinical Lectures and Reports, 3,* 259–262.

4. Shuttleworth, G. E. (1886). Clinical lecture on idiocy and imbecility. *British Medical Journal*, 1, 183.
5. *Encyclopedia Britannica*. (1970).
6. Crookshank, F. (1924). *The mongol in our midst*. London: Kegan, Paul, Treuch & Trubner.
7. Bard, B., & Fletcher, J. (1968). The right to die. *Atlantic Monthly*, April, 59–64.
8. Centerwall, S., & Centerwall, W. (1960). A study of children with mongolism reared in the home compared to those reared away from the home. *Pediatrics*, 25, 678–685.
9. Stedman, D., & Eichorn, D. (1964). A comparison of the growth and development of institutionalized and home-reared mongoloids during infancy and early childhood. *Journal of Mental Deficiency*, 69, 391–401.
10. Adams, M. (1969). Siblings of the retarded: Their problems and treatment. In W. Wolfensberger & R. Kurtz (Eds.), *Management of the family of the mentally retarded* (pp. 444–452). Chicago: Follett.
11. Jones, O. (1977). Mother–child communication with prelinguistic Down's syndrome and normal infants. In H. R. Schaffer (Ed.), *Studies in mother–child interaction*. New York: Academic Press.
12. Cicchetti, D., & Sroufe, L. (1976). The relationship between affective and cognitive development in Down's syndrome infants. *Child Development*, 47, 920–929.
13. Mans, L., Cicchetti, C., & Sroufe, L. (1978). Mirror reactions of Down's syndrome infants and toddlers: Cognitive underpinnings of self-recognition. *Child Development*, 49, 1247–1250.
14. Bidder, R., Bryant, G., & Gray, O. (1975). Benefits to Down's syndrome children through training their mothers. *Archives of Disease in Childhood*, 50, 383–386.
15. Jeffree, D., Wheldall, K., & Mittler, P. (1973). Facilitating two-word utterances in two Down's syndrome boys. *American Journal of Mental Deficiency*, 78, 117–122.
16. MacDonald, J., Blott, J., Gordon, K., Spiegel, B., & Hartmann, M. (1974). An experimental parent-assisted treatment program for preschool language-delayed children. *Journal of Speech and Hearing Disorders*, 39(4), 395–415.
17. Piper, M., & Pless, I. (1980). Early intervention for infants with Down syndrome: A controlled trial. *Pediatrics*, 65, 463–468.
18. Pothier, P., Morrison, D., & Gorman, F. (1974). Effects of receptive language training on receptive and expressive language development. *Journal of Abnormal Child Psychology*, 2, 153–164.
19. Rynders, J., & Horrobin, J. M. (1980). Educational provisions for young children with Down's syndrome. In J. Gottlieb (Ed.), *Educating mentally retarded persons in the mainstream*. Baltimore: University Park Press.
20. Aronson, M., & Fallstrom, K. (1977). Immediate and long-term effects of developmental training in children with Down's syndrome. *Developmental Medicine and Child Neurology*, 19, 489–494.
21. Harris, S. (1981). Effects of neurodevelopmental therapy on motor performance of infants with Down's syndrome. *Developmental Medicine and Child Neurology*, 23, 477–483.
22. Rynders, J., & Stealey, D. (1985). Early education: A strategy for producing a less (least) restrictive environment for young children with severe handicaps. In K.

Lakin & R. Bruininks (Eds.), *Strategies for achieving community integration of developmentally disabled citizens*. Baltimore: Brookes.

CHAPTER 9

1. Berry, P., Gunn, V., & Andrews, R. (1984). Development of Down's syndrome children from birth to five years. In J. Berg (Ed.), *Perspectives and progress in mental retardation* (Vol. 1). Baltimore: University Park Press.
2. Down, J. L. (1866). *Clinical lectures and reports*. London: London Hospital.
3. Restak, R. (1975). Genetic counseling for defective parents: The danger of knowing too much. *Psychology Today, 9*(21), 92–93.
4. Rynders, J., Spiker, D., & Horrobin, J. M. (1978). Underestimating the educability of Down's syndrome children: Examination of methodological problems in recent literature. *American Journal of Mental Deficiency, 82*, 440–448.
5. Brown, L., Jones, S., Troccolo, E., Heiser, C., Bellamy, T., & Sontag, E. (1972). Teaching functional reading to young trainable students: Toward longitudinal objectives. *Journal of Special Education, 3*, 237–246.
6. Dalton, A., Rubino, C., & Hislop, M. (1973). Some effects of token rewards on school achievement of children with Down's syndrome. *Journal of Applied Behavior Analysis, 6*, 251–259.
7. Miller, J. (1987). Language and communication characteristics of children with Down syndrome. In S. Pueschel, C. Tingey, J. Rynders, A. Crocker, & D. Crutcher (Eds.), *New perspectives on Down syndrome* (pp. 233–262). Baltimore: Brookes.
8. Till, M., Rynders, J., Messer, L., & Rynders, P. (1985). Review of "Home dental care: An audio visual training program for parents of children with handicaps." *Exceptional Children, 52*, 181–184.
9. Rynders, J., Behlen, K., & Horrobin, M. (1979). Performance characteristics of preschool Down's syndrome children receiving augmented or repetitive verbal instruction. *American Journal of Mental Deficiency, 84*, 67–73.
10. Penrose, L. S. (1949). The incidence of mongolism in the general population. *Journal of Mental Science, 95*, 685.
11. Smith, G. F. (1975). Present approaches to therapy in Down's syndrome. In R. Koch & F. F. de la Cruz (Eds.), *Down's syndrome (mongolism): Research, prevention, and management*. New York: Brunner/Mazel.
12. Wehman, P., & Schleien, S. (1981). *Leisure programs for handicapped persons: Adaptations, techniques, and curriculum*. Austin, TX: Pro-Ed.
13. Rynders, J., Johnson, R., Johnson, D., & Schmidt, B. (1980). Effects of cooperative goal structuring in producing positive interaction between Down syndrome and nonhandicapped teenagers: Implications for mainstreaming. *American Journal of Mental Deficiency, 85*, 268–273.
14. Johnson, D. W., & Johnson, R. (1975). *Learning together and alone: Cooperation, competition, and individualization*. Englewood Cliffs, NJ: Prentice-Hall.
15. Pendler, B. (1979). My daughter is leaving home. What do I do now? *Exceptional Parent, 9*, 14–16.
16. Ellis, W. G., McCulloch, J. R., & Corley, C. L. (1974). Presenile dementia in Down's

syndrome: Ultrastructural identity with Alzheimer's disease. *Neurology, 24,* 101–106.

17. Benda, C. E. (1969). *Down's syndrome: Mongolism and its management.* New York: Grune and Stratton.
18. Dybwad, G., & Dybwad, R. (1977). A personalized situation report: Lifestyles of individuals with severe intellectual deficits. *International Child Welfare Review, 32,* 55–61.
19. Smith, G. F., & Berg, J. M. (1976). *Down's anomaly.* New York: Churchill Livingston.
20. Corcoran, E. L. (1979). Campus life for retarded citizens. *Education Unlimited, 1,* 22–24.
21. Nelson, M. (1978). Educational achievements of Down's syndrome children. *Down Syndrome News, 2,* 142–143.
22. Wieck, C. (1979). David Kaul. *Education Unlimited, 1,* 29–32.
23. Lewis, M. (1979). Horticulture—A therapy that leads toward independence. *Down Syndrome News, 10,* 134–135.
24. Gold, M. (1980). Personal communication.
25. Bellamy, G. T., Rhodes, L. E., Wilcox, B., Ablin, J., Mank, D. M., Boles, S. M., Horner, R. H., Collins, M., & Turner, J. (1984). *Quality and equality in employment services for adults with severe disabilities.* Unpublished manuscript, University of Oregon—Eugene.
26. U.S. Department of Health and Human Services. (1981). *Final report: Training and employment services for handicapped individuals.* Washington, DC: Office of the Assistant Secretary for Planning and Evaluation.
27. Moss, J. W. (1979). *Post secondary vocational education for mentally retarded adults* (Final report to the Division of Developmental Disabilities, Rehabilitation Services Administration, U.S. Department of Health, Education, and Welfare, Grant No. 56P 50281/0).
28. Wehman, P. (1981). *Competitive employment: New horizons for severely disabled individuals.* Baltimore: Brookes.
29. Beebe, P. D., & Karan, O. C. (1986). A methodology for a community-based vocational program for adults. In R. H. Horner, L. H. Meyer, & H. D. B. Fredericks (Eds.), *Education of learners with severe handicaps: Exemplary service strategies* (pp. 3–28). Baltimore: Brookes.
30. Hill, M., & Wehman, P. (1983). Cost benefit analysis of placing moderately and severely handicapped individuals into competitive employment. *Journal of the Association for the Severely Handicapped, 8,* 30–38.
31. Rudrud, E. H., Ziarnik, J. P., Bernstein, G. S., & Ferrara, J. M. (1984). *Proactive vocational habilitation.* Baltimore: Brookes.
32. Will, M. (1984). *OSERS programming for the transition of youth with disabilities: Bridges from school to working life.* Washington, DC: Office of Special Education and Rehabilitative Services.
33. Bellamy, G. T., Sheehan, M. R., Horner, R. H., & Boles, S. M. (1980). Community programs for severely handicapped adults: An analysis of vocational opportunities. *TASH Review, 5*(4), 307–324.
34. Schleien, S., & Larson, A. (1986). Adult leisure education for the independent use of a community recreation center. *Journal of the Association for Persons with Severe Handicaps, 11*(1), 39–44.

CHAPTER 10

1. Mearig, J. S. (1982). *Ethical and psychological aspects of surgical intervention for D.S. children.* Paper presented at the IASSMD conference, Toronto.
2. Mearig, J. S. (1985). Facial surgery and an active modification approach for children with Down syndrome: Some psychological and ethical issues. *Rehabilitation Literature, 46,* 72–77.
3. Otterman-Aquire, J. A. (1969). Mongolism and plastic surgery. *Plastic and Reconstructive Surgery, 45,* 411–418.
4. Lemperle, G., & Radu, D. (1980). Facial plastic surgery in children with Down's syndrome. *Plastic and Reconstructive Surgery, 66,* 337–342.
5. Olbrisch, R. R. (1979). Plastische Chirurgie bei mongoloiden Kindern. *Fortschritte der Medizin, 97,* 1475–1479.
6. Olbrisch, R. R. (1982). Plastic surgical management of children with Down's syndrome. *Plastic and Reconstructive Surgery, 35,* 195–198.
7. Wexler, M. R., Peled, I. J., & Shapiro, J. (1984). Facial plastic surgery for Down's syndrome. *Harefua, 106,* 439–443. (Hebrew)
8. Rosner, L. (1983). Facial plastic surgery for Down's syndrome. *Lancet, 1,* 1320–1323.
9. Feuerstein, R. (1982). *Structural cognitive modifiability: Theory and its application with low-functioning persons.* Paper presented at the IASSMD Conference, Toronto.
10. Rand, Y. (1982). *Mediated learning experiences: Emotional aspects of Down's syndrome subjects in pre- and post-reconstructive facial surgery.* Paper presented at the IASSMD Conference, Toronto.
11. Mintzker, Y. (1982). *Research issues following surgery in children with Down's syndrome.* Paper presented at the IASSMD Conference, Toronto.
12. Feuerstein, R., Rand, Y., & Mintzker, Y. (1984). *Reconstructive plastic surgery in Down's syndrome children and adults.* Jerusalem: HWCRI.
13. Rand, Y., Mintzker, Y., Feuerstein, R., Strauss, R. P., Wexler, M. R., & Peled, I. J. (1987). The evaluation of the outcomes of plastic surgery with children with Down's syndrome. In M. R. Wexler & R. Feuerstein (Eds.), *Rehabilitative plastic surgery with Down's syndrome persons* (pp. 54–63). Jerusalem: S. Zack. (Hebrew)
14. Feuerstein, R., & Krasilowsky, D. (1971). The treatment group technique. In M. Wollins & M. Gottesman (Eds.), *Group care—An Israeli approach.* New York: Gordon & Breach.
15. Aviad, Y. (1983). *The success of labeling mental retardates, prevalence of severe mental retardation and an estimate of their needs.* Doctoral dissertation, Tel Aviv University.
16. Rand, Y., Mintzker, Y., & Feuerstein, R. (with Wexler, M. R., & Peled, I. Y., as medical authors). (1986). Rehabilitation of the face in patients with Down's syndrome. *Plastic and Reconstructive Surgery, 77*(3), 383–391.
17. Strauss, R. P., Mintzker, Y., Feuerstein, R., Wexler, M. R., & Rand, Y. (1987). Social perceptions of the effects of Down's syndrome facial surgery: A school-based study of ratings by normal adolescents. *Plastic and Reconstructive Surgery,* in press.
18. Parsons, C. L., Iacono, T. A., & Rozner, L (1987). Effect of tongue reduction on articulation in children with Down's syndrome. *American Journal of Mental Deficiency, 91*(3).

CHAPTER 11

1. Sternberg, R. J. (1984). Macrocomponents and microcomponents of intelligence: Some proposed loci of mental retardation. In P. H. Brooks, R. Sperber, & C. McCauley (Eds.), *Learning and cognition in the mentally retarded.* Hillsdale, NJ: Erlbaum.
2. de Bono, E. (1980). *Teaching thinking.* New York: Penguin Books.
3. Whimbey, A., & Lockhead, J. (1980). *Problem solving and comprehension: A short course in analytical reasoning* (2nd ed.). Philadelphia: Franklin Institute Press.
4. Lockhead, J. (1985). Teaching analytic reasoning skills through pair problem solving. In J. W. Segal, S. F. Chapman, & A. Glaser (Eds.), *Thinking and learning skills, Vol. 1: Relating instruction to research.* Hillsdale, NJ: Erlbaum.
5. Feuerstein, R., Rand, Y., & Hoffman, M. B. (1979). *The dynamic assessment of retarded performers: The learning potential assessment device—Theory, instruments and techniques.* Baltimore: University Park Press.
6. Rand, Y., Feuerstein, R., Ben Shahar, N., & Tzuriel, D. (1982). *LPAD tests: New versions. Some empirical data.* Paper presented at the IASSMD Conference, Toronto.
7. Jensen, A. (1969). How much can we boost IQ and scholastic achievement? *Harvard Educational Review, 39,* 1–123.
8. Raven, J. C. (1956). *Coloured Progression Matrices, sets A, Ab and B.* London: H. K. Lewis.
9. Bryant, P. E. (1974). *Perception and understanding in young children.* London: Methuen.
10. Mearig, J. (1987). Assessing the learning potential of kindergarten and primary age children. In C. S. Lidz (Ed.), *Dynamic assessment, foundations and fundamentals.* New York: Guilford Press.
11. Lidz, C. S. (1987). *Dynamic assessment: An interactional approach to evaluating learning potential.* New York: Guilford Press.
12. Tzuriel, D., & Klein, P. S. (1985). The assessment of analogical thinking modifiability among regular, special education, disadvantaged, and mentally retarded children. *Journal of Abnormal Child Psychology, 13*(4).
13. Rand, Y., & Kaniel, S. (1987). Dynamic assessment: Theoretical considerations. Group testing and educational implications. In C. S. Lidz (Ed.), *Dynamic assessment, foundations and fundamentals.* New York: Guilford Press.

CHAPTER 12

1. Feuerstein, R., Rand, Y., Hoffman, M. B., & Miller, R. (1980). *Instrumental enrichment: An intervention program for cognitive modifiability.* Baltimore: University Park Press.
2. Rand, Y., Mintzker, Y., Miller, R., & Hoffman, M. B. (1981). Instrumental enrichment program: Immediate and long term effects. In P. Mittler (Ed.), *Frontiers of knowledge in mental retardation* (Vol. 1). Baltimore: University Park Press.
3. Harth, R. (1981). *The Sedalia project: Modifying cognitive performance.* Columbia: University of Missouri.
4. Klein, P. S., Raziel, P., Brisk, M., & Birenbaum, E. (1984). *Cognitive performance of three-year olds born at a very low birth weight.* Ramat-Gan, Israel: Bar Ilan University and Sheba Medical Center.

5. Mintzker, Y., Kaniel, Sh., Brodsky, B., Narrol, H., & Tzuriel, D. (1987). (Numerous publications, parents guides, and presentations available upon request). Jerusalem, Hasbro Paradigmatic Clinic for Persons with Down Syndrome.
6. Haywood, H. C., Brooks, P., & Burns, S. (1986). Stimulating cognitive development at developmental level: A tested, non-remedial preschool curriculum for preschoolers and older retarded children. In M. Schwebel & C. A. Maher (Eds.), *Facilitating cognitive development: International perspectives, programs, and practice* (pp. 127–147). New York and London: Haworth Press.
7. Ruiz-Bolivar, C. J. (1985, January) *Modificabilidad cognoscitiva e irreversibilidad: Un estudio.* Guayana, Venezuela: Universidad de Guayana.

CHAPTER 13

1. Nirje, B. (1969). The normalization principle and its human management implications. *Journal of Mental Subnormality, 16*, 62–70.
2. Selye, H. *Stress without distress.*
3. Carew, J. (1980). *Monographs in Child Development.*
4. Broussard, E. (1979). Assessment of the adaptive potential of the mother–infant system: The Neonatal Perception Inventories. *Seminars in Perinatology, 3*, 91–100.
5. Klein, P., & Feuerstein, R. (1985). Environmental variables and cognitive development. In S. Harel & N. Anastasiow (Eds.), *The at-risk infant: Psycho/social/medical aspects* (pp. 369–377). Baltimore: Brookes.
6. Schaeffer, E., & Emerson, P. (1964). The development of social attachments in infancy. *Monograph of the Society for Research in Child Development, 29*, 1–77.
7. Denenberg, V., & Thoman, E. (1976). From animal to infant research. In T. Tjossem (Ed.), *Intervention strategies for high-risk infants and young children.* Baltimore: University Park Press.
8. Taft, T. (1981). Intervention programs for infants with cerebral palsy. In C. Brown (Ed.), *Infants at risk: Assessment and intervention. An update for health care professionals and parents.* Palm Beach: Johnson & Johnson Baby Products.
9. Adelson, E., & Fraiberg, S. (1974). Gross motor development in infants blind from birth. *Child Development, 45*, 114–126.
10. Fraiberg, S. (1971). Intervention in infancy: A program for blind infants. *Journal of the American Academy of Child Psychiatry, 10*(3), 381–405.
11. Fraiberg, S., Smith, M., & Adelson, E. (1969). An educational program for blind infants. *Journal of Special Education, 3*(2), 121–139.
12. Meyer, L. H. (1987). *Why integration?* Syracuse: Syracuse University School of Education.
13. Brown, L., Nietupski, J., & Hamre-Nietupski, S. (1976). The criterion of ultimate functioning. In M. A. Thomas (Ed.), *Hey, don't forget about me!* Reston, VA: CEC Information Center.
14. Hamre-Nietupski, S., & Nietupski, J. (1981). Integral involvement of severely handicapped students within regular public schools. *Journal of the Association for the Severely Handicapped, 6*(2), 30–39.
15. Meyer, L. H., & Kishi, G. S. (1985). School integration strategies. In K. C. Lakin & R. H. Bruininks (Eds.), *Strategies for achieving community integration of developmentally disabled citizens* (pp. 231–252). Baltimore: Brookes.

16. Biklen, D. (1985). *Achieving the complete school.* New York: Teachers College, Columbia University.
17. Stetson, F. (1984). Critical factors that facilitate integration: A theory of administrative responsibility. In N. Certo, N. Haring, & R. York (Eds.), *Public school integration of severely handicapped students* (pp. 65–81). Baltimore: Brookes.
18. Taylor, S. J. (1982). From segregation to integration: Strategies for integrating severely handicapped students in normal school and community settings. *Journal of the Association of the Severely Handicapped, 7*(3), 42–49.
19. Sailor, W., & Guess, D. (1983). *Severely handicapped students: An instructional design.* Boston: Houghton Mifflin.
20. Rynders, J., Meyer, L., Vandercook, T., Schleien, S., & Mustonen, T. (1988). *Integration of learners with severe disabilities in regular schools and community recreation settings: Implementing research findings.* Minneapolis: University of Minnesota Consortium Institute for the Education of Learners with Severe Handicaps.
21. Voeltz, L. J., Hemphill, N. J., Brown, S., Kishi, G., Klein, R., Fruehling, R., Collie, J., Levy, G., & Kube, C. (1983). *The Special Friends program: A trainer's manual for integrated school settings* (rev. ed.). Honolulu: University of Hawaii Department of Special Education.
22. Cole, D., Vandercook, T., & Rynders, J. (in press) Programming social integration between children with and without severe disabilities. *American Educational Research Journal.*
23. Meyer, L. H., Fox, A., Schermer, A., Ketelsen, D., Montan, N., Maley, K., & Cole, D. (1987). The effects of teacher intrusion on social play interactions between children with autism and their nonhandicapped peers. *Journal of Autism and Developmental Disorders, 17,* 315–332.
24. Cole, D. A., Meyer, L. H., Vandercook, T., & McQuarter, R. (1986). Interactions between peers with and without severe handicaps: Dynamics of teacher intervention. *American Journal of Mental Deficiency, 91,* 160–169.
25. Rynders, J., Behlen, K., & Horrobin, M. (1979). Performance characteristics of preschool Down's syndrome children receiving augmented or repetitive verbal instruction. *American Journal of Mental Deficiency, 84,* 67–73.
26. Schleien, S., Rynders, J., & Mustonen, T. (1986). *Using applied behavior analysis approaches to integrate children with severe handicaps into an outdoor education environment.* Minneapolis: University of Minnesota Consortium Institute for the Education of Learners with Severe Handicaps.
27. Schleien, S., Mustonen, T., & Rynders, J. (1987). *Integrating children with severe handicaps into various art activities.* Minneapolis: University of Minnesota Consortium Institute for the Education of Learners with Severe Handicaps.
28. Schleien, S., Ray, M., Soderman-Olson, M., & McMahon, K. (in press). Integrating children with moderate to severe cognitive deficits into a community museum program. *Education and Training of the Mentally Retarded.*
29. Rynders, J., Johnson, R., Johnson, D., & Schmidt, B. (1980). Effects of cooperative goal structuring in producing positive interaction between Down's syndrome and nonhandicapped teenagers: Implications for mainstreaming. *American Journal of Mental Deficiency, 85,* 268–273.
30. Vandercook, T. (1987). *Performance in the criterion situation for learners with severe disabilities.* Unpublished doctoral dissertation, University of Minnesota, Department of Educational Psychology, Special Education Programs.
31. Cole, D. A., Vandercook, T., & Rynders, J. (1987). Dyadic interactions between

children with and without mental handicaps: The effects of age discrepancy. *American Journal of Mental Deficiency, 92,* 194–202.

32. Meyer, L. H., & Putnam, J. (in press). Social integration. In V. B. Van Hasselt, P. S. Strain, & M. Hersen (Eds.), *Handbook of developmental and physical disabilities.* New York: Pergamon.

33. Schleien, S., Olson, K., Rogers, N., & McLafferty, M. (1985). Integrating children with severe handicaps into recreation and physical education programs. *Journal of Park and Recreation Administration, 3*(1), 50–66.

34. Schleien, S., Rynders, J., Mustonen, T., Fox, A., & Kelterborn, B. (1986). *Effects of integrated recreation on learners with severe disabilities across four social levels of play.* Minneapolis: University of Minnesota Consortium Institute for the Education of Learners with Severe Handicaps.

35. Schleien, S., Krotee, M., Mustonen, T., Kelterborn, B., & Schermer, A. (in press). The effects of integrating children with autism into a physical activity and recreation setting. *Therapeutic Recreation Journal.*

36. Meyer, L. H., & Kishi, G. S. (1985). School integration strategies. In K. C. Lakin & R. H. Bruininks (Eds.), *Strategies for achieving community integration of developmentally disabled citizens* (pp. 231–252). Baltimore: Brookes.

37. Voeltz, L. M. (1980). Children's attitudes toward handicapped peers. *American Journal of Mental Deficiency, 85,* 268–283.

38. Voeltz, L. M. (1982). Effects of structured interactions with severely handicapped peers on children's attitudes. *American Journal of Mental Deficiency, 86,* 180–190.

39. Schleien, S., & Ray, M. T. (1988). *Community recreation and persons with disabilities: Strategies for integration.* Baltimore: Brookes.

40. Johnson, R., Rynders, J., Johnson, D. W., Schmidt, B., & Haider, S. (1979). Producing positive interaction between handicapped and nonhandicapped teenagers through cooperative goal structuring: Implications for mainstreaming. *American Educational Research Journal, 16,* 161–168.

41. Vandercook, T. (1987). *Teacher intervention to facilitate peer interactions: Definitions and examples.* Unpublished manuscript, University of Minnesota.

42. Schleien, S., Rynders, J., & Mustonen, T. (submitted). *Social and horticulture skill training in young adults with severe and mild mental retardation.*

43. Schleien, S., Mustonen, T., & Rynders, J. (in preparation). *Integrating children with severe handicaps into various art activities.*

44. Voeltz, L. M., & Brennan, J. (1984). Analysis of interactions between nonhandicapped and severely handicapped peers using multiple measures. In J. M. Berg (Ed.), *Perspectives and progress in mental retardation, Vol. I: Social, psychological, and educational aspects.* Baltimore: University Park Press.

45. Breen, C., Haring, T., Pitts-Conway, V , & Gaylord-Ross, R. (1985). The training and generalization of social interaction during breaktime at two job sites in the natural environment. *Journal of the Association for Persons with Severe Handicaps, 10*(1), 41–50.

EPILOGUE

1. Kamin, L. J. (1977). *The science and politics of IQ.* Hillsdale, NJ: Erlbaum.

2. Coles, G. (1987). *The learning mystique.* New York: Pantheon Books.

CONTRIBUTIONS OF INDIVIDUAL AUTHORS BY CHAPTER

Chapter 1	Yaacov Rand, Reuven Feuerstein, and John E. Rynders
Chapter 2	Yaacov Rand, Reuven Feuerstein, and John E. Rynders
Chapter 3	Reuven Feuerstein, Yaacov Rand, and John E. Rynders
Chapter 4	Reuven Feuerstein, Yaacov Rand, and John E. Rynders
Chapter 5	Reuven Feuerstein, Yaacov Rand, and John E. Rynders
Chapter 6	Reuven Feuerstein, Yaacov Rand, and John E. Rynders
Chapter 7	Yaacov Rand, John E. Rynders, and Reuven Feuerstein
Chapter 8	John E. Rynders, Yaacov Rand, Reuven Feuerstein, and Pnina Klein
Chapter 9	John E. Rynders, Yaacov Rand, and Reuven Feuerstein
Chapter 10	Yaacov Rand, Reuven Feuerstein, John E. Rynders, and Yael Mintzker
Chapter 11	Reuven Feuerstein, Yaacov Rand, and John E. Rynders
Chapter 12	Reuven Feuerstein, Yaacov Rand, and John E. Rynders
Chapter 13	John E. Rynders, Reuven Feuerstein, and Yaacov Rand
Epilogue	Reuven Feuerstein, Yaacov Rand, and John E. Rynders
Appendixes	John E. Rynders, Reuven Feuerstein, Yaacov Rand, and Pnina Klein

Index

305